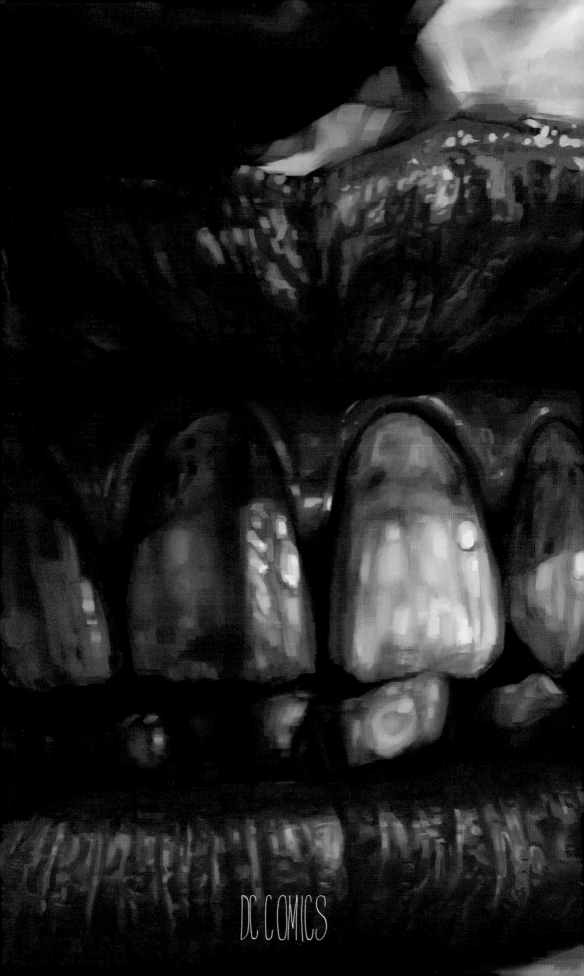

DC COMICS

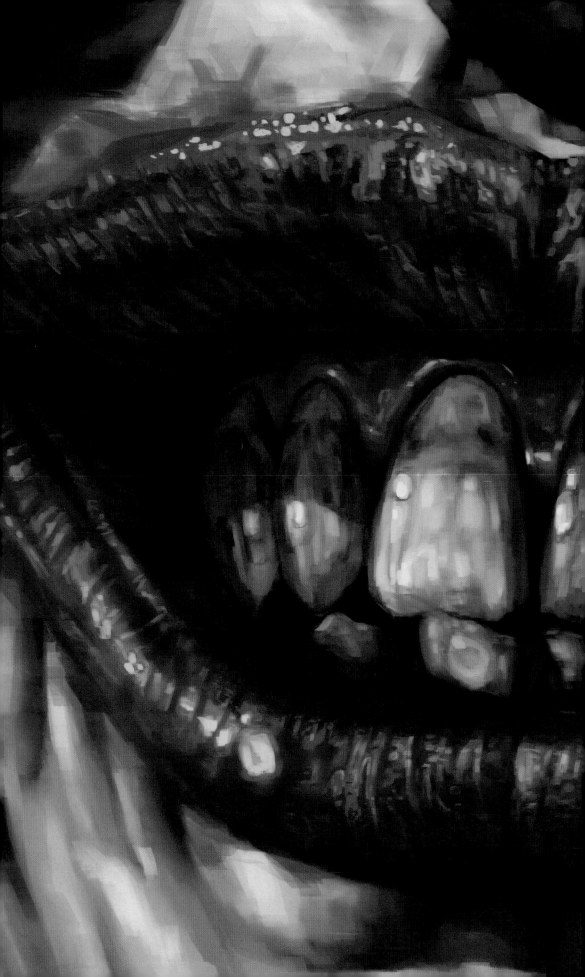

JOKER

BRIAN AZZARELLO
writer

LEE BERMEJO
PENCILS and COVERS
INKS 1,4,14,16,18-23,48,49,66,73,
115,117,119,120,and 121

MICK GRAY INKS

PATRICIA MULVIHILL
COLORS

ROBERT CLARK
LETTERS

Dan DiDio Sr. VP-Executive Editor   Will Dennis Editor   Louis Prandi Art Director   Paul Levitz President & Publisher   Georg Brewer VP-Design & DC Direct Creative   Richard Bruning Sr. VP-Creative Director   Patrick Caldon Exec. VP-Finance & Operations   Chris Caramalis VP-Finance   John Cunningham VP-Marketing   Terri Cunningham VP-Managing Editor   Amy Genkins Sr. VP-Business & Legal Affairs   Alison Gill VP-Manufacturing   David Hyde VP-Publicity   Hank Kanalz VP-General Manager, WildStorm   Jim Lee, Editorial Director-WildStorm   Gregory Noveck Sr. VP-Creative Affairs   Sue Pohja VP-Book Trade Sales   Steve Rotterdam Senior VP-Sales & Marketing   Cheryl Rubin Sr. VP-Brand Management   Jeff Trojan VP-Business Development, DC Direct   Alysse Soll VP-Advertising & Custom Publishing   Bob Wayne VP-Sales

SUSTAINABLE
FORESTRY
INITIATIVE
Certified Chain of Custody
Promoting Sustainable
Forest Management
www.sfiprogram.org

Fiber used in this product line meets the
sourcing requirements of the SFI program.
www.sfiprogram.org SGS-SFI/COC-US10/81072

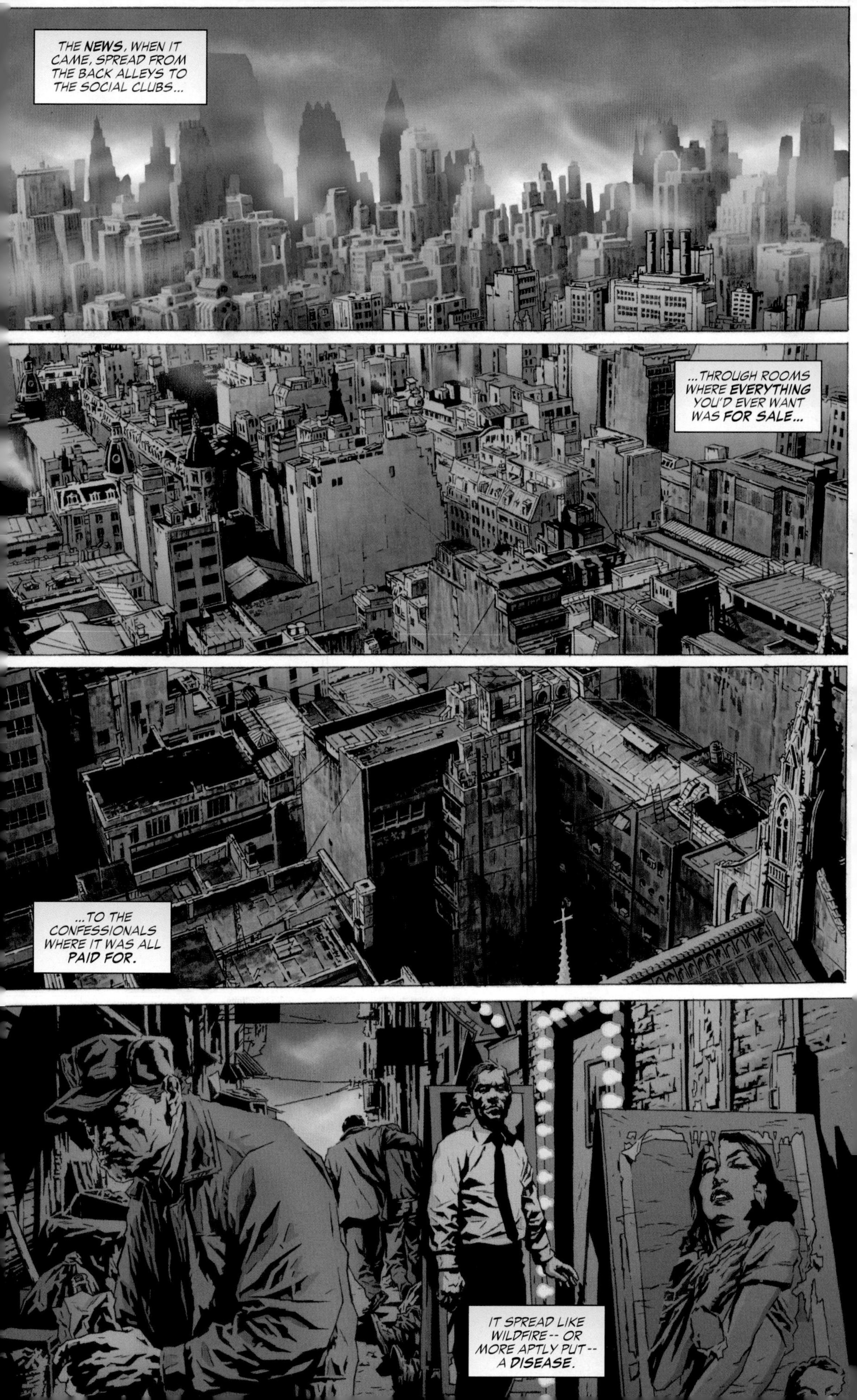
THE NEWS, WHEN IT CAME, SPREAD FROM THE BACK ALLEYS TO THE SOCIAL CLUBS...
...THROUGH ROOMS WHERE EVERYTHING YOU'D EVER WANT WAS FOR SALE...
...TO THE CONFESSIONALS WHERE IT WAS ALL PAID FOR.
IT SPREAD LIKE WILDFIRE -- OR MORE APTLY PUT -- A DISEASE.

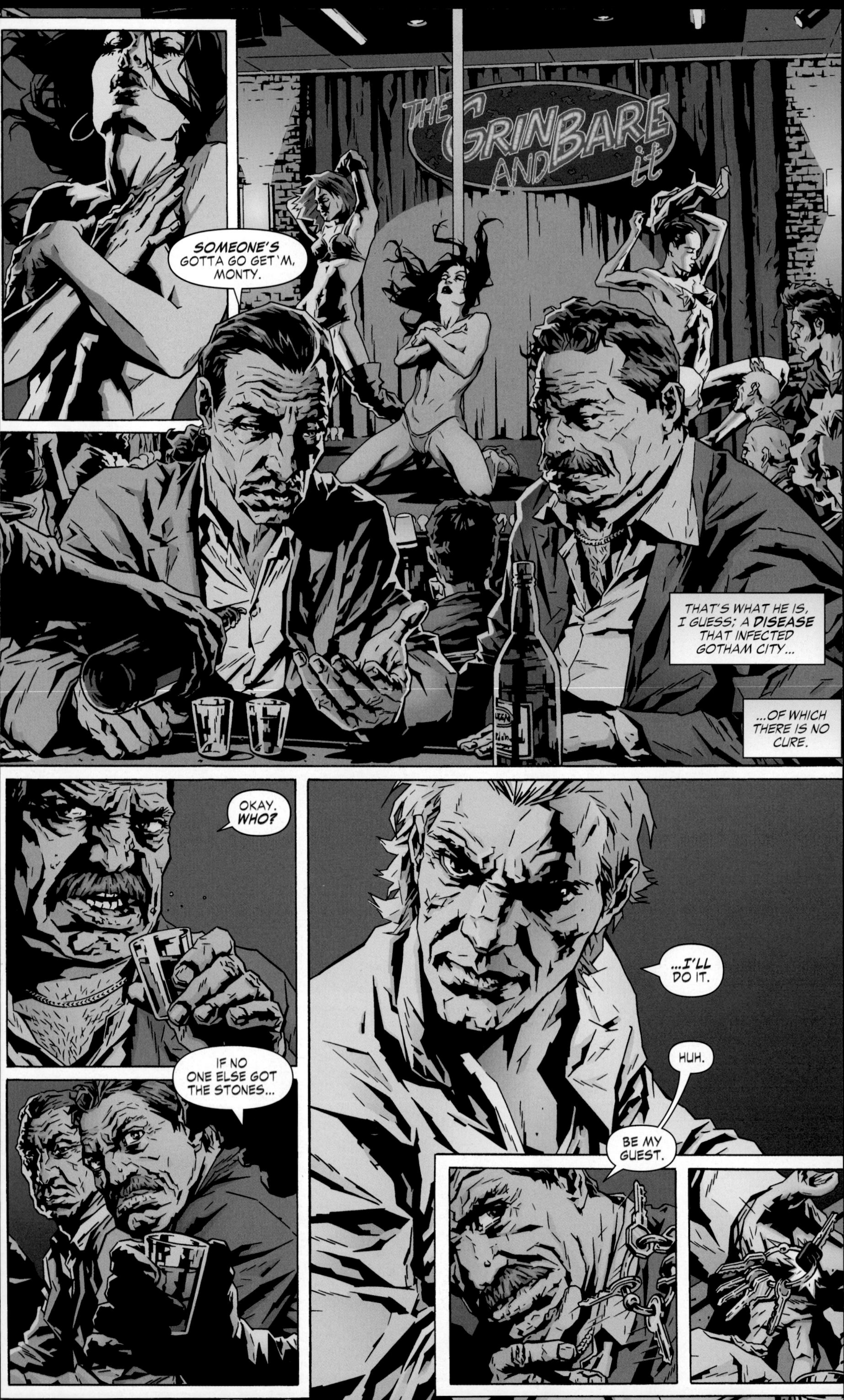
THE GRIN AND BARE it
SOMEONE'S GOTTA GO GET 'M, MONTY.
THAT'S WHAT HE IS, I GUESS; A DISEASE THAT INFECTED GOTHAM CITY...
...OF WHICH THERE IS NO CURE.
OKAY. WHO?
IF NO ONE ELSE GOT THE STONES...
...I'LL DO IT.
HUH.
BE MY GUEST.

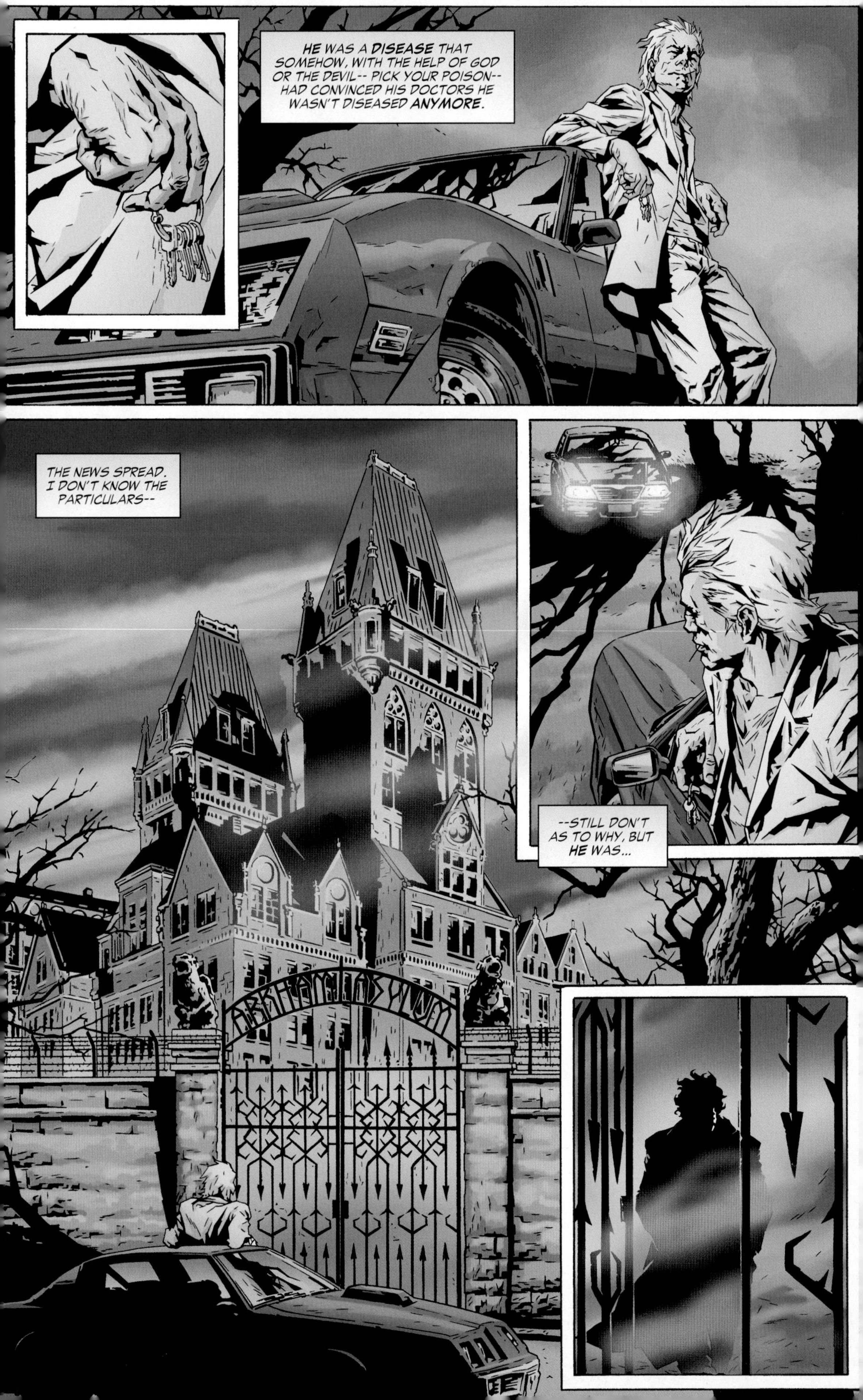
HE WAS A DISEASE THAT SOMEHOW, WITH THE HELP OF GOD OR THE DEVIL-- PICK YOUR POISON-- HAD CONVINCED HIS DOCTORS HE WASN'T DISEASED ANYMORE.
THE NEWS SPREAD. I DON'T KNOW THE PARTICULARS--
--STILL DON'T AS TO WHY, BUT HE WAS...

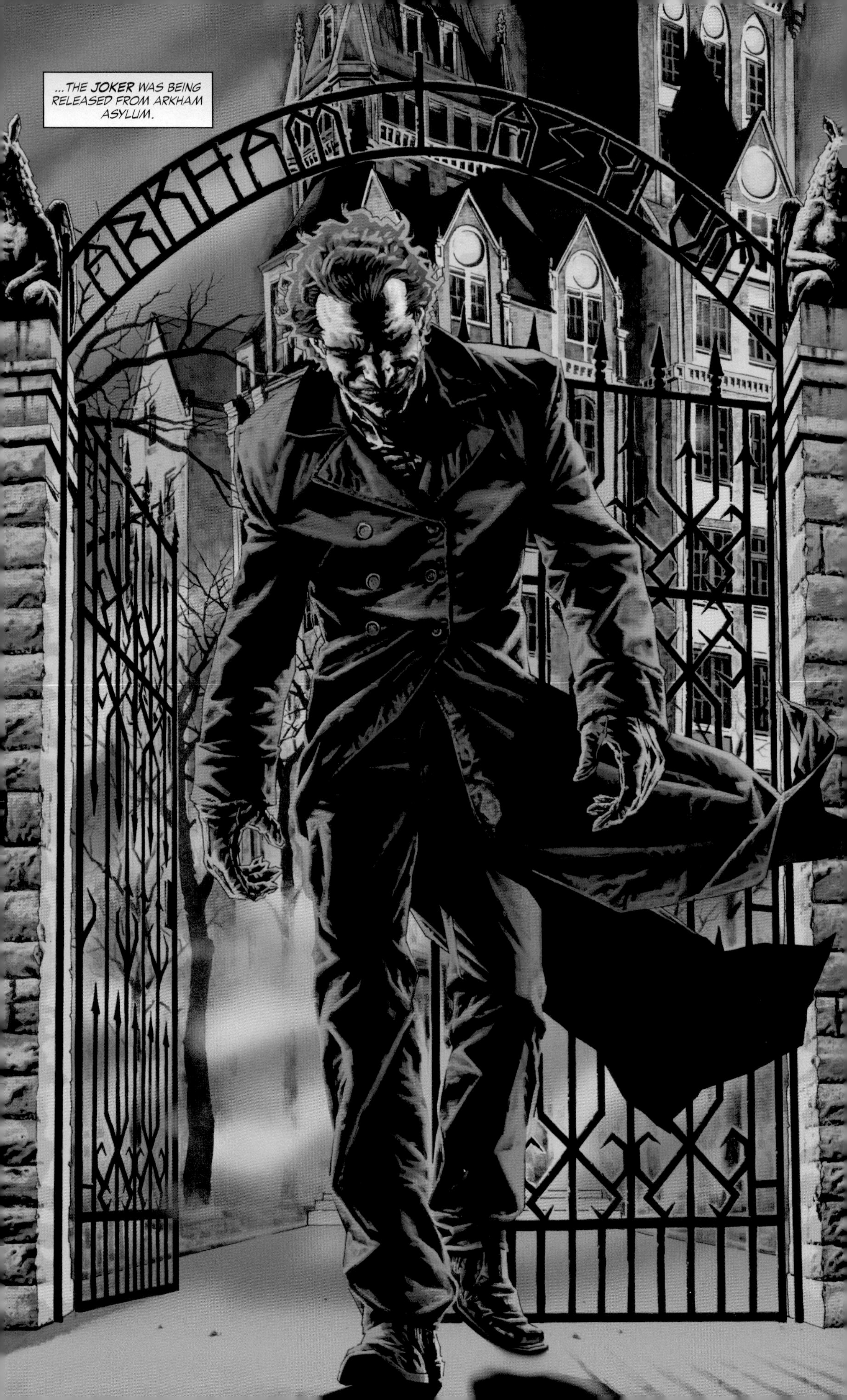
...THE JOKER WAS BEING RELEASED FROM ARKHAM ASYLUM.
ARKHAM ASYLUM

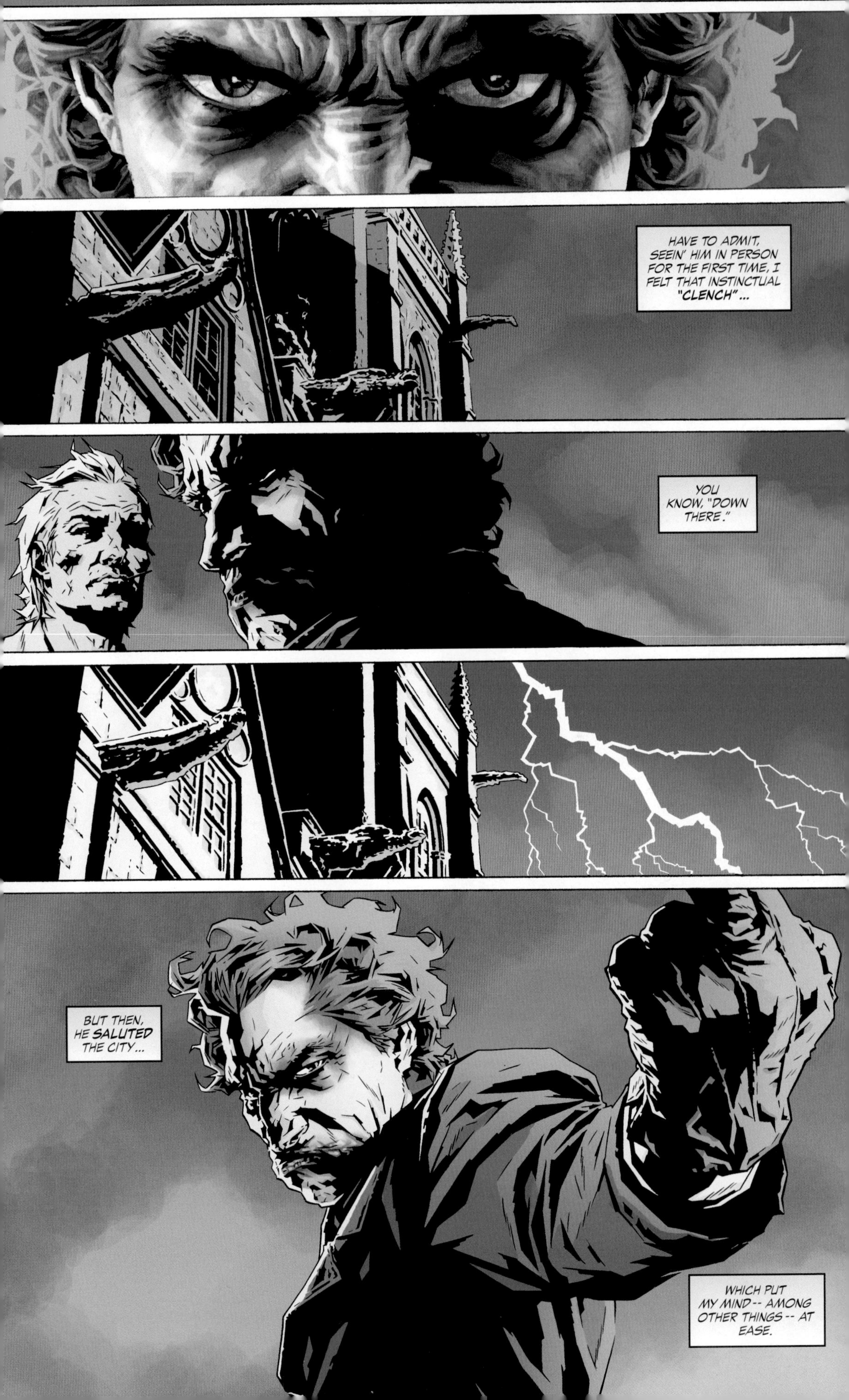
HAVE TO ADMIT, SEEIN' HIM IN PERSON FOR THE FIRST TIME, I FELT THAT INSTINCTUAL "CLENCH"...
YOU KNOW, "DOWN THERE."
BUT THEN, HE SALUTED THE CITY...
WHICH PUT MY MIND -- AMONG OTHER THINGS -- AT EASE.

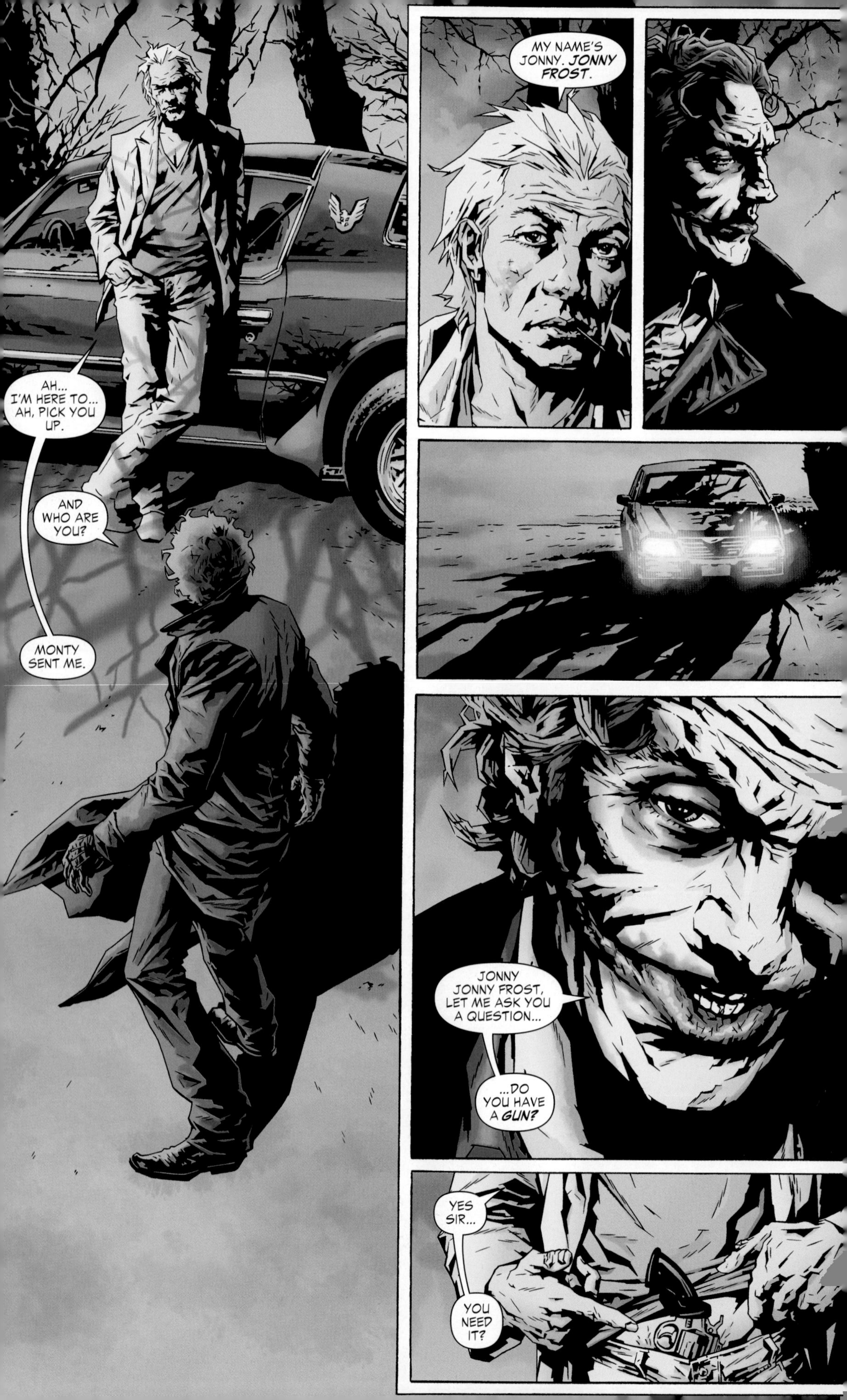
AH... I'M HERE TO... AH, PICK YOU UP.
AND WHO ARE YOU?
MONTY SENT ME.
MY NAME'S JONNY. JONNY FROST.
JONNY JONNY FROST, LET ME ASK YOU A QUESTION...
...DO YOU HAVE A GUN?
YES SIR...
YOU NEED IT?

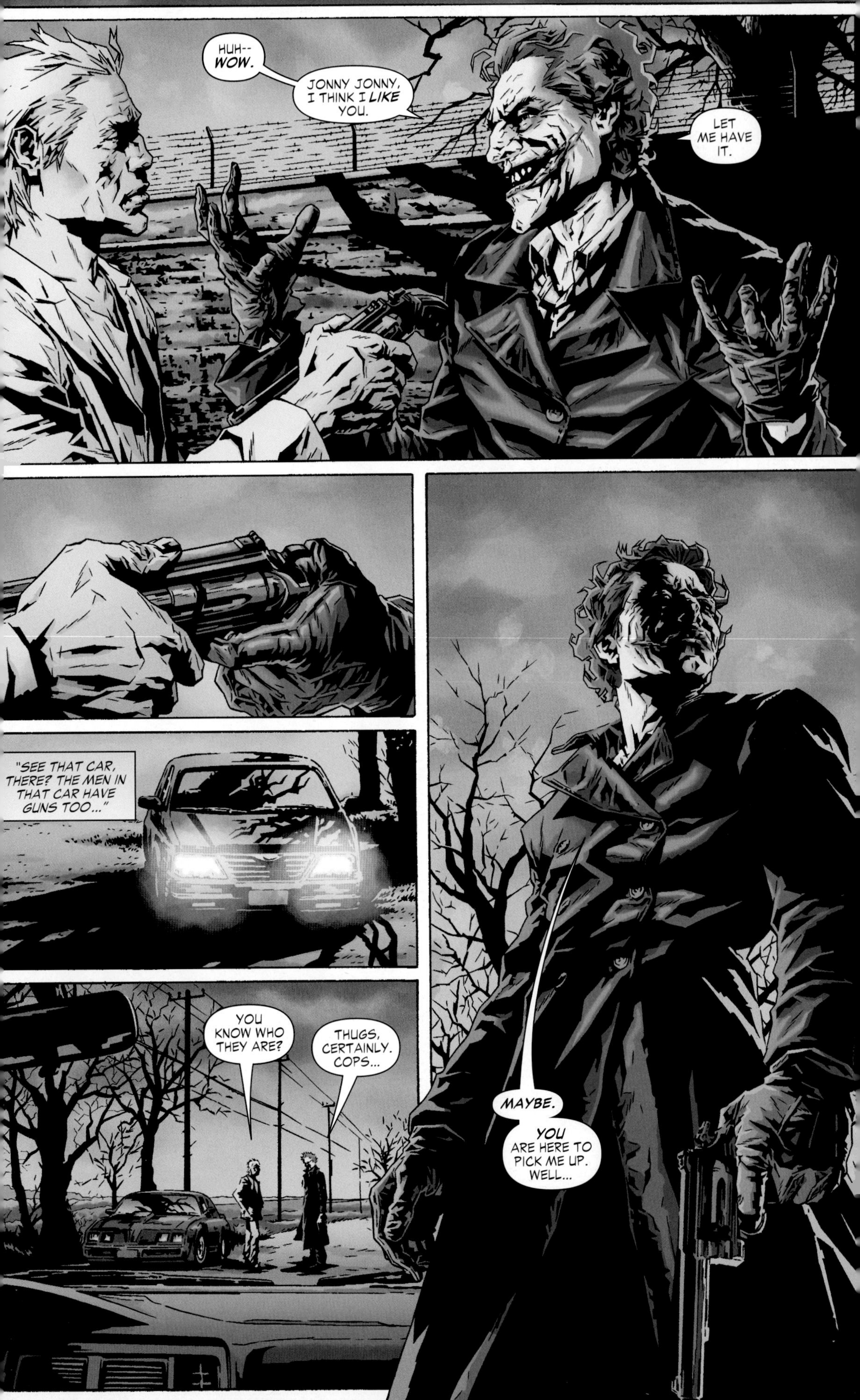
HUH--
WOW.
JONNY JONNY, I THINK I LIKE YOU.
LET ME HAVE IT.
"SEE THAT CAR, THERE? THE MEN IN THAT CAR HAVE GUNS TOO..."
YOU KNOW WHO THEY ARE?
THUGS, CERTAINLY. COPS...
MAYBE.
YOU ARE HERE TO PICK ME UP. WELL...

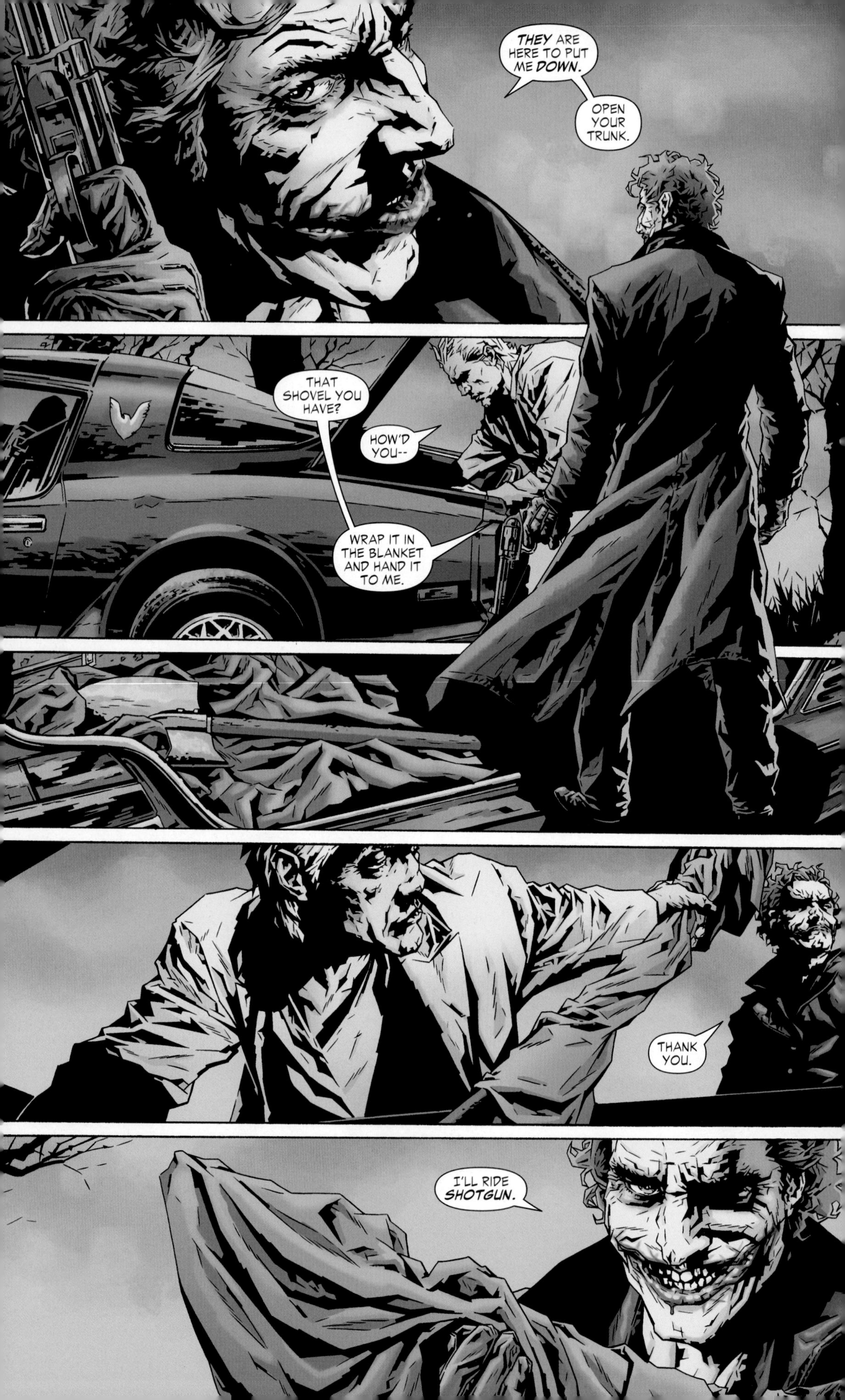
THEY ARE HERE TO PUT ME DOWN.
OPEN YOUR TRUNK.
THAT SHOVEL YOU HAVE?
HOW'D YOU--
WRAP IT IN THE BLANKET AND HAND IT TO ME.
THANK YOU.
I'LL RIDE SHOTGUN.

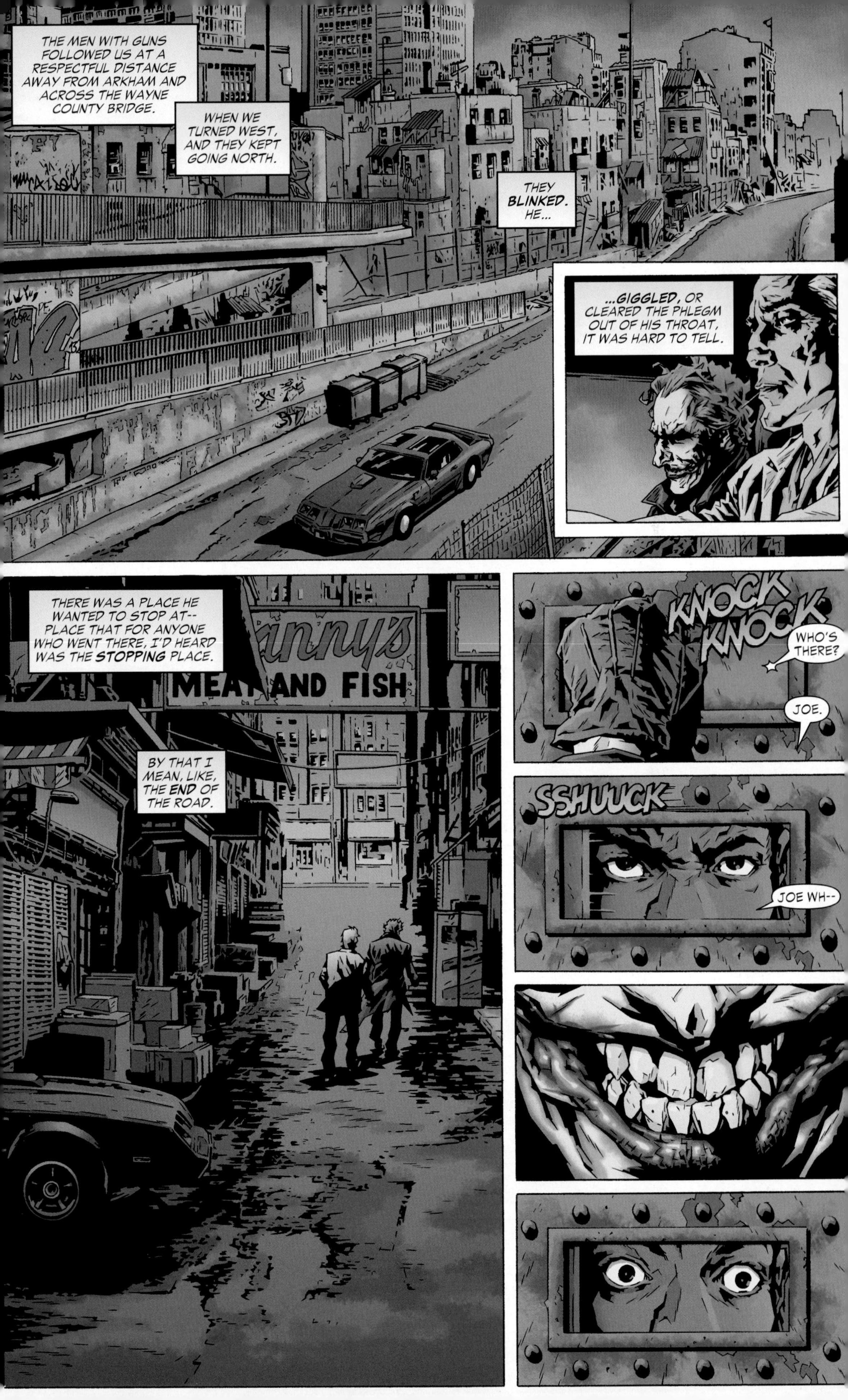
THE MEN WITH GUNS FOLLOWED US AT A RESPECTFUL DISTANCE AWAY FROM ARKHAM AND ACROSS THE WAYNE COUNTY BRIDGE.
WHEN WE TURNED WEST, AND THEY KEPT GOING NORTH.
THEY BLINKED. HE...
...GIGGLED, OR CLEARED THE PHLEGM OUT OF HIS THROAT, IT WAS HARD TO TELL.
THERE WAS A PLACE HE WANTED TO STOP AT-- PLACE THAT FOR ANYONE WHO WENT THERE, I'D HEARD WAS THE STOPPING PLACE.
MEAT AND FISH
BY THAT I MEAN, LIKE, THE END OF THE ROAD.
KNOCK KNOCK
WHO'S THERE?
JOE.
SSHUUCK
JOE WH--

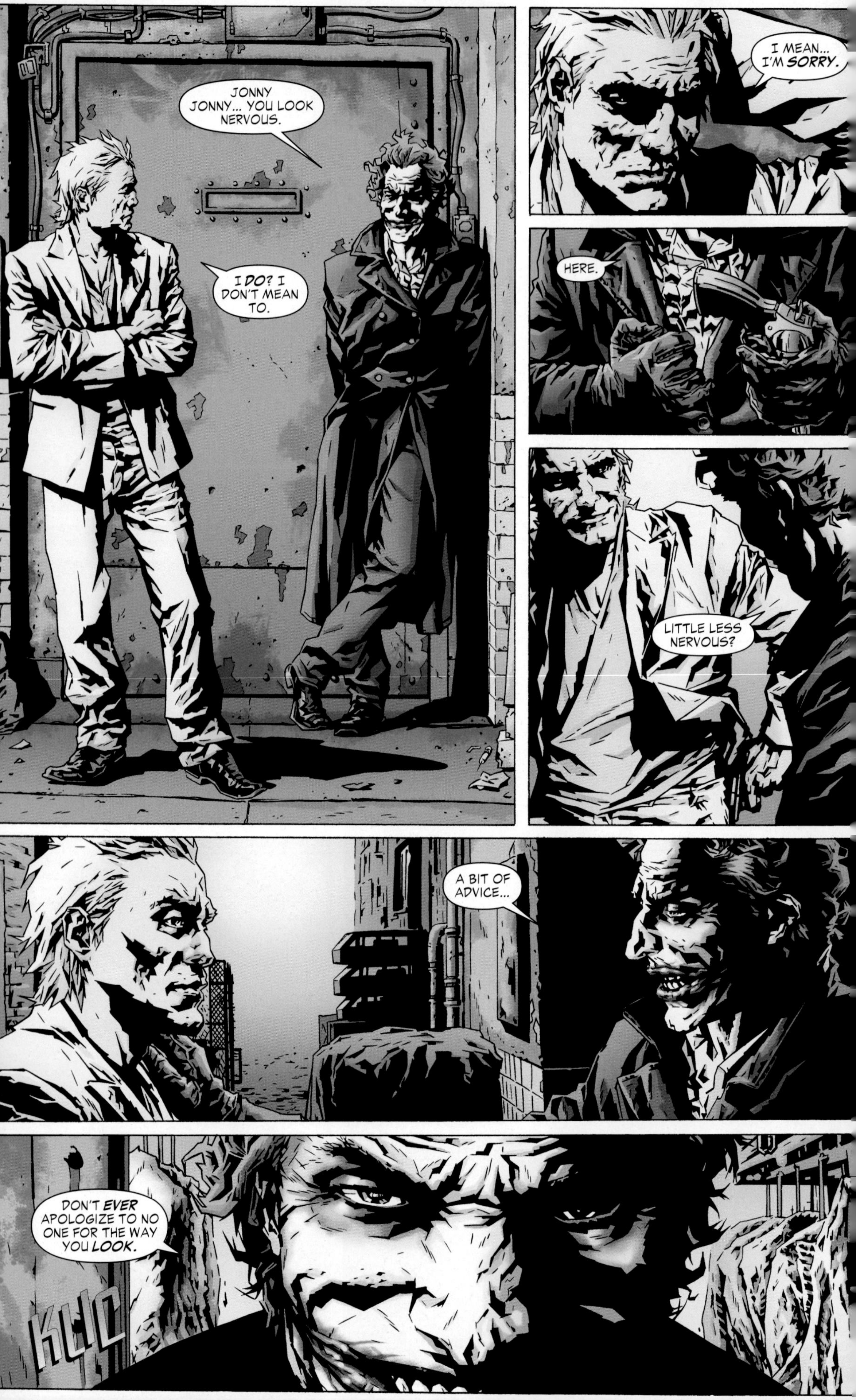
JONNY JONNY... YOU LOOK NERVOUS.
I DO? I DON'T MEAN TO.
I MEAN... I'M SORRY.
HERE.
LITTLE LESS NERVOUS?
A BIT OF ADVICE...
DON'T EVER APOLOGIZE TO NO ONE FOR THE WAY YOU LOOK.
KLIC

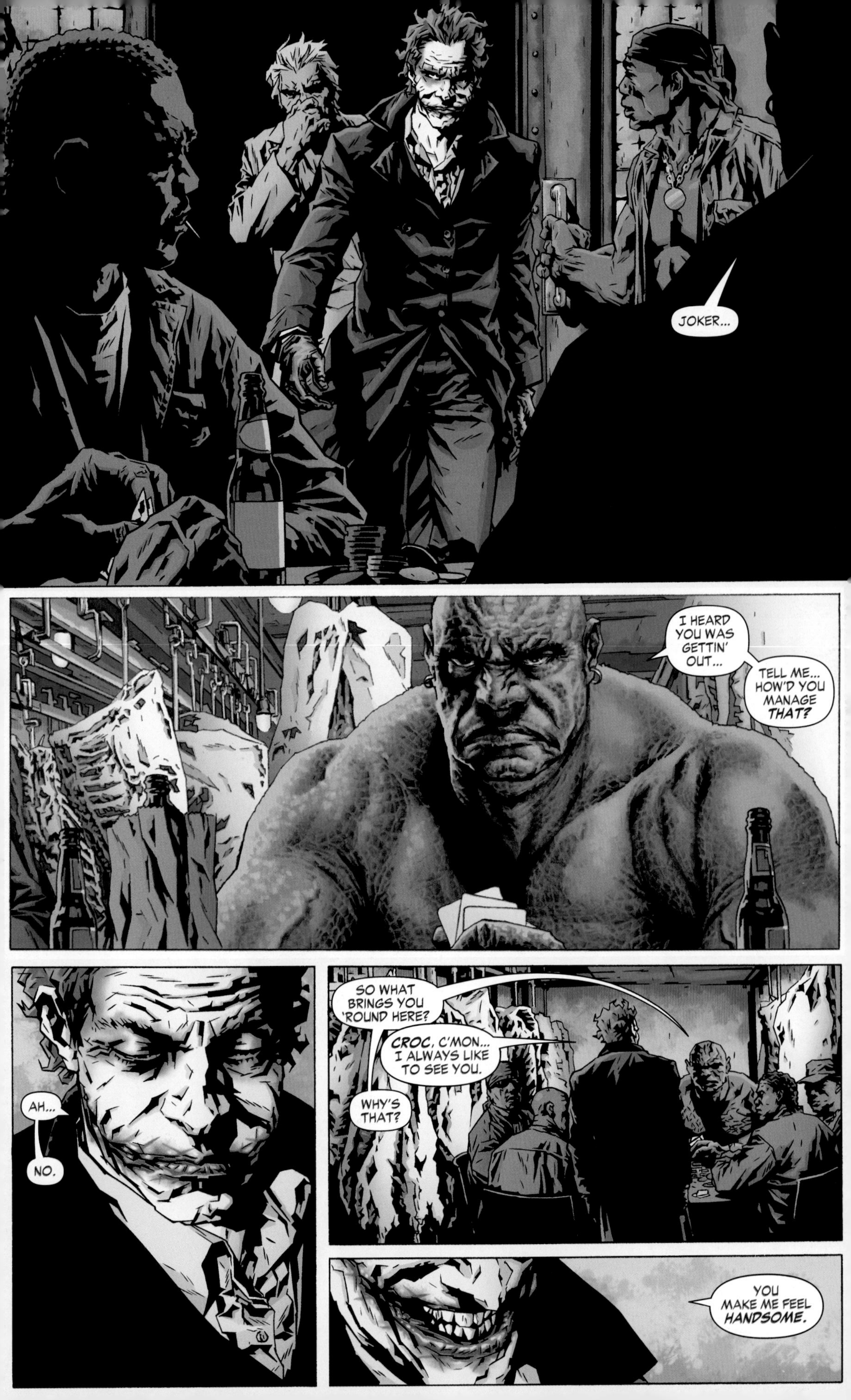
JOKER...
I HEARD YOU WAS GETTIN' OUT...
TELL ME... HOW'D YOU MANAGE THAT?
AH...
NO.
SO WHAT BRINGS YOU 'ROUND HERE?
CROC, C'MON... I ALWAYS LIKE TO SEE YOU.
WHY'S THAT?
YOU MAKE ME FEEL HANDSOME.

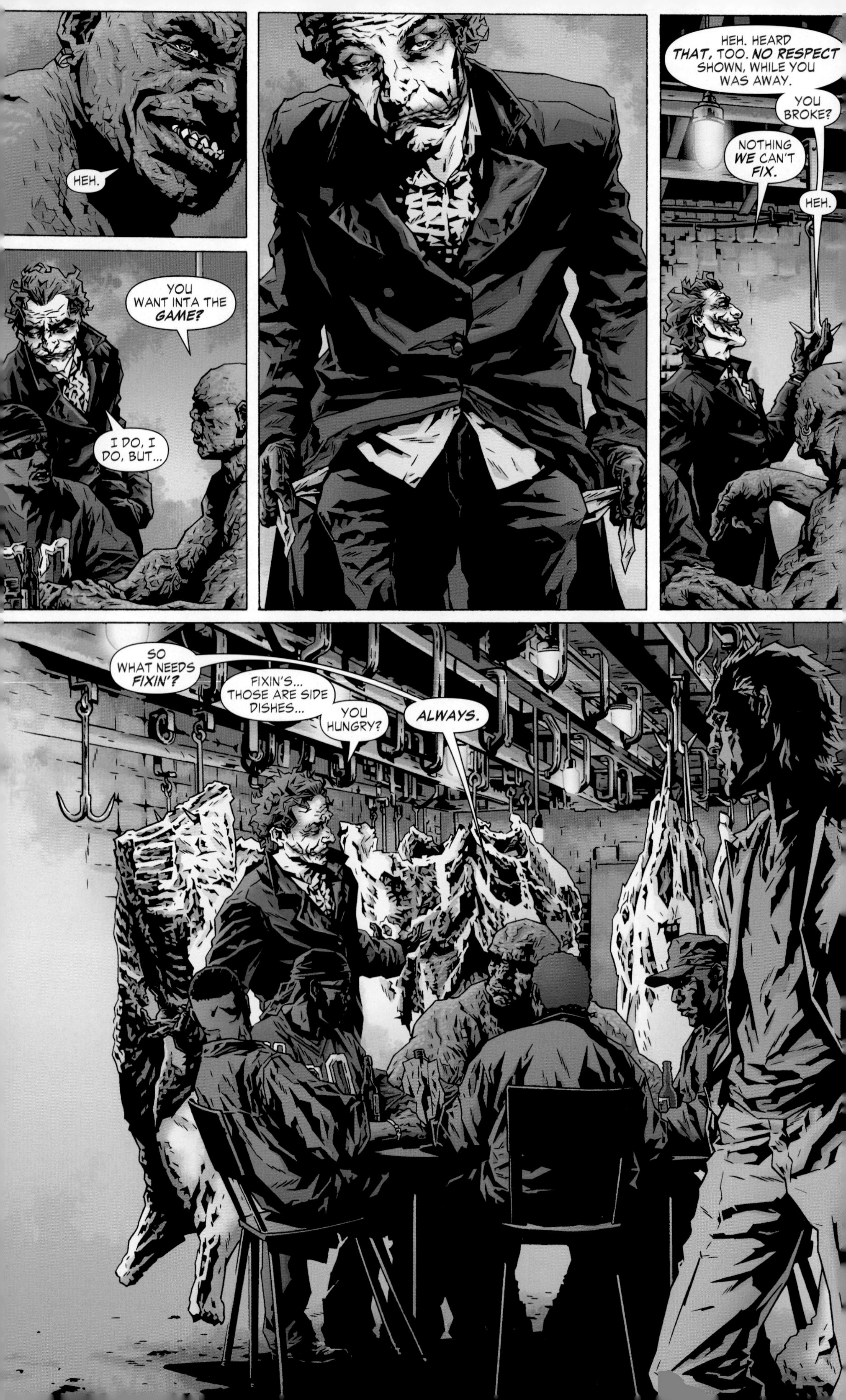
HEH.
YOU WANT INTA THE GAME?
I DO, I DO, BUT...
HEH. HEARD THAT, TOO. NO RESPECT SHOWN, WHILE YOU WAS AWAY.
YOU BROKE?
NOTHING WE CAN'T FIX.
HEH.
SO WHAT NEEDS FIXIN'?
FIXIN'S... THOSE ARE SIDE DISHES...
YOU HUNGRY?
ALWAYS.

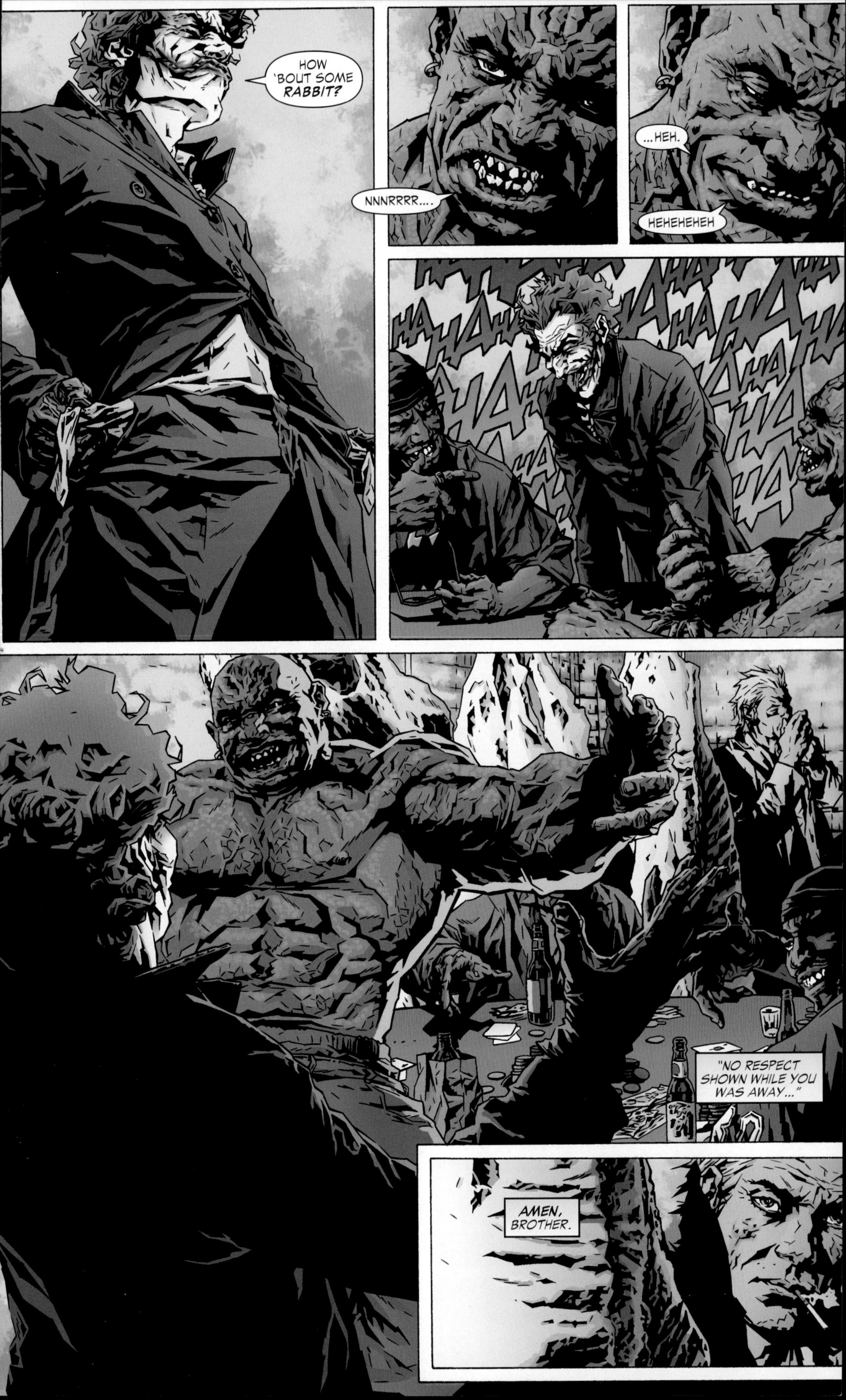
HOW 'BOUT SOME RABBIT?
NNNRRRR....
...HEH.
HEHEHEHEH
"NO RESPECT SHOWN WHILE YOU WAS AWAY..."
AMEN, BROTHER.

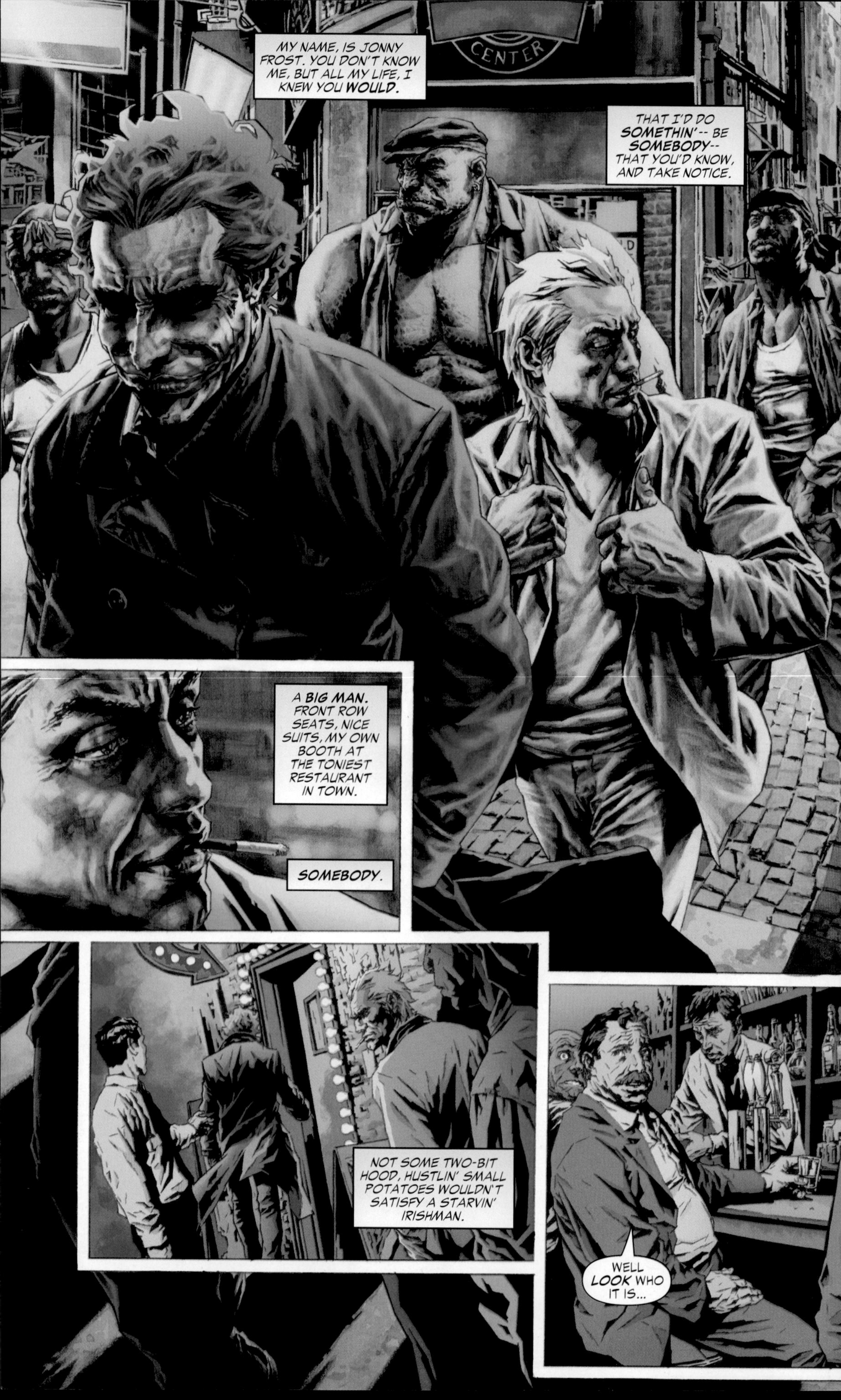

MY NAME, IS JONNY FROST. YOU DON'T KNOW ME, BUT ALL MY LIFE, I KNEW YOU WOULD.
THAT I'D DO SOMETHIN'-- BE SOMEBODY-- THAT YOU'D KNOW, AND TAKE NOTICE.
A BIG MAN. FRONT ROW SEATS, NICE SUITS, MY OWN BOOTH AT THE TONIEST RESTAURANT IN TOWN.
SOMEBODY.
NOT SOME TWO-BIT HOOD, HUSTLIN' SMALL POTATOES WOULDN'T SATISFY A STARVIN' IRISHMAN.
WELL LOOK WHO IT IS...

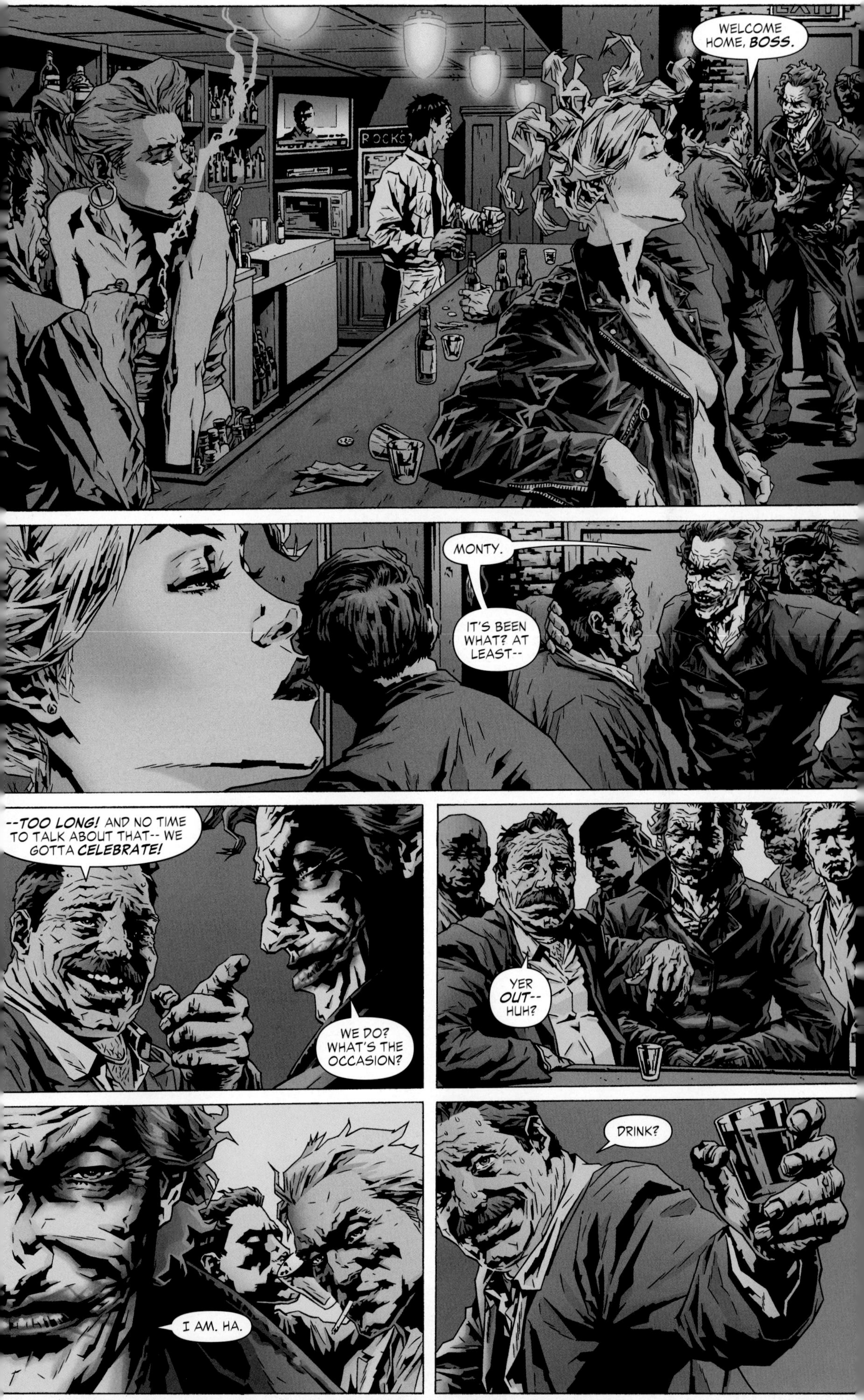
WELCOME HOME, BOSS.
MONTY.
IT'S BEEN WHAT? AT LEAST--
--TOO LONG! AND NO TIME TO TALK ABOUT THAT-- WE GOTTA CELEBRATE!
WE DO? WHAT'S THE OCCASION?
YER OUT-- HUH?
I AM. HA.
DRINK?

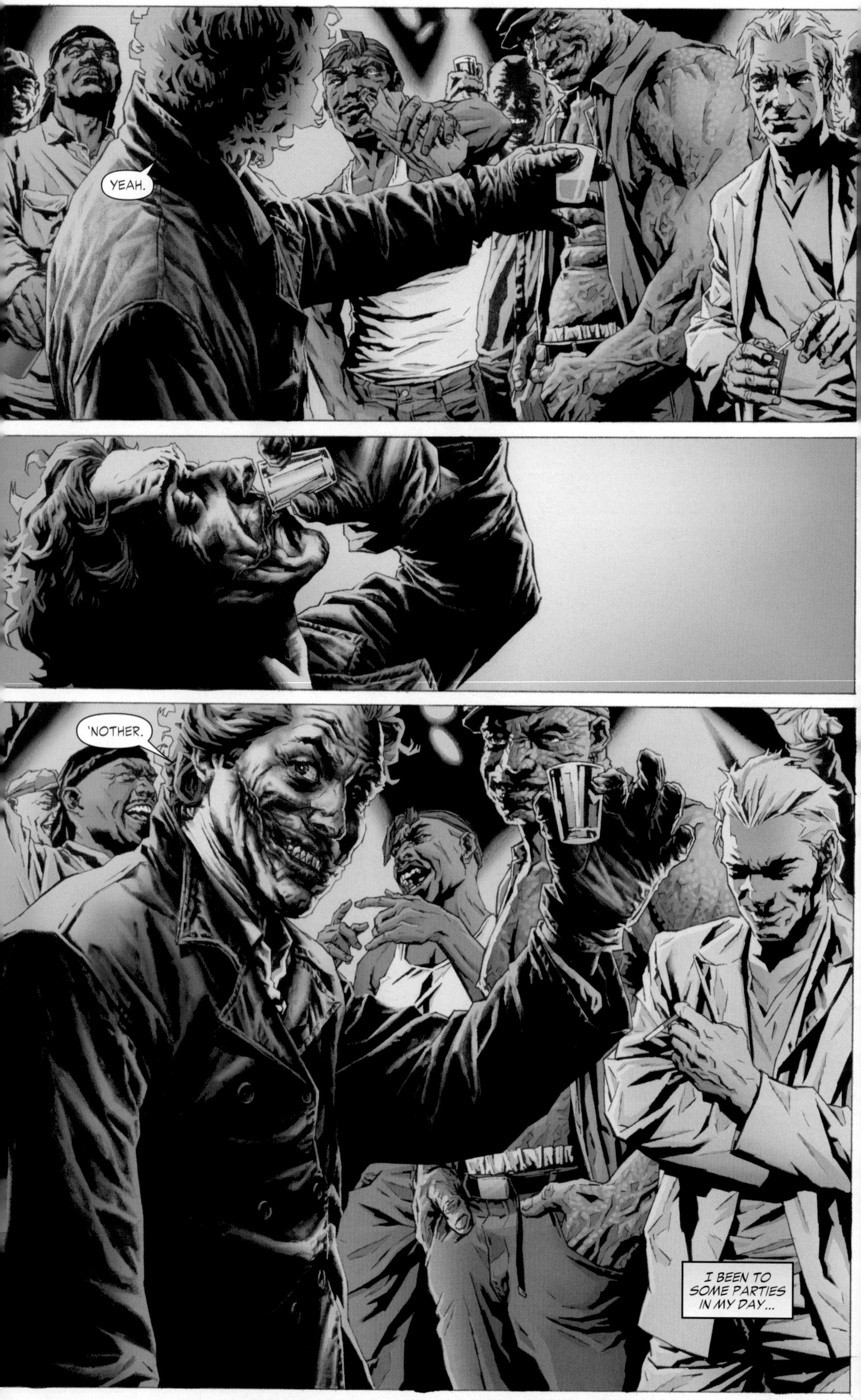
YEAH.
'NOTHER.
I BEEN TO SOME PARTIES IN MY DAY...

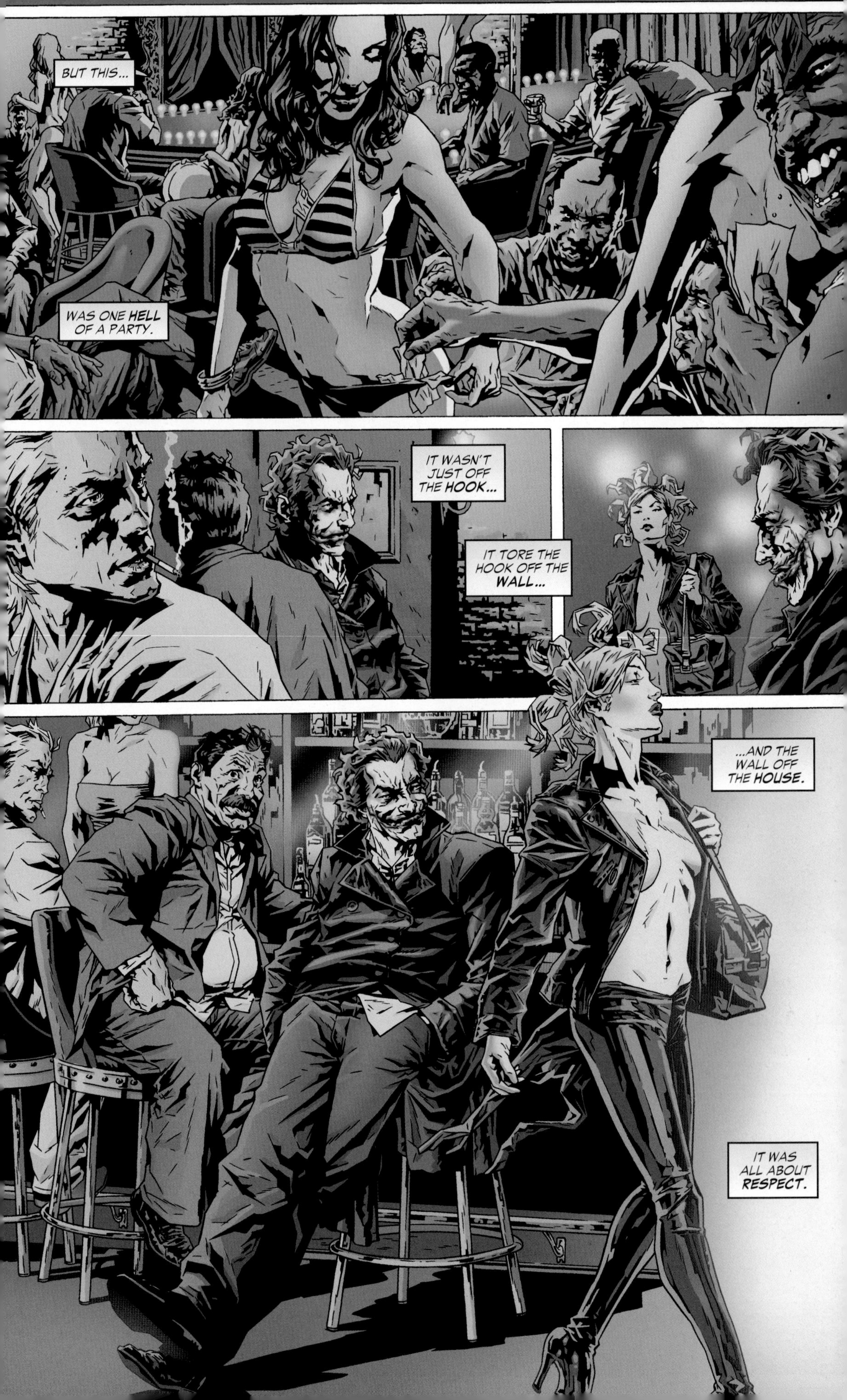
BUT THIS...
WAS ONE HELL OF A PARTY.
IT WASN'T JUST OFF THE HOOK...
IT TORE THE HOOK OFF THE WALL...
...AND THE WALL OFF THE HOUSE.
IT WAS ALL ABOUT RESPECT.

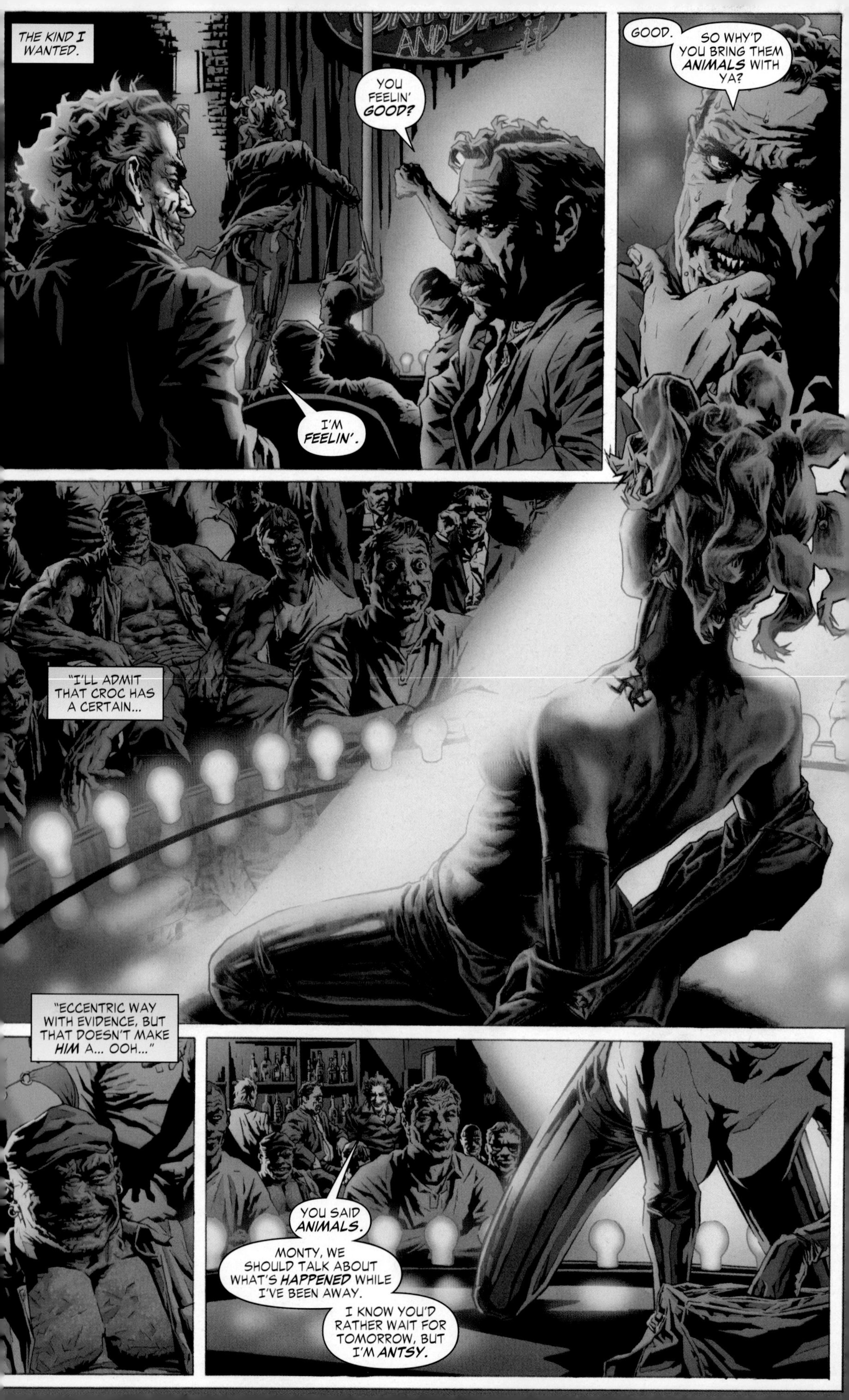
THE KIND I WANTED.
YOU FEELIN' GOOD?
I'M FEELIN'.
GOOD.
SO WHY'D YOU BRING THEM ANIMALS WITH YA?
"I'LL ADMIT THAT CROC HAS A CERTAIN...
"ECCENTRIC WAY WITH EVIDENCE, BUT THAT DOESN'T MAKE HIM A... OOH..."
YOU SAID ANIMALS.
MONTY, WE SHOULD TALK ABOUT WHAT'S HAPPENED WHILE I'VE BEEN AWAY.
I KNOW YOU'D RATHER WAIT FOR TOMORROW, BUT I'M ANTSY.

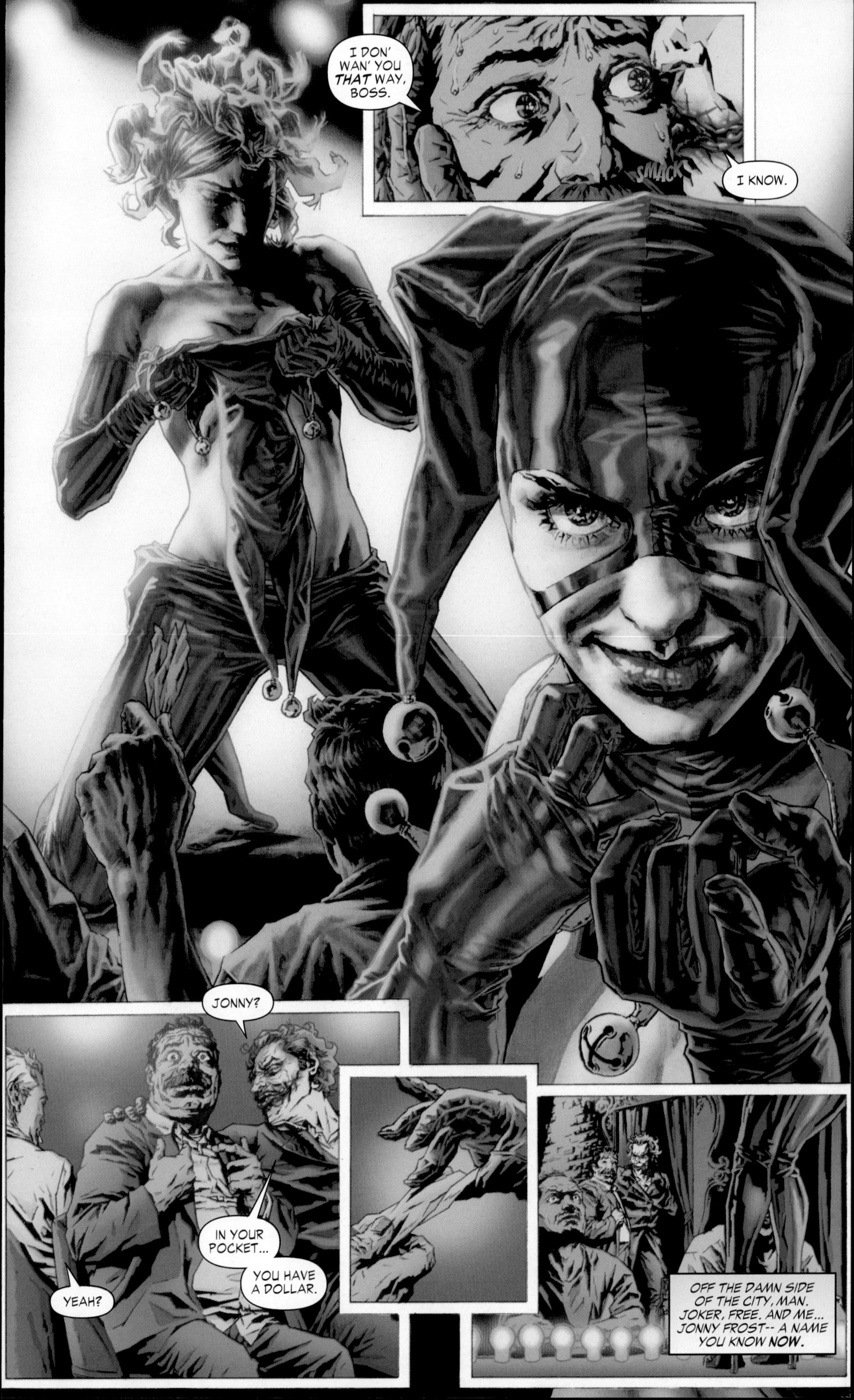
I DON' WAN' YOU THAT WAY, BOSS.
SMACK
I KNOW.
JONNY?
IN YOUR POCKET...
YOU HAVE A DOLLAR.
YEAH?
OFF THE DAMN SIDE OF THE CITY, MAN. JOKER, FREE. AND ME... JONNY FROST-- A NAME YOU KNOW NOW.

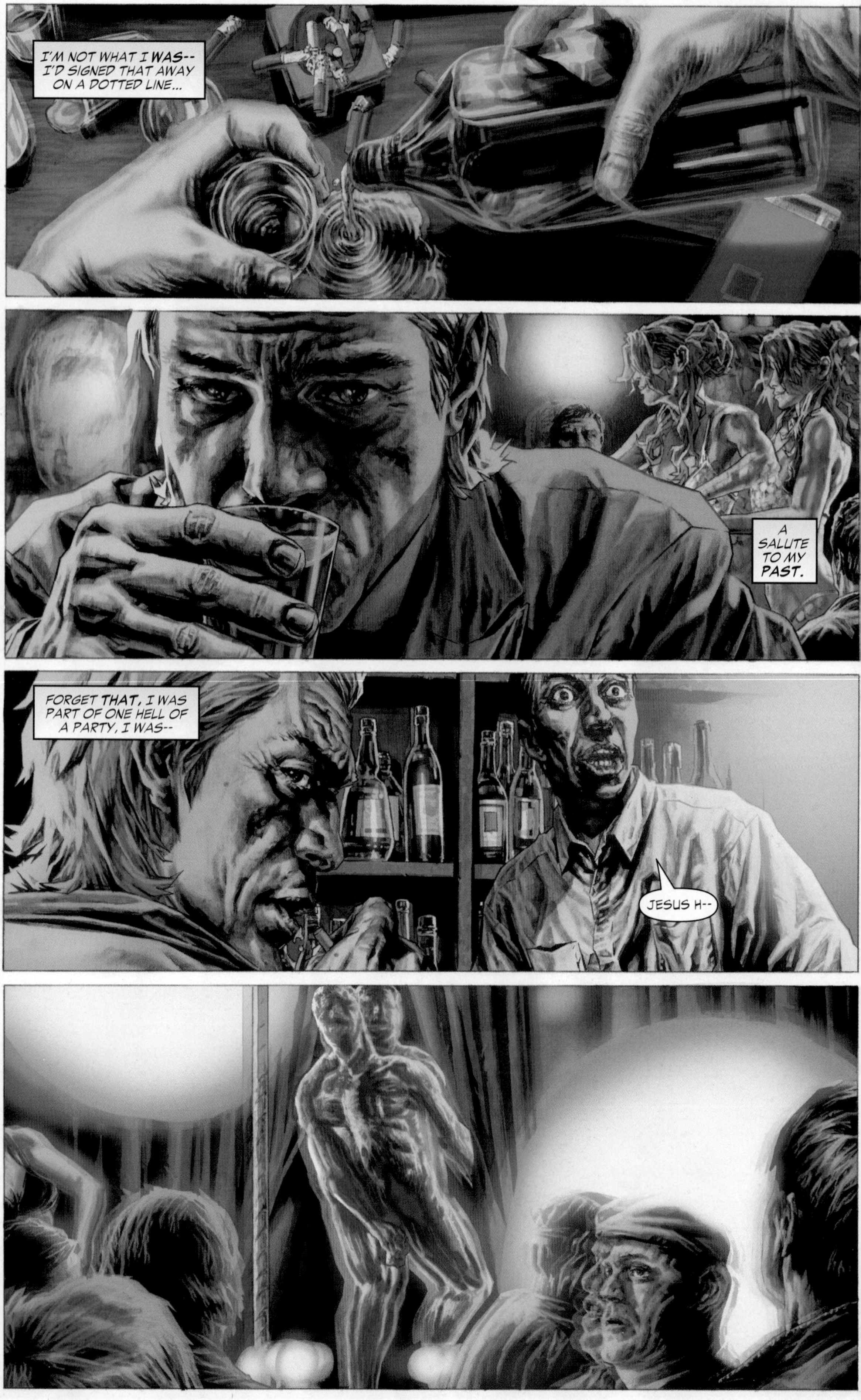
I'M NOT WHAT I WAS--
I'D SIGNED THAT AWAY ON A DOTTED LINE...
A SALUTE TO MY PAST.
FORGET THAT, I WAS PART OF ONE HELL OF A PARTY, I WAS--
JESUS H--

SLACK

SHLLUMP!

HEH.

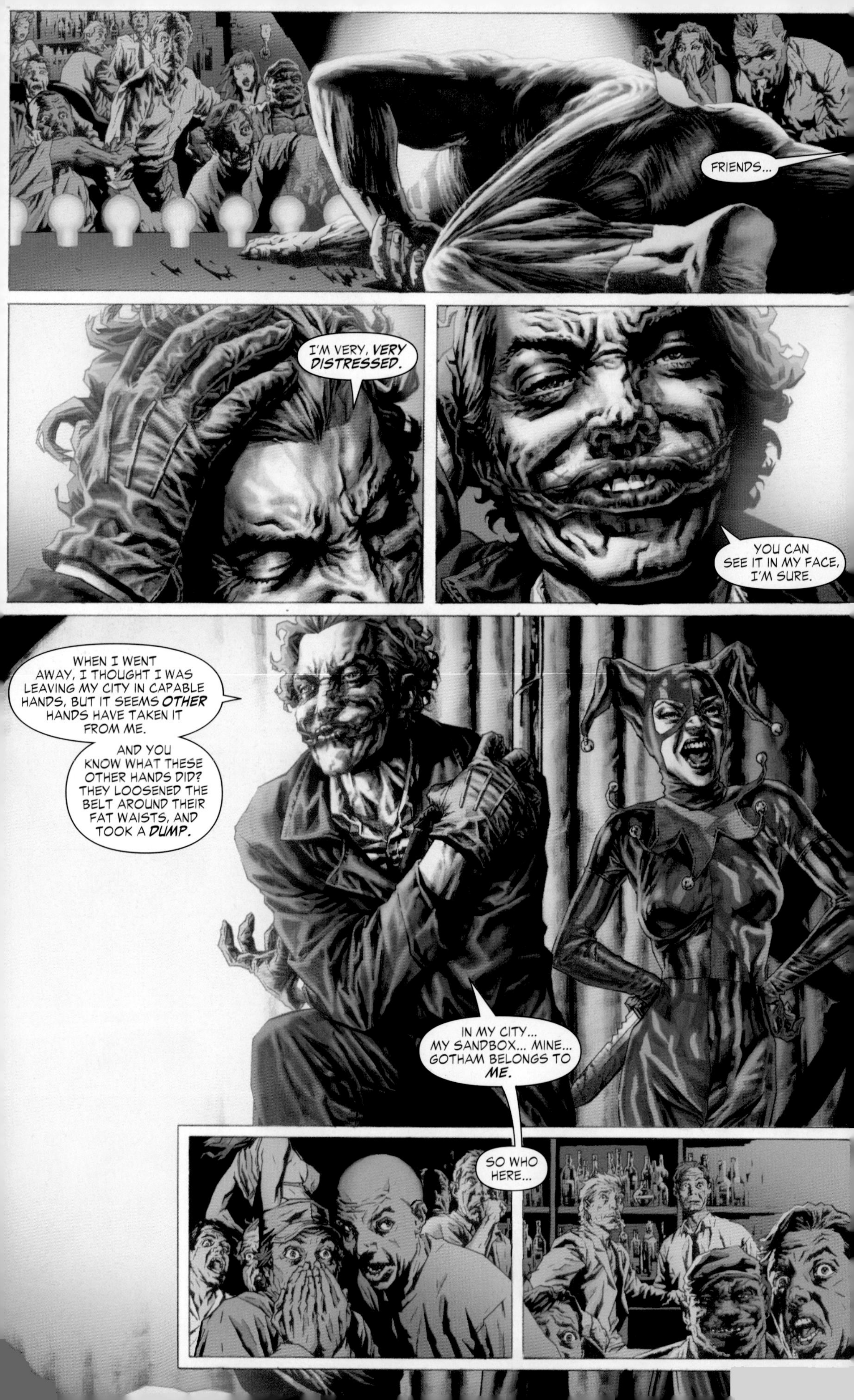
FRIENDS...
I'M VERY, VERY DISTRESSED.
YOU CAN SEE IT IN MY FACE, I'M SURE.
WHEN I WENT AWAY, I THOUGHT I WAS LEAVING MY CITY IN CAPABLE HANDS, BUT IT SEEMS OTHER HANDS HAVE TAKEN IT FROM ME.
AND YOU KNOW WHAT THESE OTHER HANDS DID? THEY LOOSENED THE BELT AROUND THEIR FAT WAISTS, AND TOOK A DUMP.
IN MY CITY... MY SANDBOX... MINE... GOTHAM BELONGS TO ME.
SO WHO HERE...

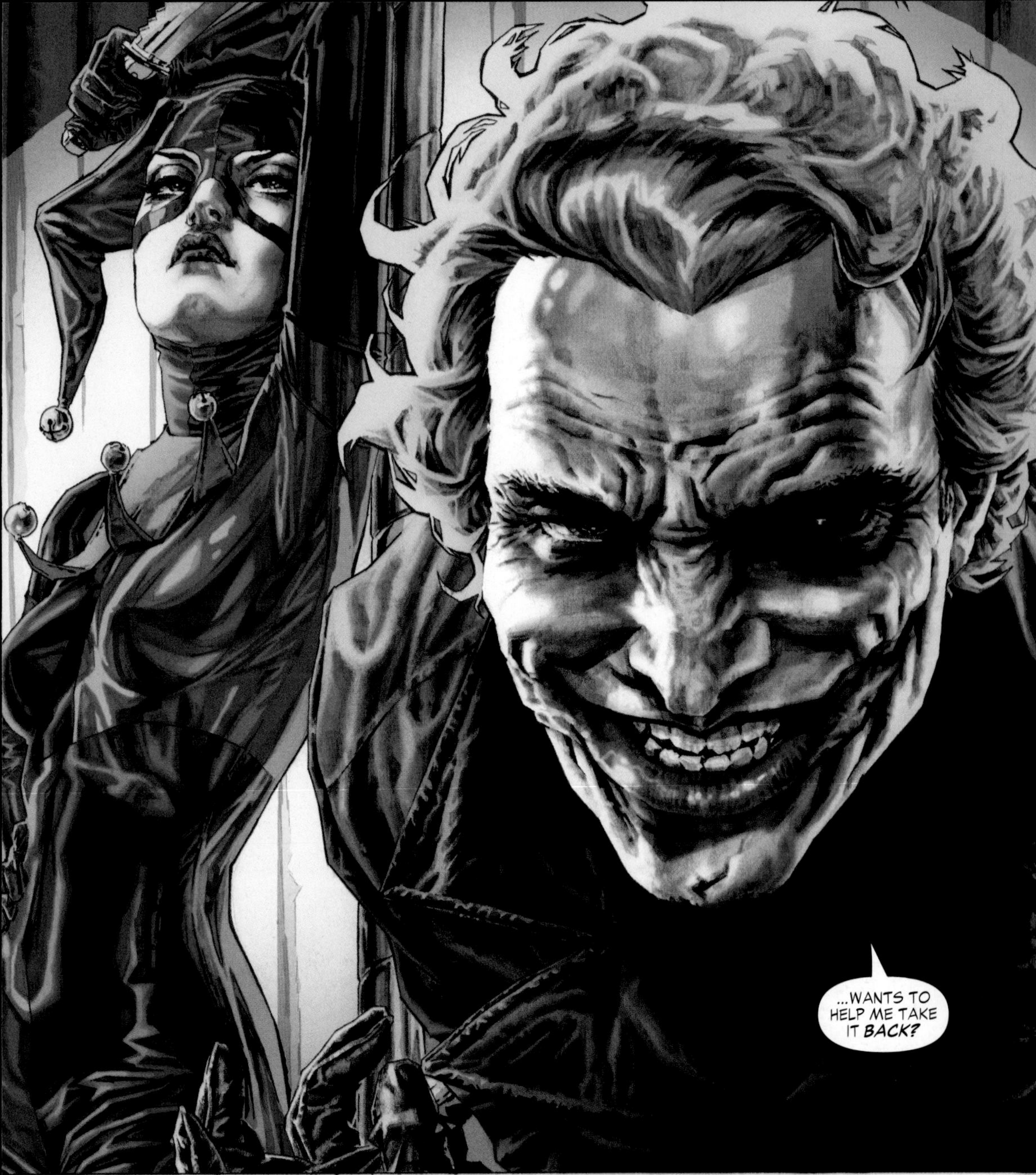
...WANTS TO HELP ME TAKE IT BACK?

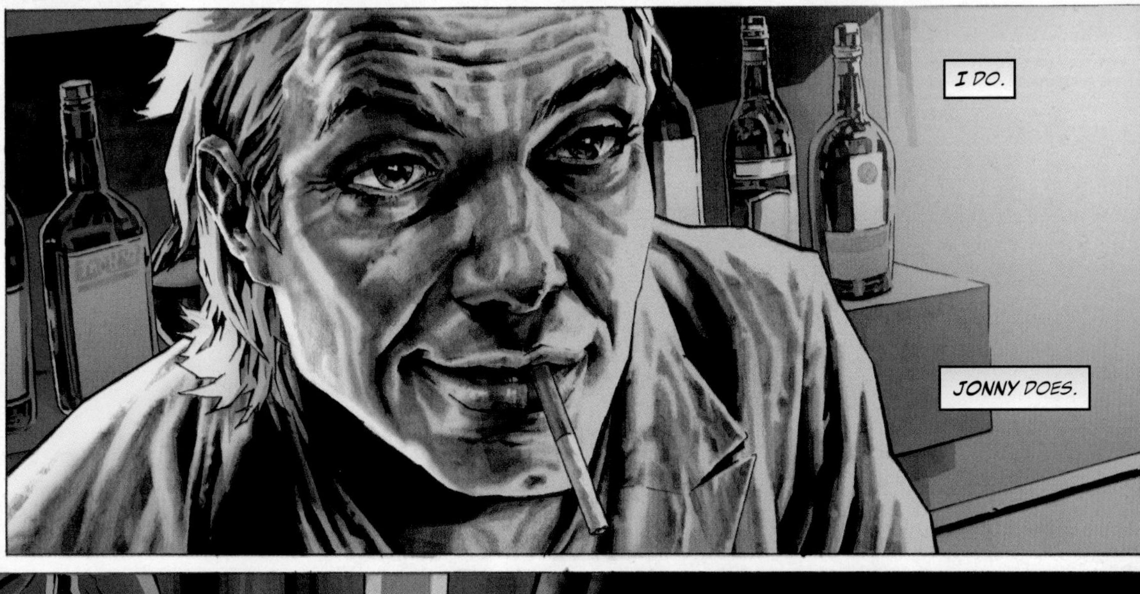
I DO.
JONNY DOES.

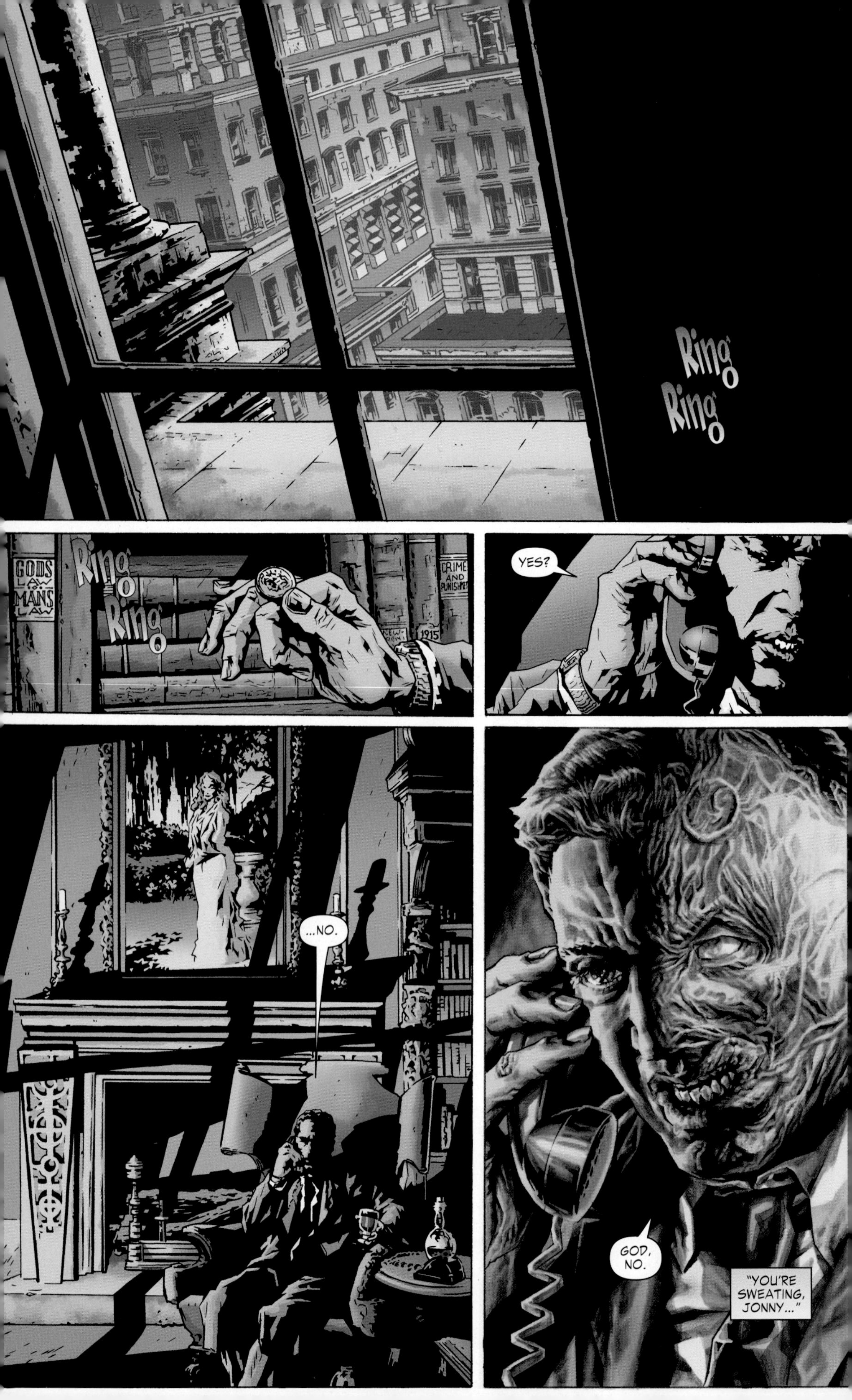
RING RING
GODS LAW MANS LAW
CRIME AND PUNISHMENT
1915
RING RING
YES?
...NO.
GOD, NO.
"YOU'RE SWEATING, JONNY..."

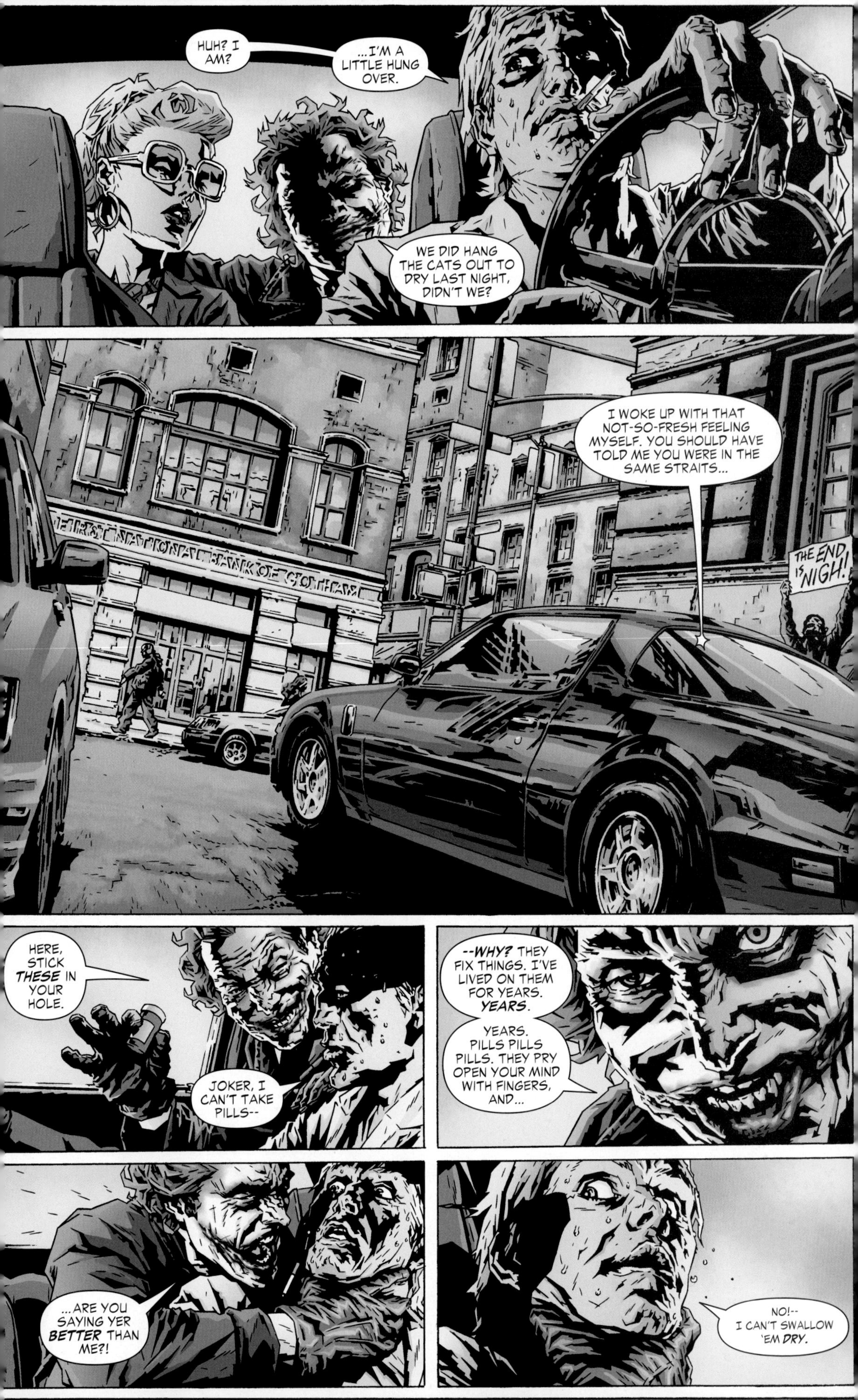
HUH? I AM?
...I'M A LITTLE HUNG OVER.
WE DID HANG THE CATS OUT TO DRY LAST NIGHT, DIDN'T WE?
FIRST NATIONAL BANK OF GOTHAM
THE END IS NIGH!
I WOKE UP WITH THAT NOT-SO-FRESH FEELING MYSELF. YOU SHOULD HAVE TOLD ME YOU WERE IN THE SAME STRAITS...
HERE, STICK THESE IN YOUR HOLE.
JOKER, I CAN'T TAKE PILLS--
--WHY? THEY FIX THINGS. I'VE LIVED ON THEM FOR YEARS. YEARS.
YEARS. PILLS PILLS PILLS. THEY PRY OPEN YOUR MIND WITH FINGERS, AND...
...ARE YOU SAYING YER BETTER THAN ME?!
NO!-- I CAN'T SWALLOW 'EM DRY.

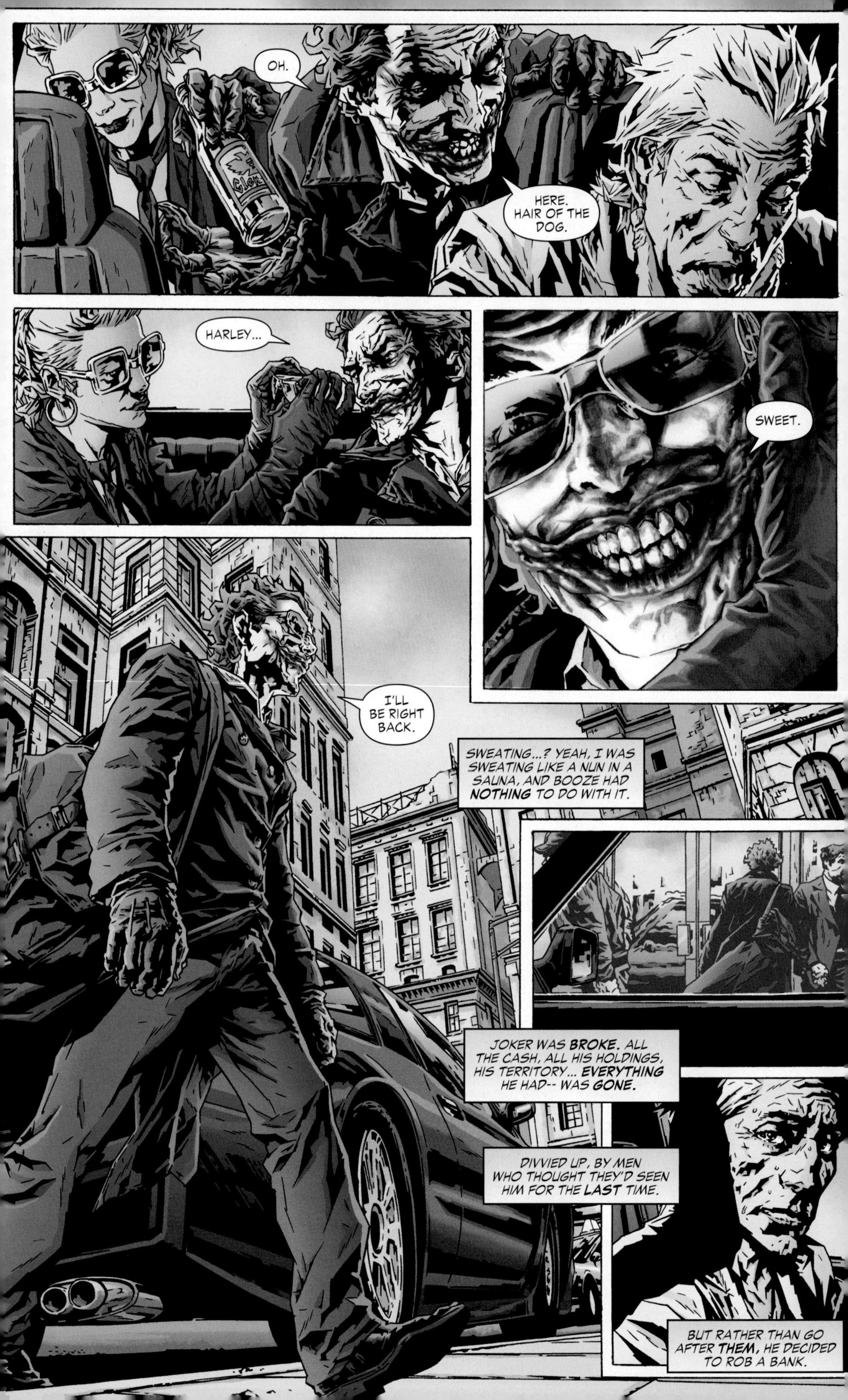
OH.
HERE. HAIR OF THE DOG.
HARLEY...
SWEET.
I'LL BE RIGHT BACK.
SWEATING...? YEAH, I WAS SWEATING LIKE A NUN IN A SAUNA, AND BOOZE HAD NOTHING TO DO WITH IT.
JOKER WAS BROKE. ALL THE CASH, ALL HIS HOLDINGS, HIS TERRITORY... EVERYTHING HE HAD-- WAS GONE.
DIVVIED UP, BY MEN WHO THOUGHT THEY'D SEEN HIM FOR THE LAST TIME.
BUT RATHER THAN GO AFTER THEM, HE DECIDED TO ROB A BANK.

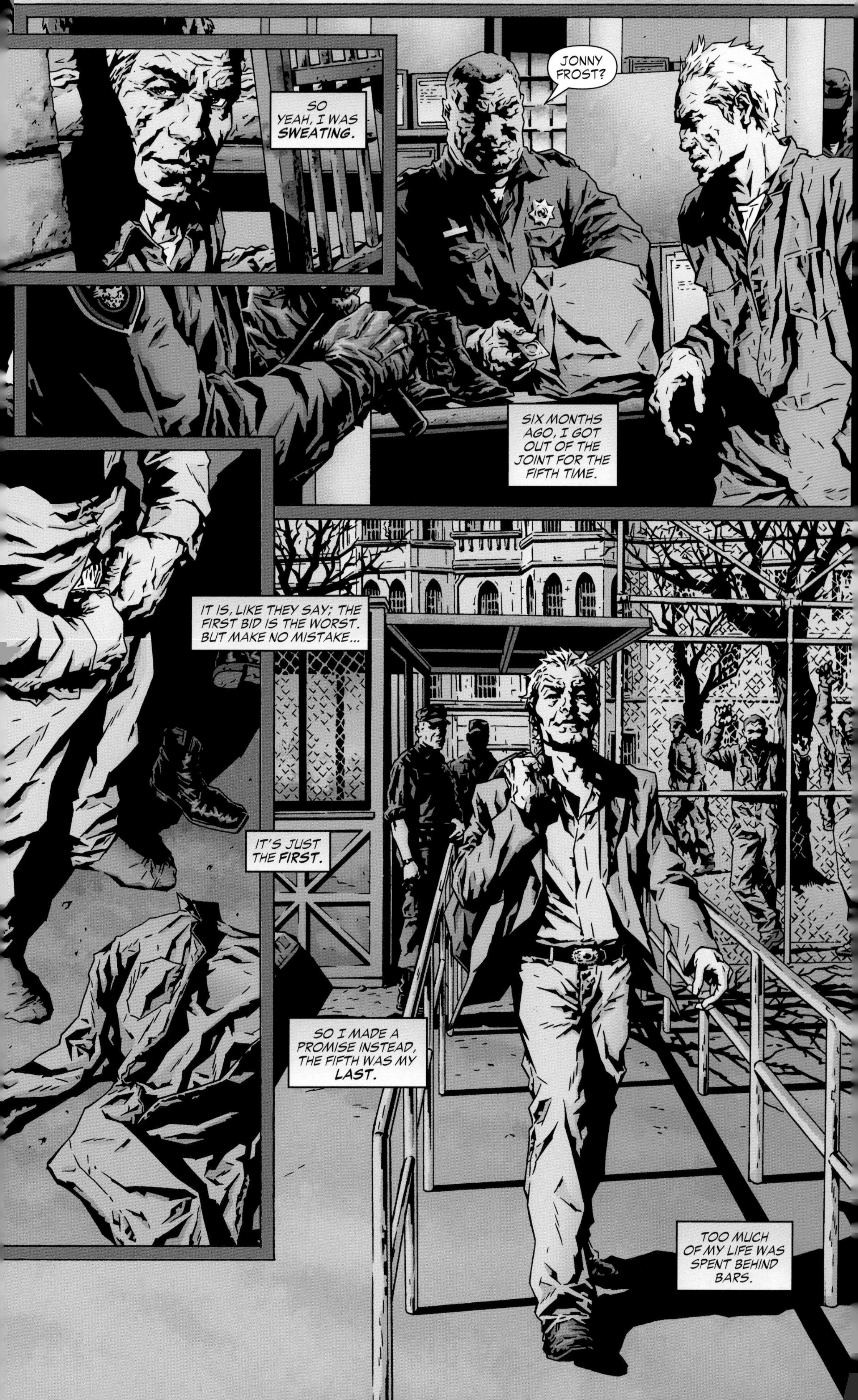

SO YEAH, I WAS SWEATING.
JONNY FROST?
SIX MONTHS AGO, I GOT OUT OF THE JOINT FOR THE FIFTH TIME.
IT IS, LIKE THEY SAY; THE FIRST BID IS THE WORST. BUT MAKE NO MISTAKE...
IT'S JUST THE FIRST.
SO I MADE A PROMISE INSTEAD, THE FIFTH WAS MY LAST.
TOO MUCH OF MY LIFE WAS SPENT BEHIND BARS.

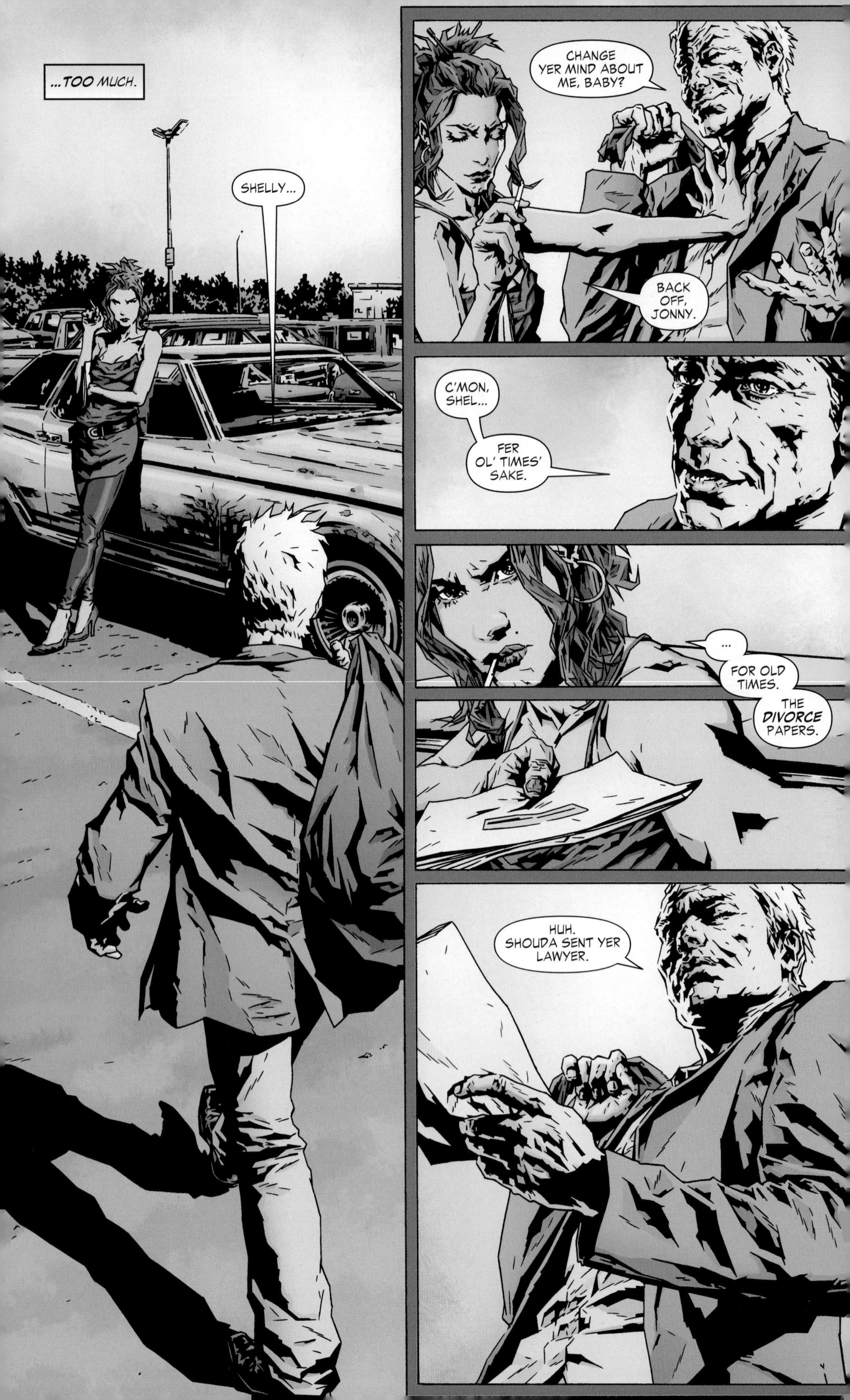
...TOO MUCH.
SHELLY...
CHANGE YER MIND ABOUT ME, BABY?
BACK OFF, JONNY.
C'MON, SHEL...
FER OL' TIMES' SAKE.
...
FOR OLD TIMES.
THE DIVORCE PAPERS.
HUH. SHOUDA SENT YER LAWYER.

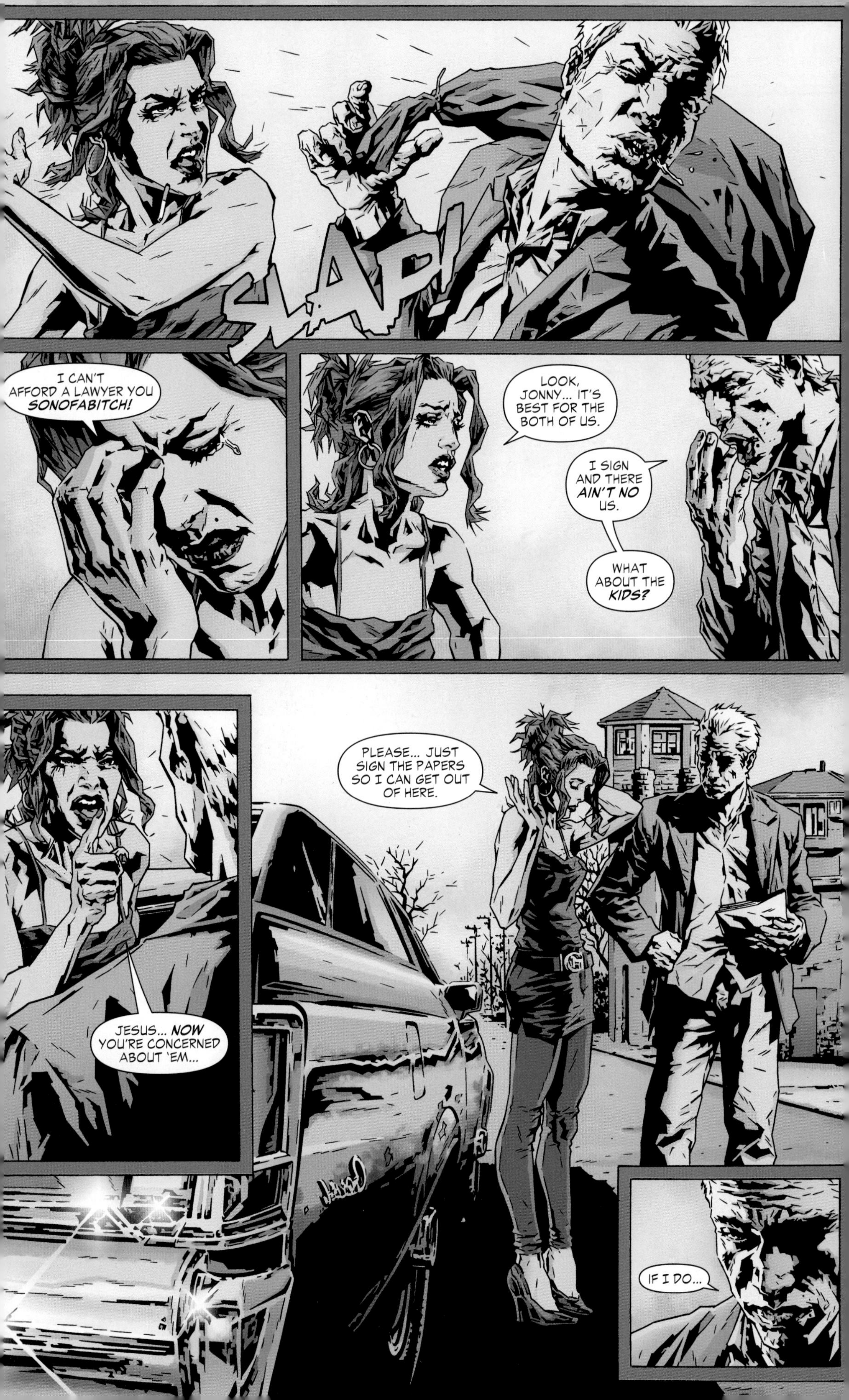
SLAP!
I CAN'T AFFORD A LAWYER YOU SONOFABITCH!
LOOK, JONNY... IT'S BEST FOR THE BOTH OF US.
I SIGN AND THERE AIN'T NO US.
WHAT ABOUT THE KIDS?
JESUS... NOW YOU'RE CONCERNED ABOUT 'EM...
PLEASE... JUST SIGN THE PAPERS SO I CAN GET OUT OF HERE.
IF I DO...

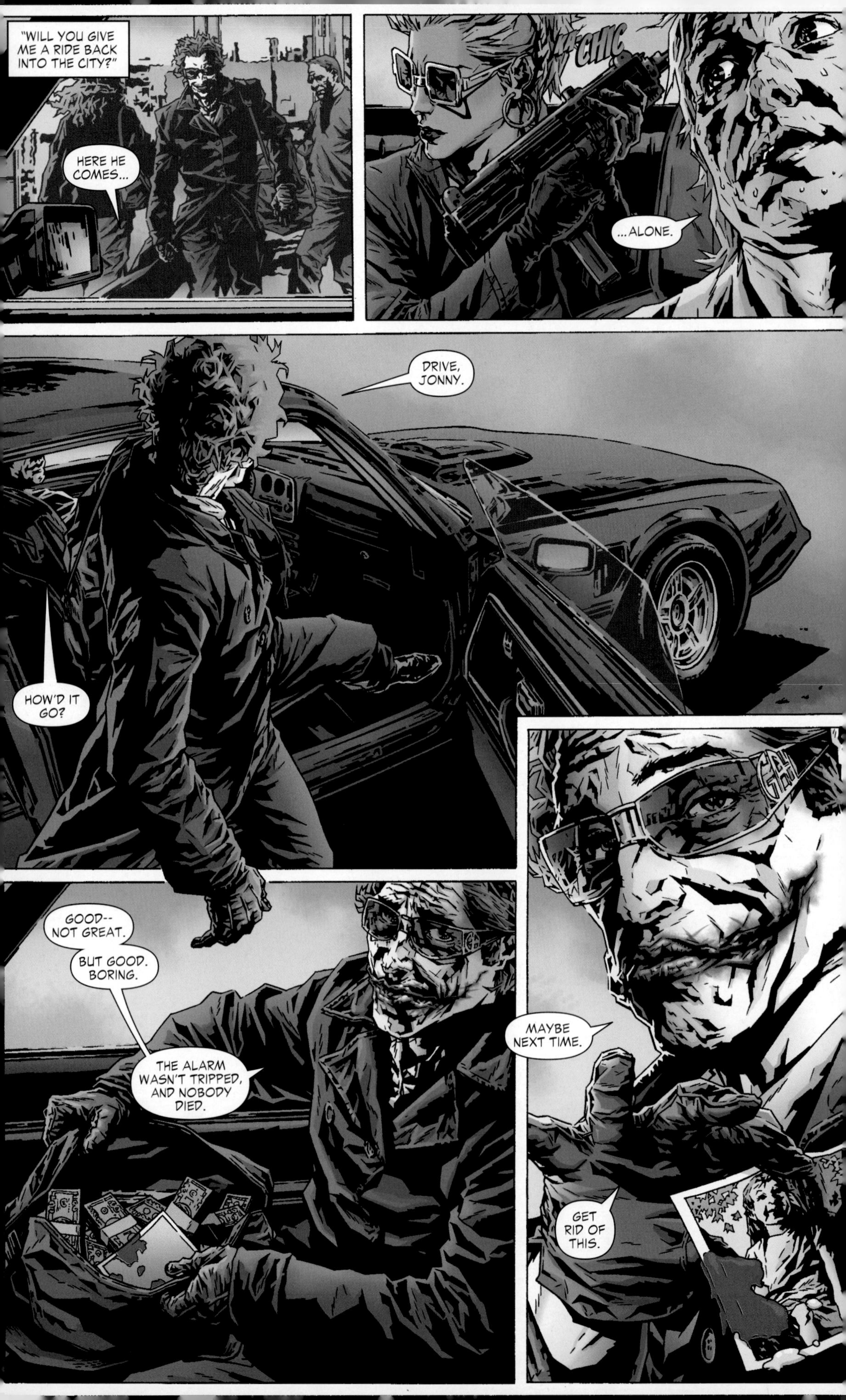
"WILL YOU GIVE ME A RIDE BACK INTO THE CITY?"
HERE HE COMES...
CHIC
...ALONE.
DRIVE, JONNY.
HOW'D IT GO?
GOOD-- NOT GREAT.
BUT GOOD. BORING.
THE ALARM WASN'T TRIPPED, AND NOBODY DIED.
MAYBE NEXT TIME.
GET RID OF THIS.

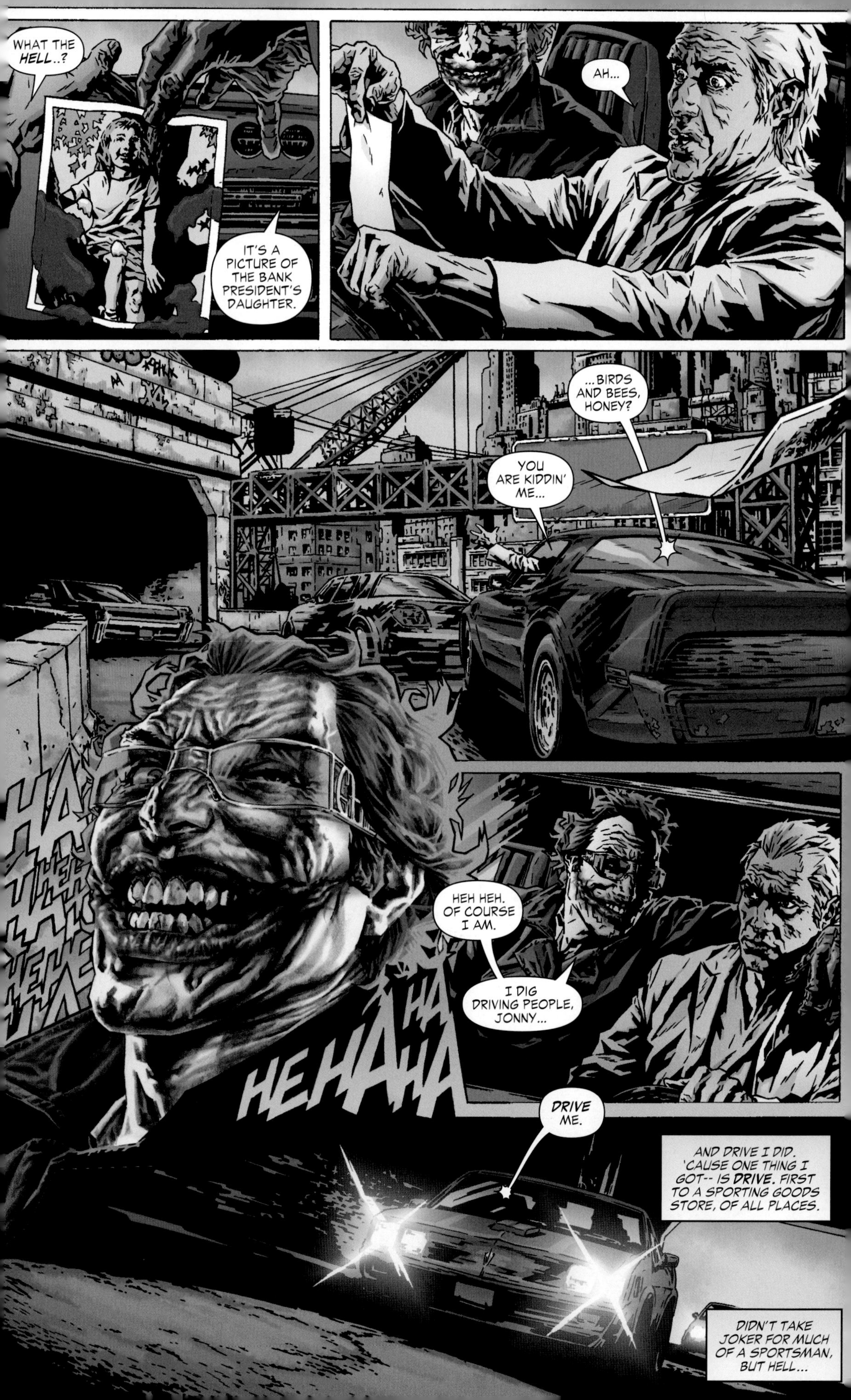
WHAT THE HELL..?
IT'S A PICTURE OF THE BANK PRESIDENT'S DAUGHTER.
AH...
...BIRDS AND BEES, HONEY?
YOU ARE KIDDIN' ME...
HEH HEH. OF COURSE I AM.
I DIG DRIVING PEOPLE, JONNY...
HEHAHA
DRIVE ME.
AND DRIVE I DID. 'CAUSE ONE THING I GOT-- IS DRIVE. FIRST TO A SPORTING GOODS STORE, OF ALL PLACES.
DIDN'T TAKE JOKER FOR MUCH OF A SPORTSMAN, BUT HELL...

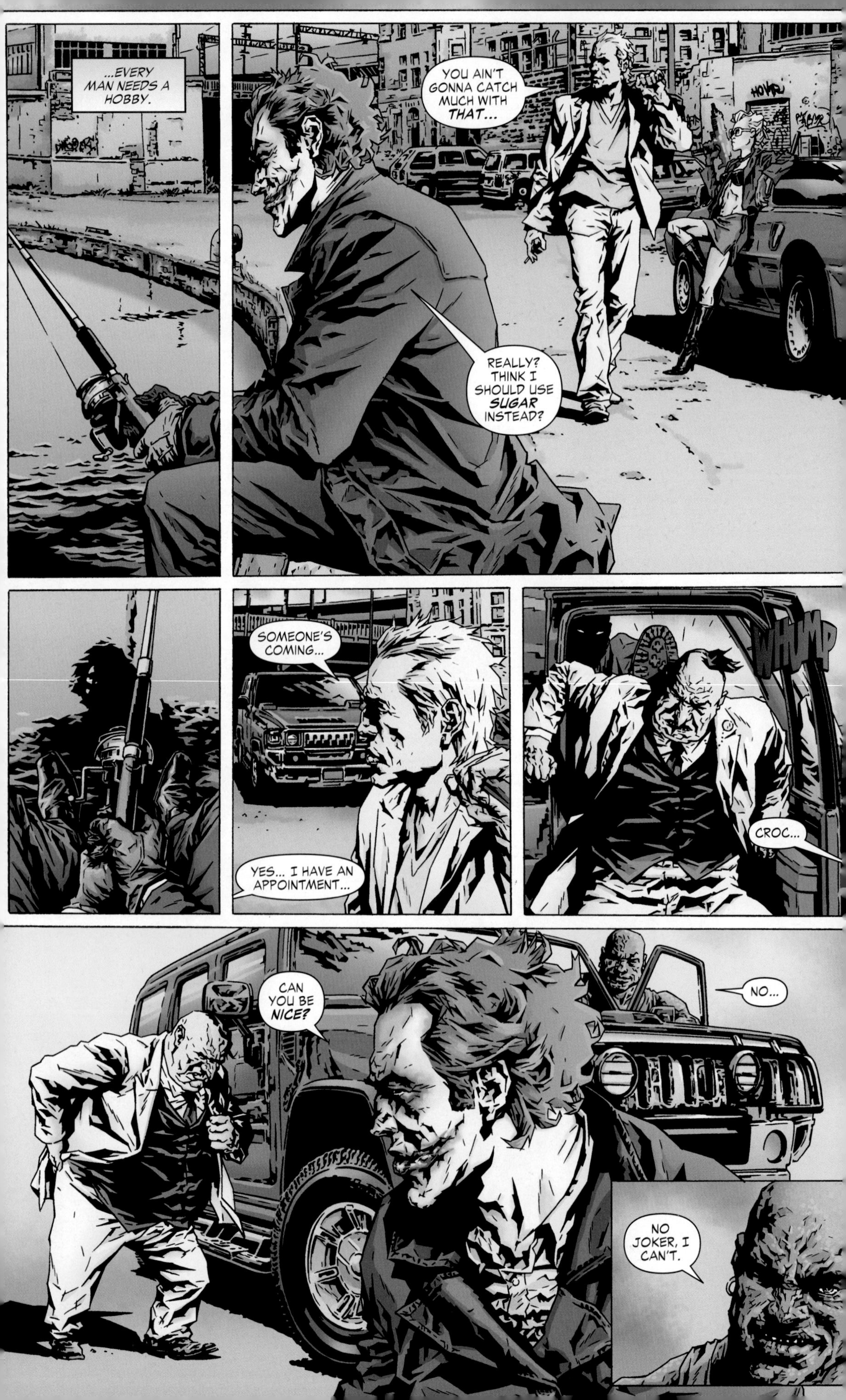
...EVERY MAN NEEDS A HOBBY.
YOU AIN'T GONNA CATCH MUCH WITH THAT...
REALLY? THINK I SHOULD USE SUGAR INSTEAD?
SOMEONE'S COMING...
YES... I HAVE AN APPOINTMENT...
WHUMP
CROC...
CAN YOU BE NICE?
NO...
NO JOKER, I CAN'T.

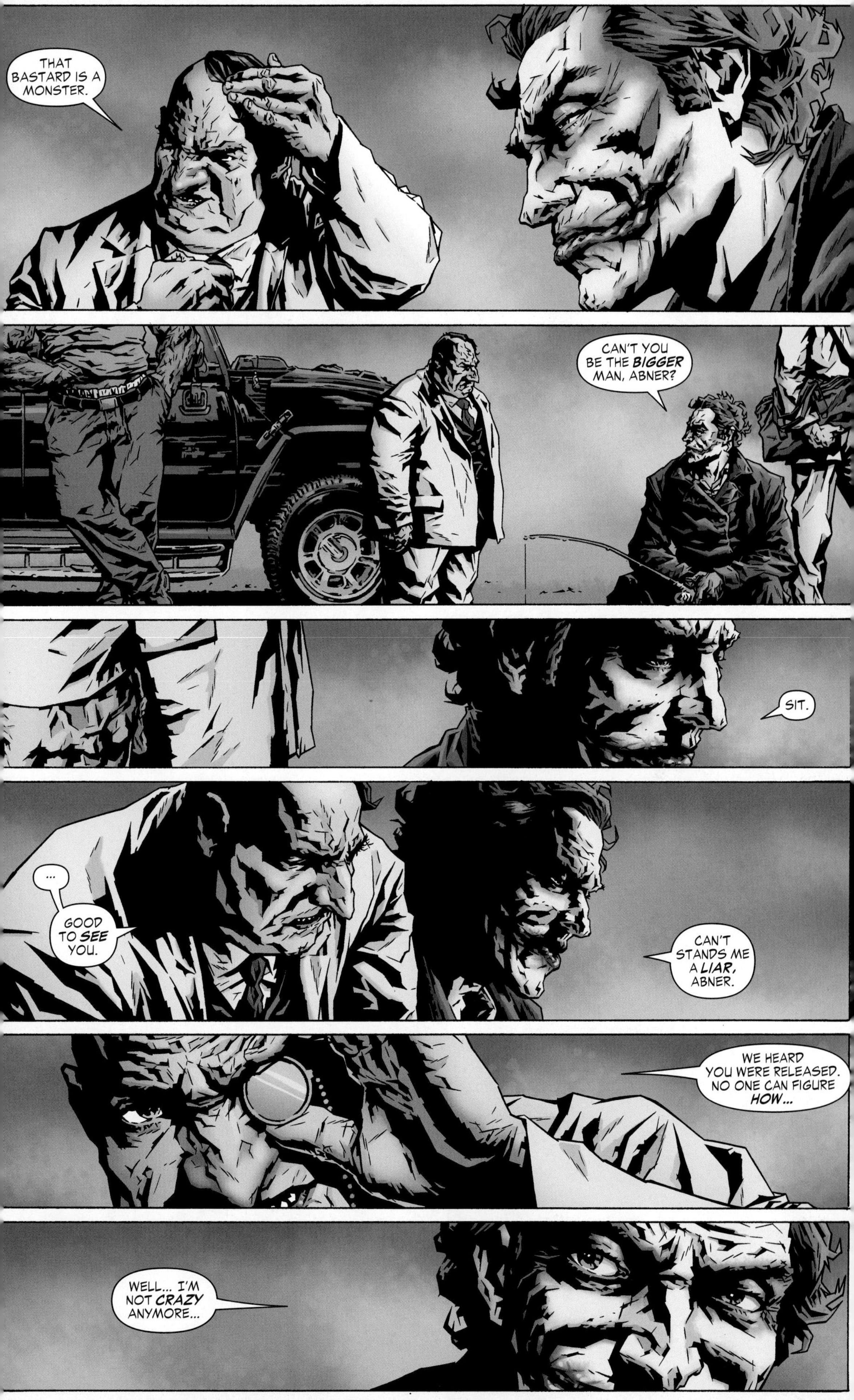
THAT BASTARD IS A MONSTER.
CAN'T YOU BE THE BIGGER MAN, ABNER?
SIT.
...
GOOD TO SEE YOU.
CAN'T STANDS ME A LIAR, ABNER.
WE HEARD YOU WERE RELEASED. NO ONE CAN FIGURE HOW...
WELL... I'M NOT CRAZY ANYMORE...

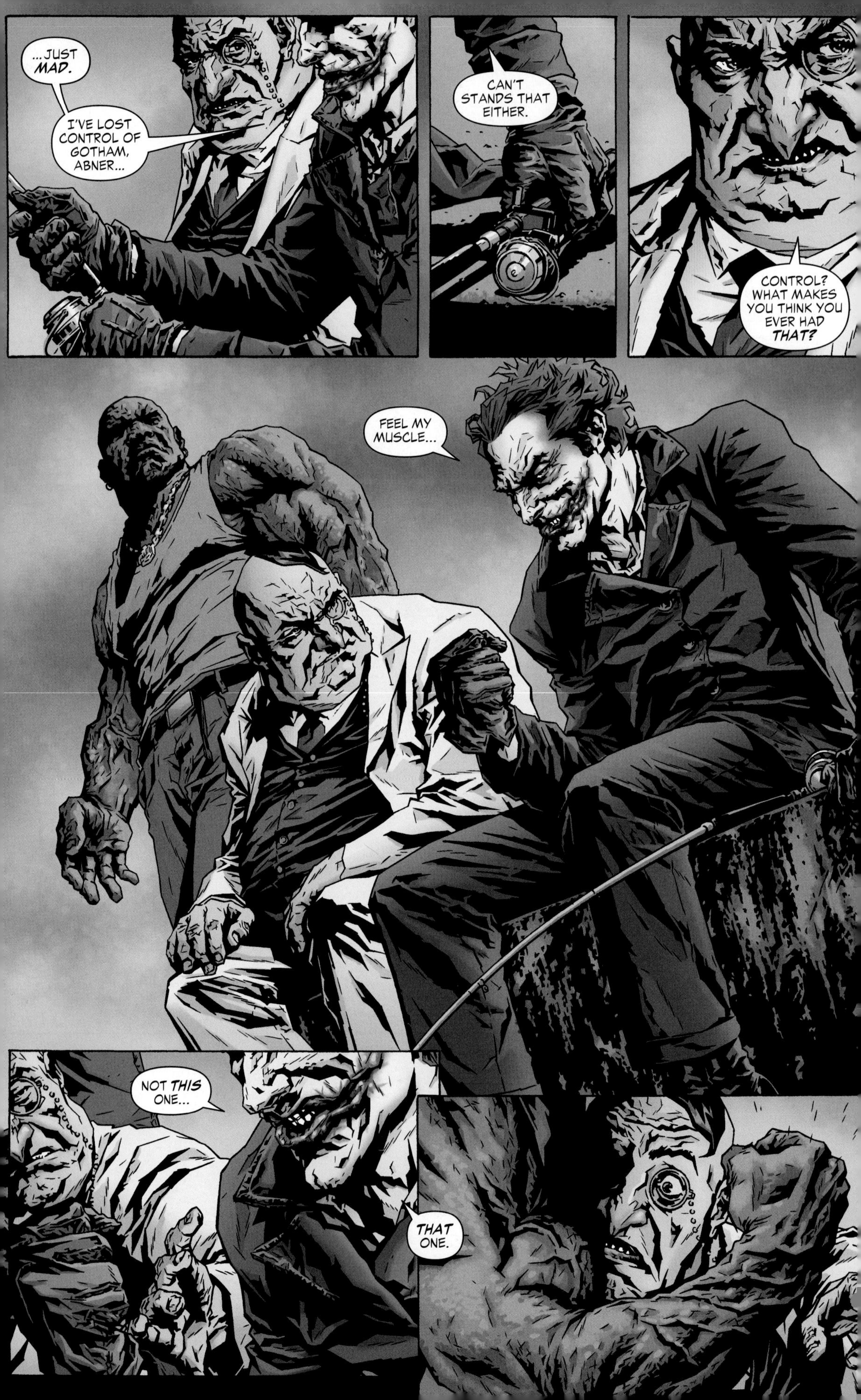
...JUST *MAD.*
I'VE LOST CONTROL OF GOTHAM, ABNER...
CAN'T STANDS THAT EITHER.
CONTROL? WHAT MAKES YOU THINK YOU EVER HAD *THAT?*
FEEL MY MUSCLE...
NOT *THIS* ONE...
THAT ONE.

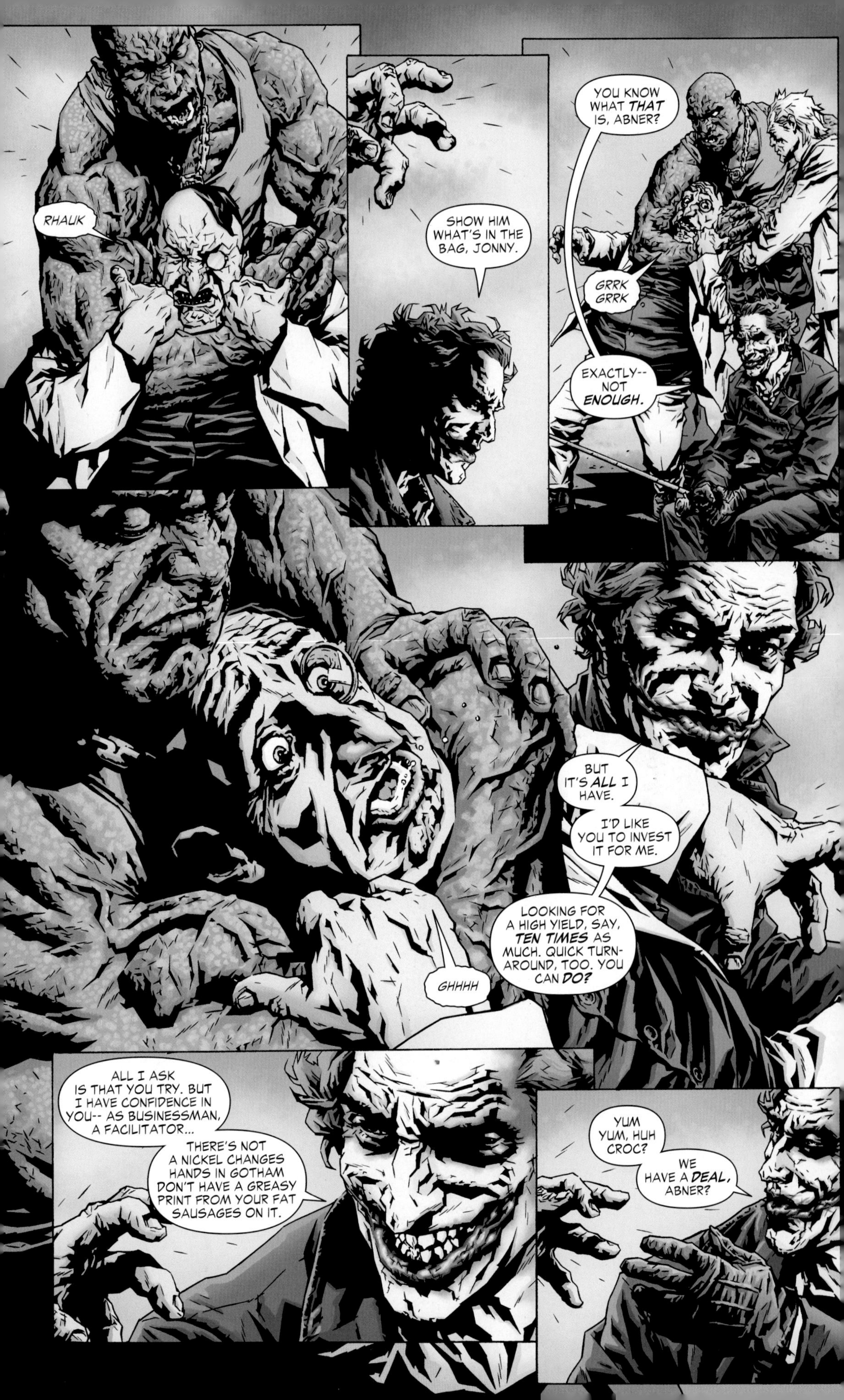
RHAUK
SHOW HIM WHAT'S IN THE BAG, JONNY.
YOU KNOW WHAT THAT IS, ABNER?
GRRK GRRK
EXACTLY--NOT ENOUGH.
BUT IT'S ALL I HAVE.
I'D LIKE YOU TO INVEST IT FOR ME.
LOOKING FOR A HIGH YIELD, SAY, TEN TIMES AS MUCH. QUICK TURN-AROUND, TOO. YOU CAN DO?
GHHHH
ALL I ASK IS THAT YOU TRY. BUT I HAVE CONFIDENCE IN YOU-- AS BUSINESSMAN, A FACILITATOR...
THERE'S NOT A NICKEL CHANGES HANDS IN GOTHAM DON'T HAVE A GREASY PRINT FROM YOUR FAT SAUSAGES ON IT.
YUM YUM, HUH CROC?
WE HAVE A DEAL, ABNER?

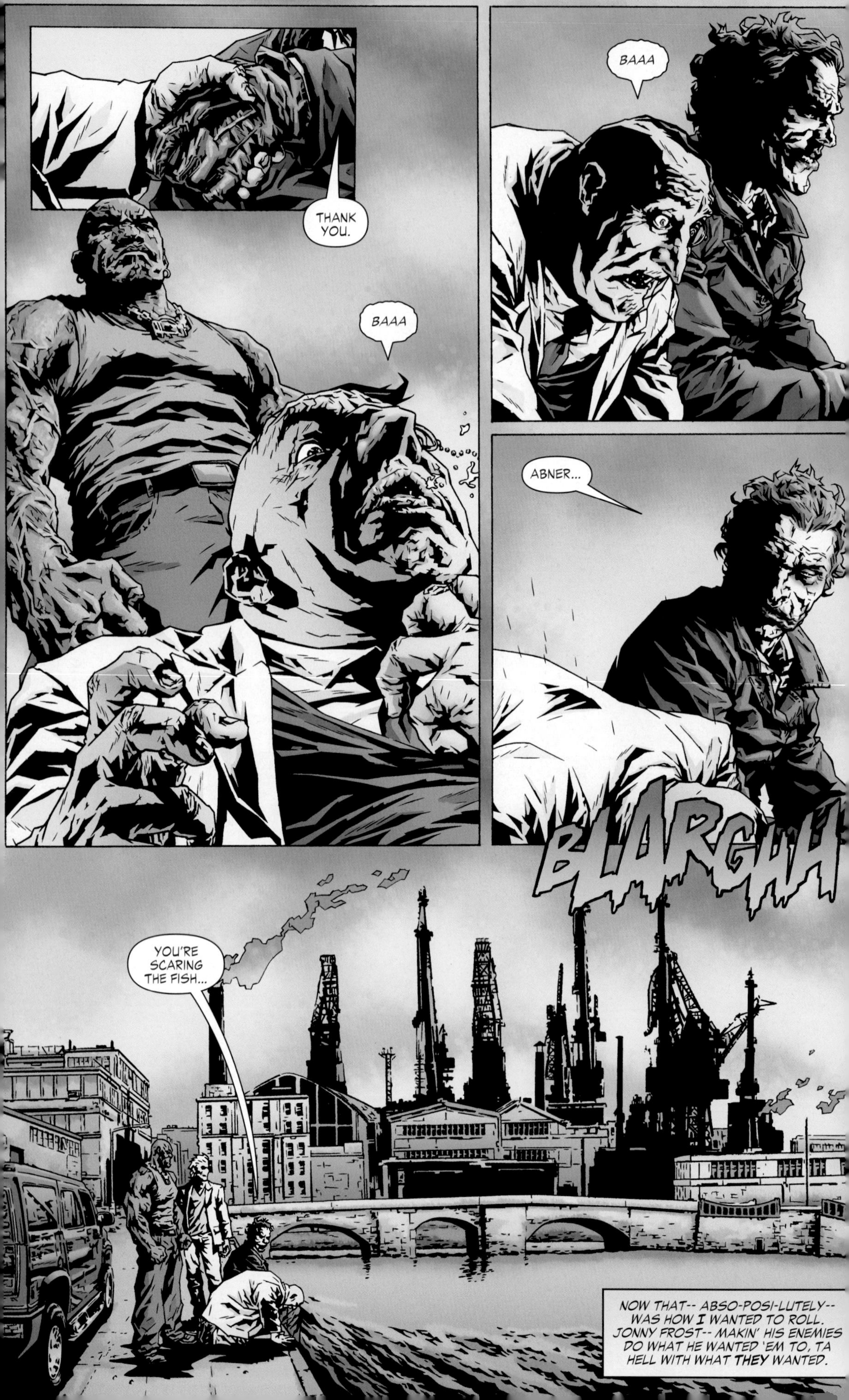
THANK YOU.
BAAA
BAAA
ABNER...
BLARGHH
YOU'RE SCARING THE FISH...
NOW THAT-- ABSO-POSI-LUTELY-- WAS HOW I WANTED TO ROLL. JONNY FROST-- MAKIN' HIS ENEMIES DO WHAT HE WANTED 'EM TO, TA HELL WITH WHAT THEY WANTED.

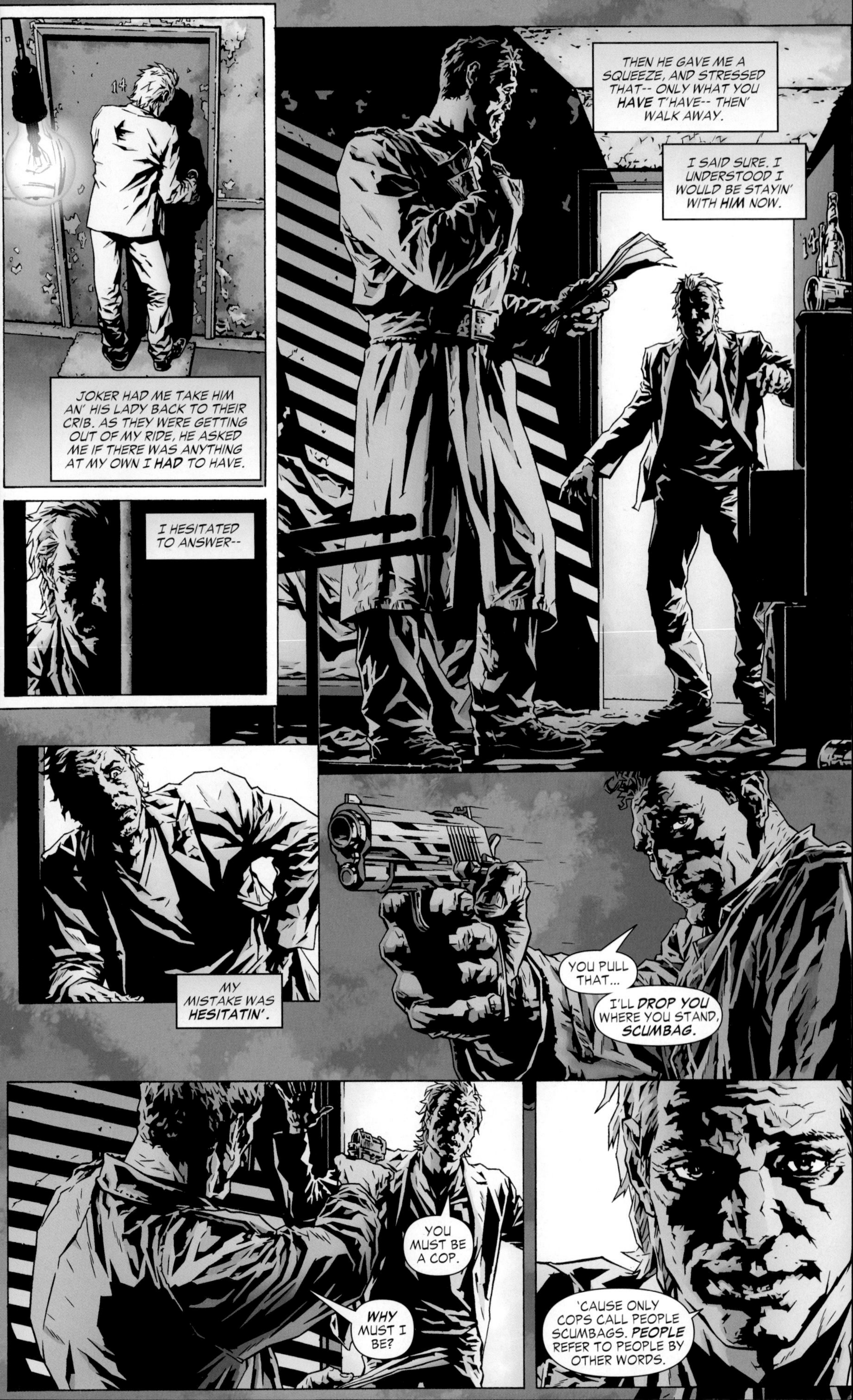
JOKER HAD ME TAKE HIM AN' HIS LADY BACK TO THEIR CRIB. AS THEY WERE GETTING OUT OF MY RIDE, HE ASKED ME IF THERE WAS ANYTHING AT MY OWN I HAD TO HAVE.
THEN HE GAVE ME A SQUEEZE, AND STRESSED THAT-- ONLY WHAT YOU HAVE T'HAVE-- THEN' WALK AWAY.
I SAID SURE. I UNDERSTOOD I WOULD BE STAYIN' WITH HIM NOW.
I HESITATED TO ANSWER--
MY MISTAKE WAS HESITATIN'.
YOU PULL THAT...
I'LL DROP YOU WHERE YOU STAND, SCUMBAG.
YOU MUST BE A COP.
WHY MUST I BE?
'CAUSE ONLY COPS CALL PEOPLE SCUMBAGS. PEOPLE REFER TO PEOPLE BY OTHER WORDS.

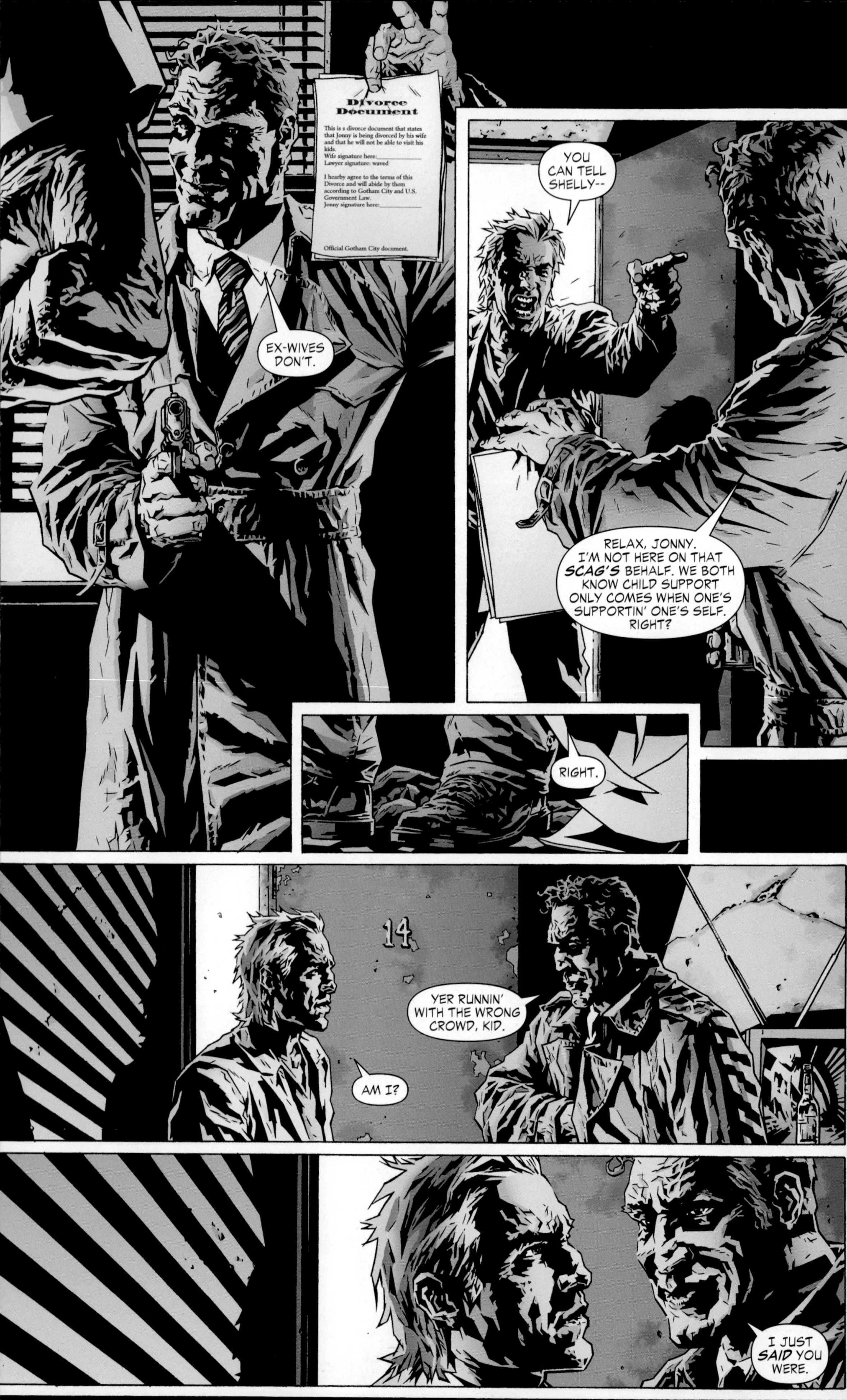
Divorce Document
This is s divorce document that states that Jonny is being divorced by his wife and that he will not be able to visit his kids.
Wife signature here:____________
Lawyer signature: waved
I hearby agree to the terms of this Divorce and will abide by them according to Gotham City and U.S. Government Law.
Jonny signature here:____________
Official Gotham City document.
EX-WIVES DON'T.
YOU CAN TELL SHELLY--
RELAX, JONNY. I'M NOT HERE ON THAT *SCAG'S* BEHALF. WE BOTH KNOW CHILD SUPPORT ONLY COMES WHEN ONE'S SUPPORTIN' ONE'S SELF. RIGHT?
RIGHT.
14
YER RUNNIN' WITH THE WRONG CROWD, KID.
AM I?
I JUST *SAID* YOU WERE.

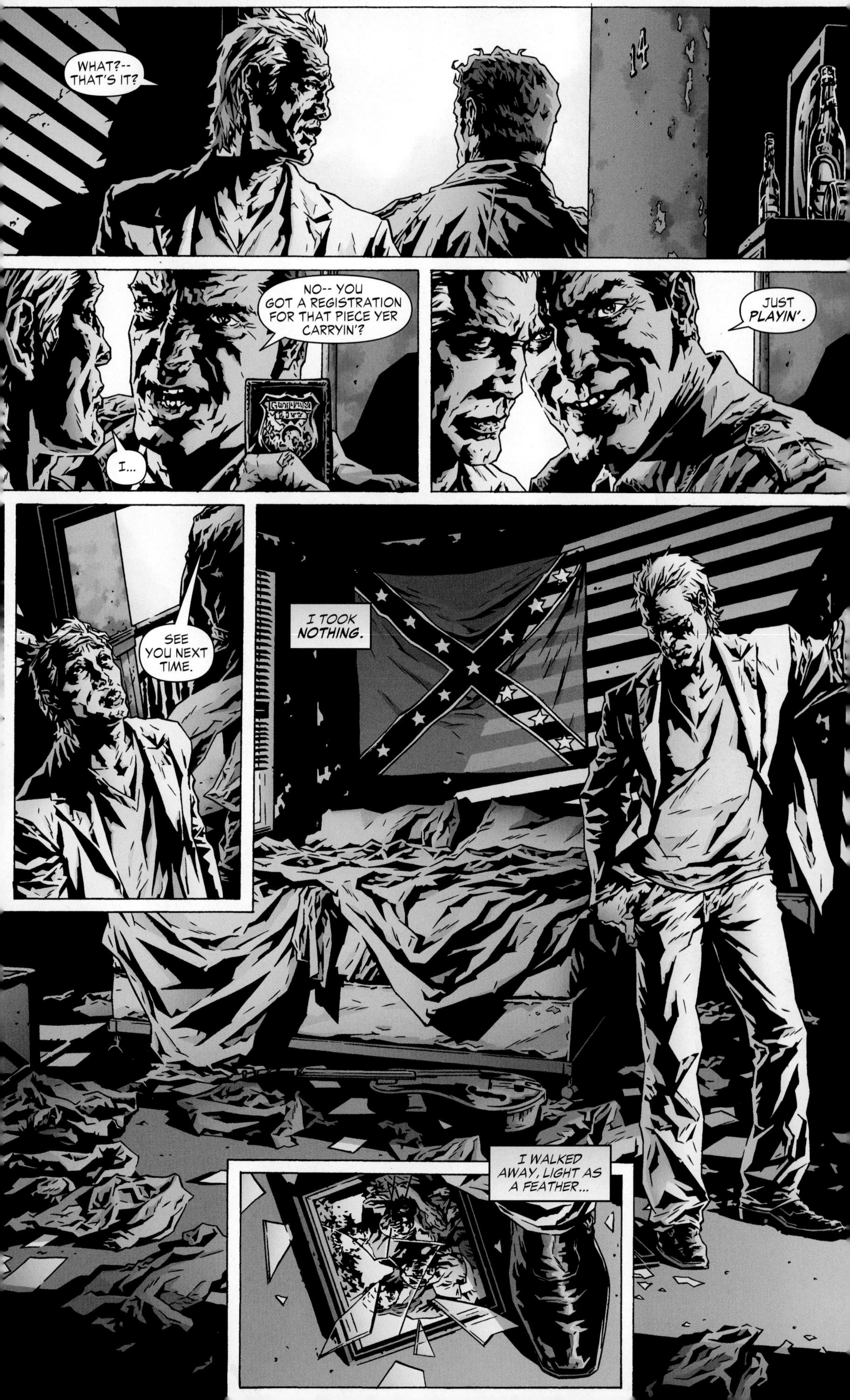
WHAT?--
THAT'S IT?
NO-- YOU GOT A REGISTRATION FOR THAT PIECE YER CARRYIN'?
I...
JUST PLAYIN'.
SEE YOU NEXT TIME.
I TOOK NOTHING.
I WALKED AWAY, LIGHT AS A FEATHER...

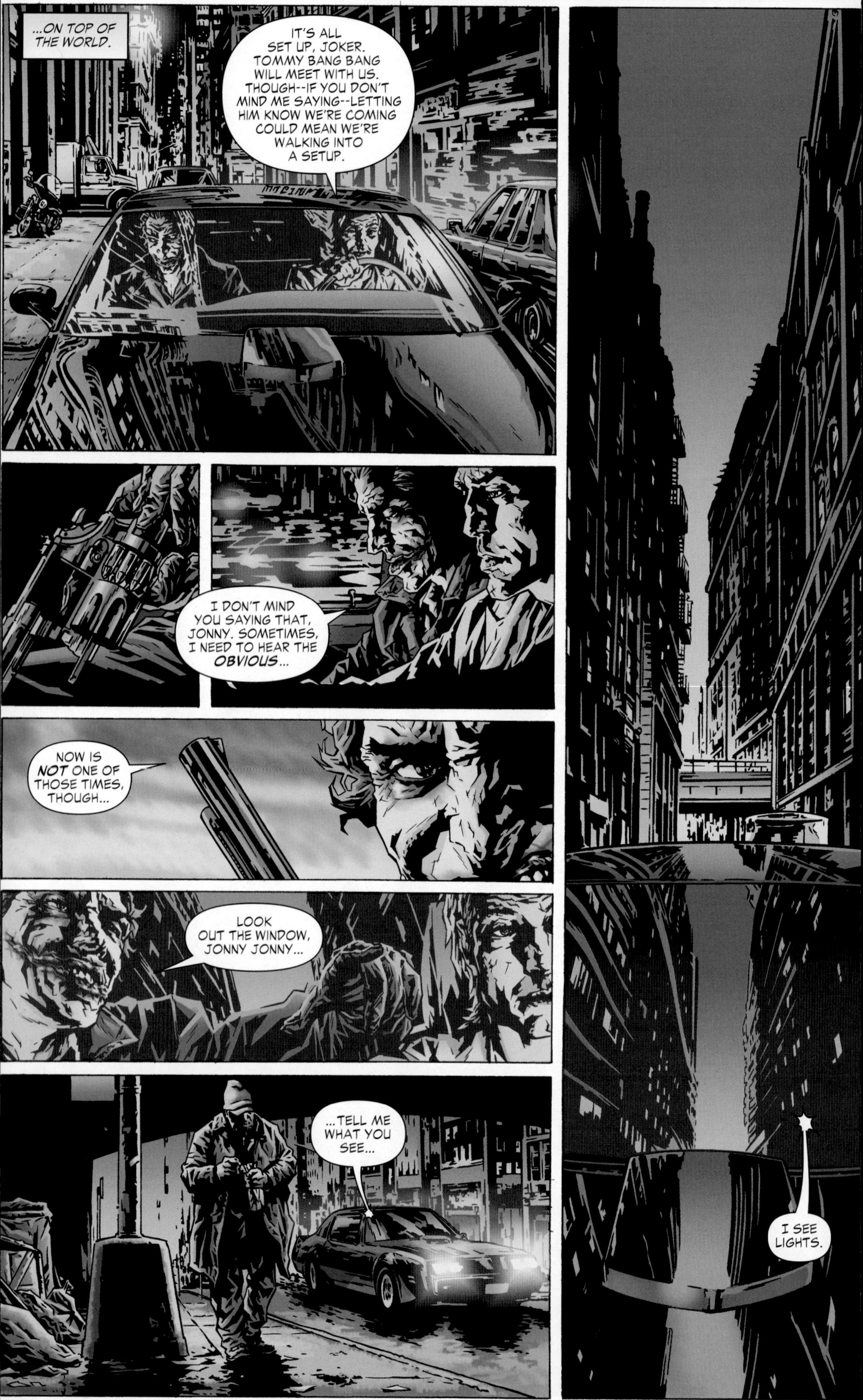
...ON TOP OF THE WORLD.
IT'S ALL SET UP, JOKER. TOMMY BANG BANG WILL MEET WITH US. THOUGH--IF YOU DON'T MIND ME SAYING--LETTING HIM KNOW WE'RE COMING COULD MEAN WE'RE WALKING INTO A SETUP.
I DON'T MIND YOU SAYING THAT, JONNY. SOMETIMES, I NEED TO HEAR THE OBVIOUS...
NOW IS NOT ONE OF THOSE TIMES, THOUGH...
LOOK OUT THE WINDOW, JONNY JONNY...
...TELL ME WHAT YOU SEE...
I SEE LIGHTS.

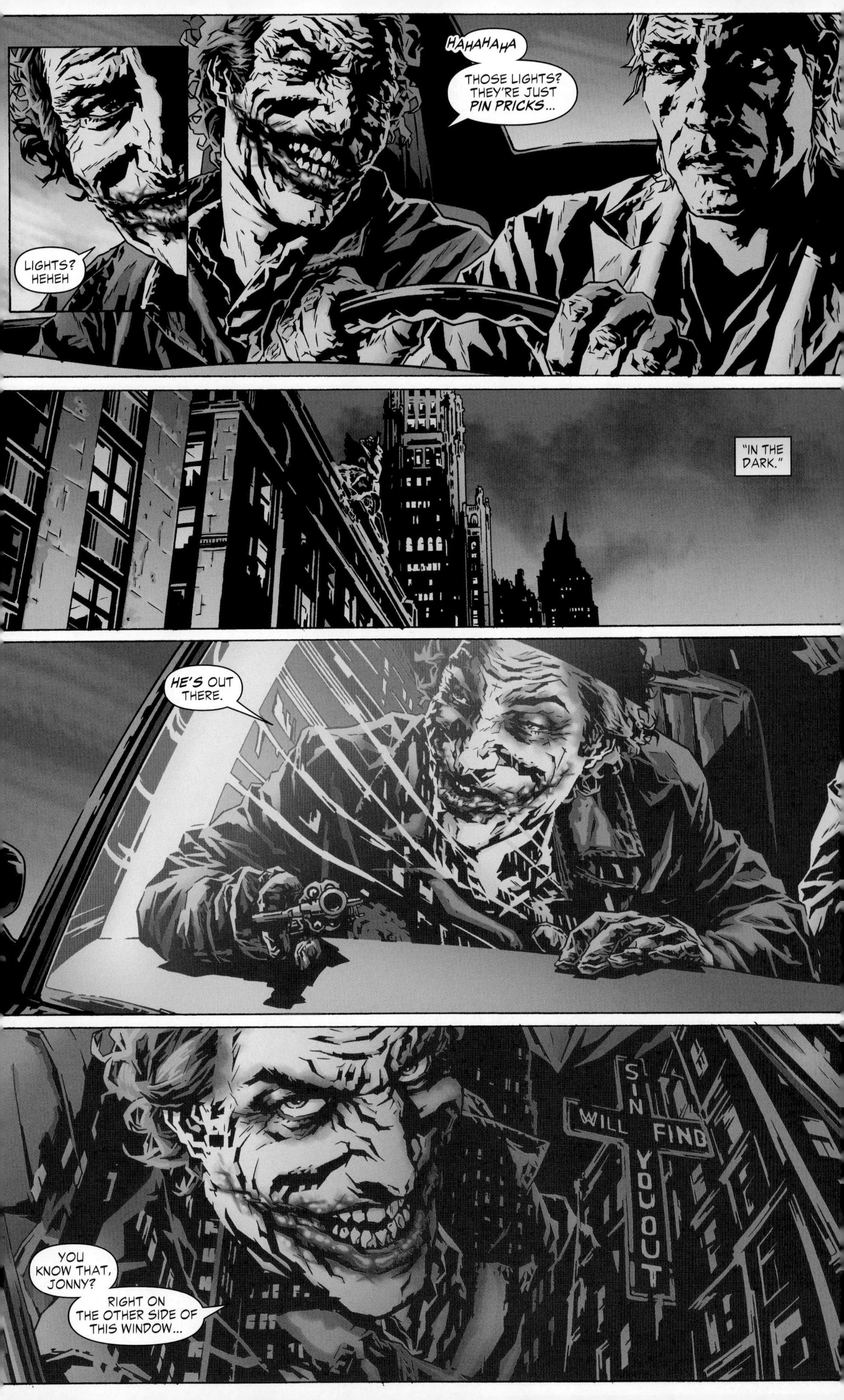
LIGHTS? HEHEH
HAHAHAHA
THOSE LIGHTS? THEY'RE JUST PIN PRICKS...
"IN THE DARK."
HE'S OUT THERE.
SIN WILL FIND YOU OUT
YOU KNOW THAT, JONNY?
RIGHT ON THE OTHER SIDE OF THIS WINDOW...

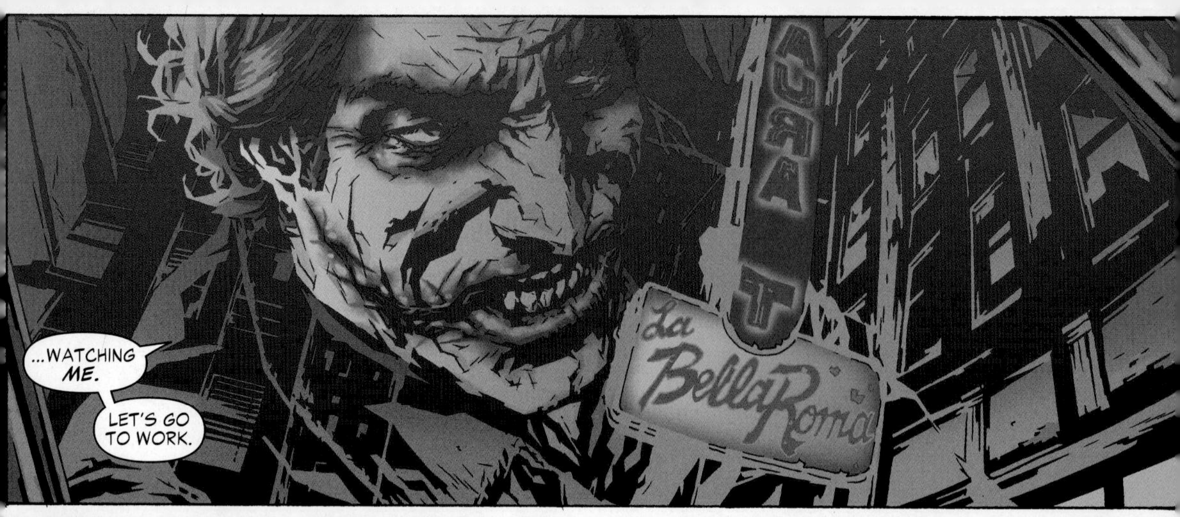
...WATCHING *ME.*
LET'S GO TO WORK.
La BellaRoma

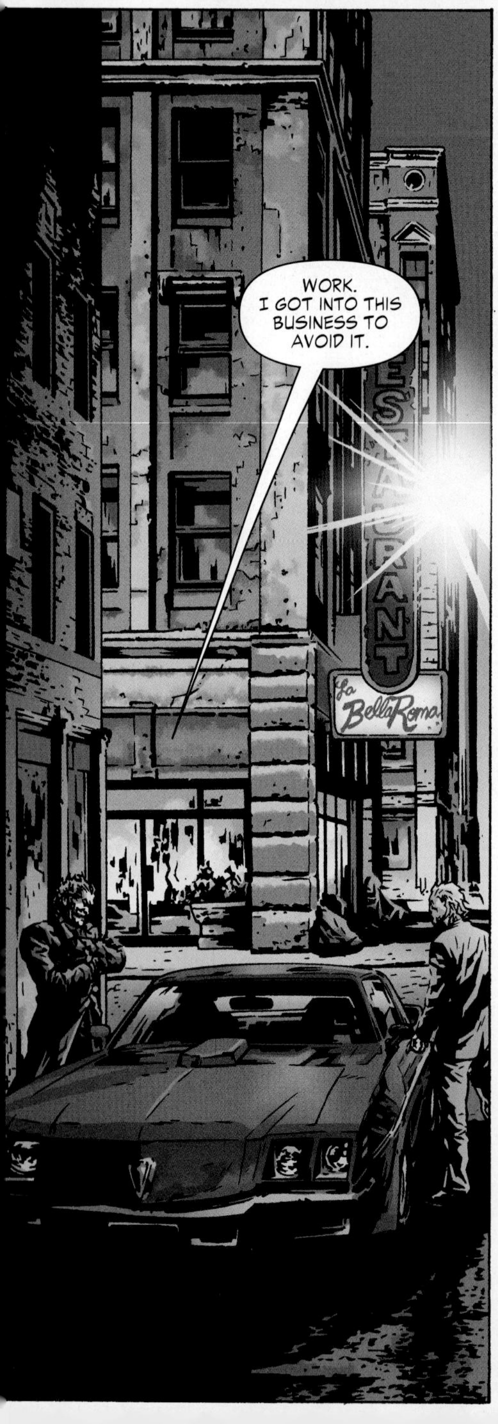
WORK. I GOT INTO THIS BUSINESS TO AVOID IT.
RESTAURANT
La BellaRoma

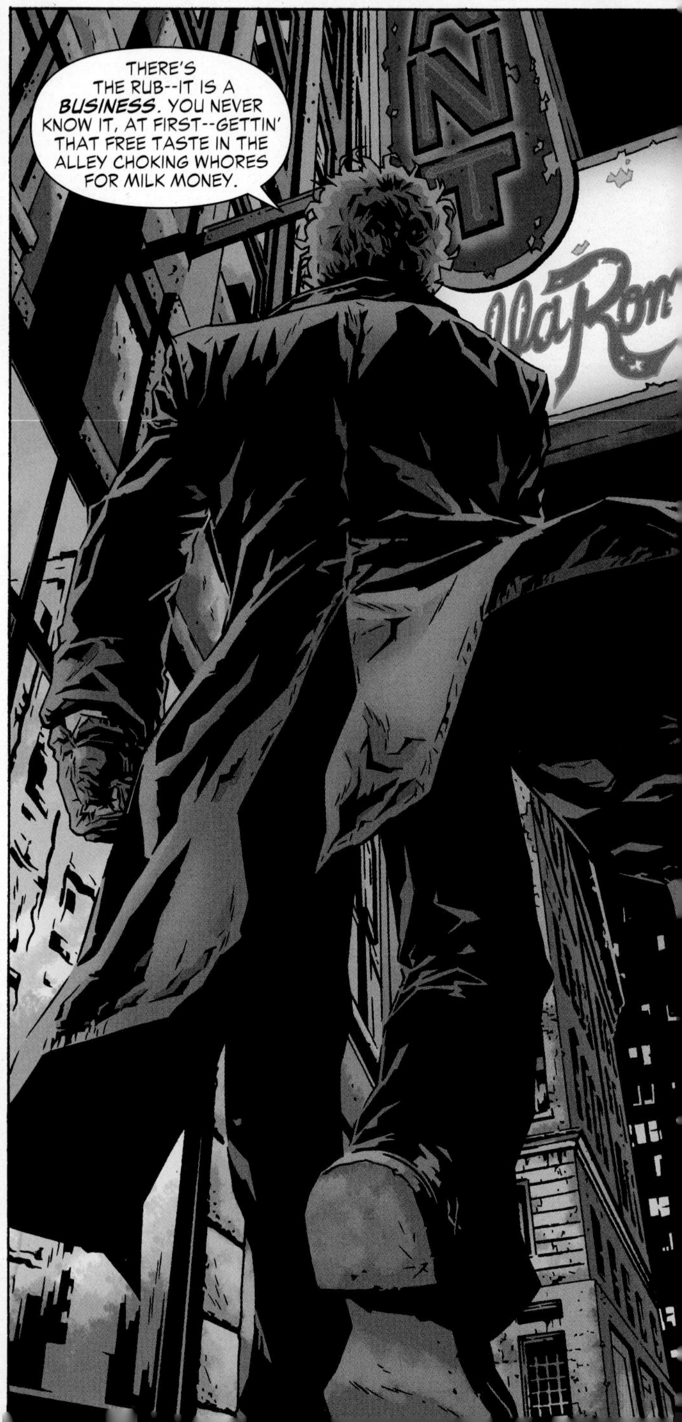
THERE'S THE RUB--IT IS A *BUSINESS*. YOU NEVER KNOW IT, AT FIRST--GETTIN' THAT FREE TASTE IN THE ALLEY CHOKING WHORES FOR MILK MONEY.

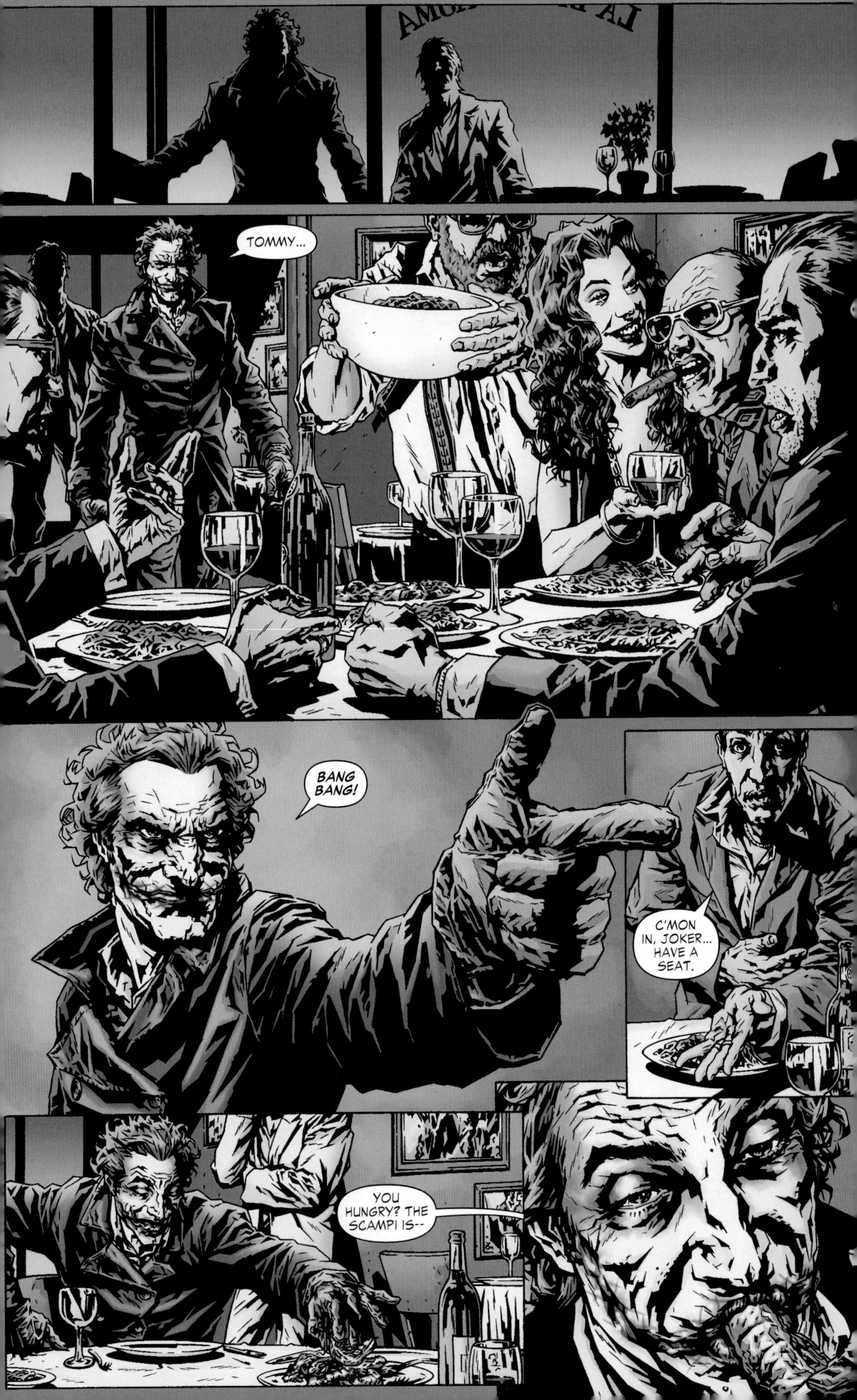
TOMMY...
BANG BANG!
C'MON IN, JOKER... HAVE A SEAT.
YOU HUNGRY? THE SCAMPI IS--

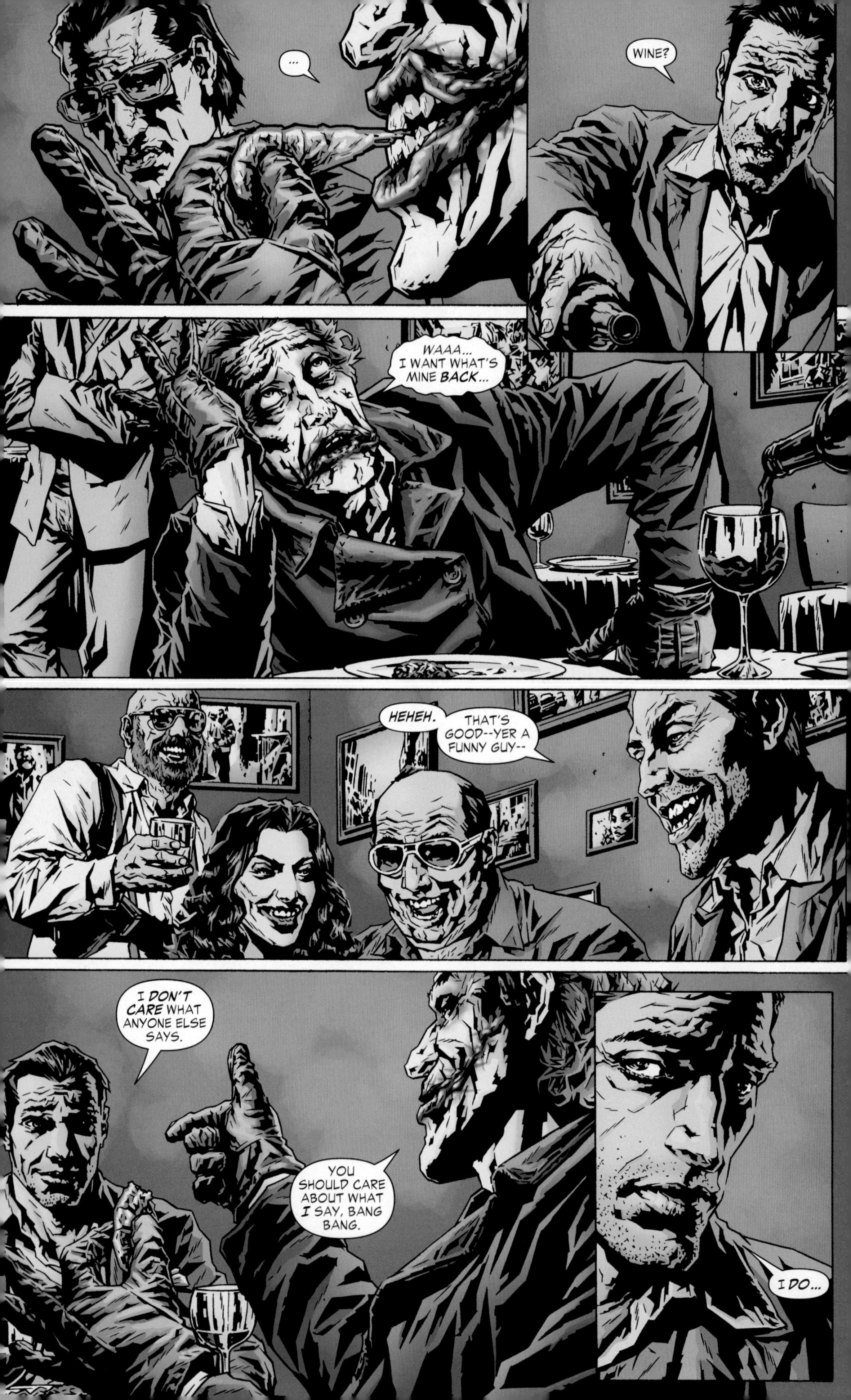
...
WINE?
WAAA... I WANT WHAT'S MINE BACK...
HEHEH.
THAT'S GOOD--YER A FUNNY GUY--
I DON'T CARE WHAT ANYONE ELSE SAYS.
YOU SHOULD CARE ABOUT WHAT I SAY, BANG BANG.
I DO...

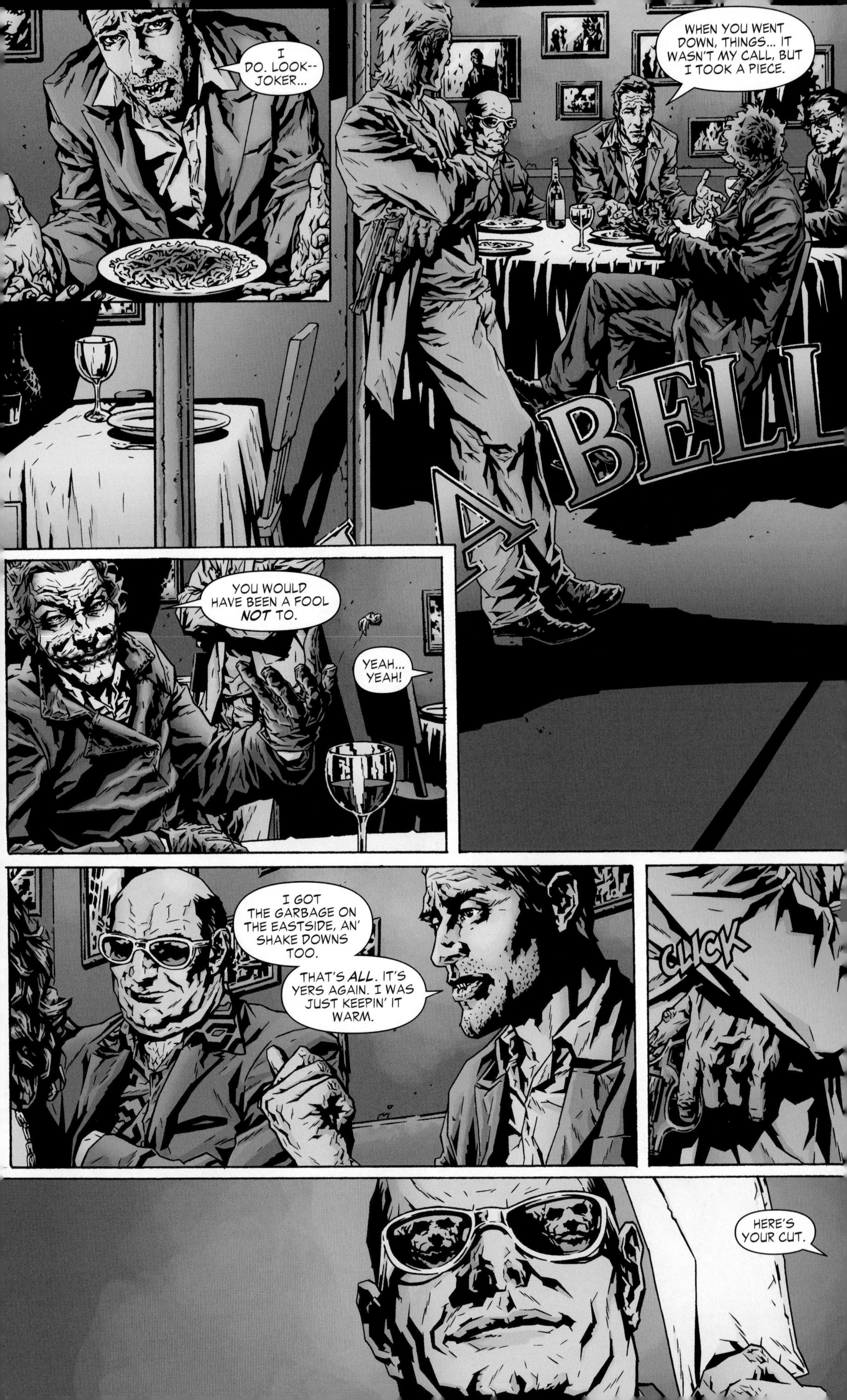
I DO. LOOK-- JOKER...
WHEN YOU WENT DOWN, THINGS... IT WASN'T MY CALL, BUT I TOOK A PIECE.
ABELL
YOU WOULD HAVE BEEN A FOOL NOT TO.
YEAH... YEAH!
I GOT THE GARBAGE ON THE EASTSIDE, AN' SHAKE DOWNS TOO.
THAT'S ALL. IT'S YERS AGAIN. I WAS JUST KEEPIN' IT WARM.
CLICK
HERE'S YOUR CUT.

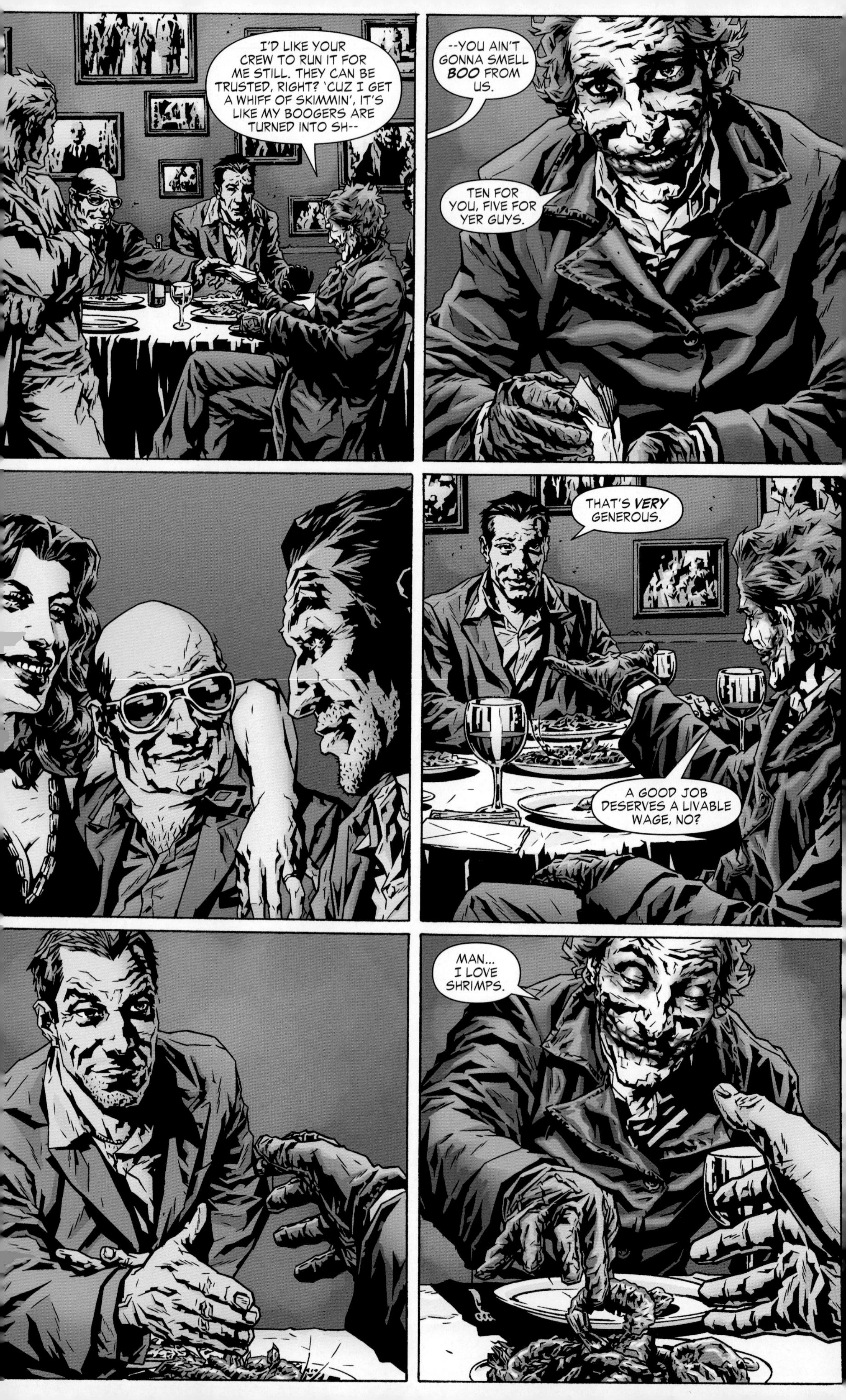
I'D LIKE YOUR CREW TO RUN IT FOR ME STILL. THEY CAN BE TRUSTED, RIGHT? 'CUZ I GET A WHIFF OF SKIMMIN', IT'S LIKE MY BOOGERS ARE TURNED INTO SH--
--YOU AIN'T GONNA SMELL BOO FROM US.
TEN FOR YOU, FIVE FOR YER GUYS.
THAT'S VERY GENEROUS.
A GOOD JOB DESERVES A LIVABLE WAGE, NO?
MAN... I LOVE SHRIMPS.

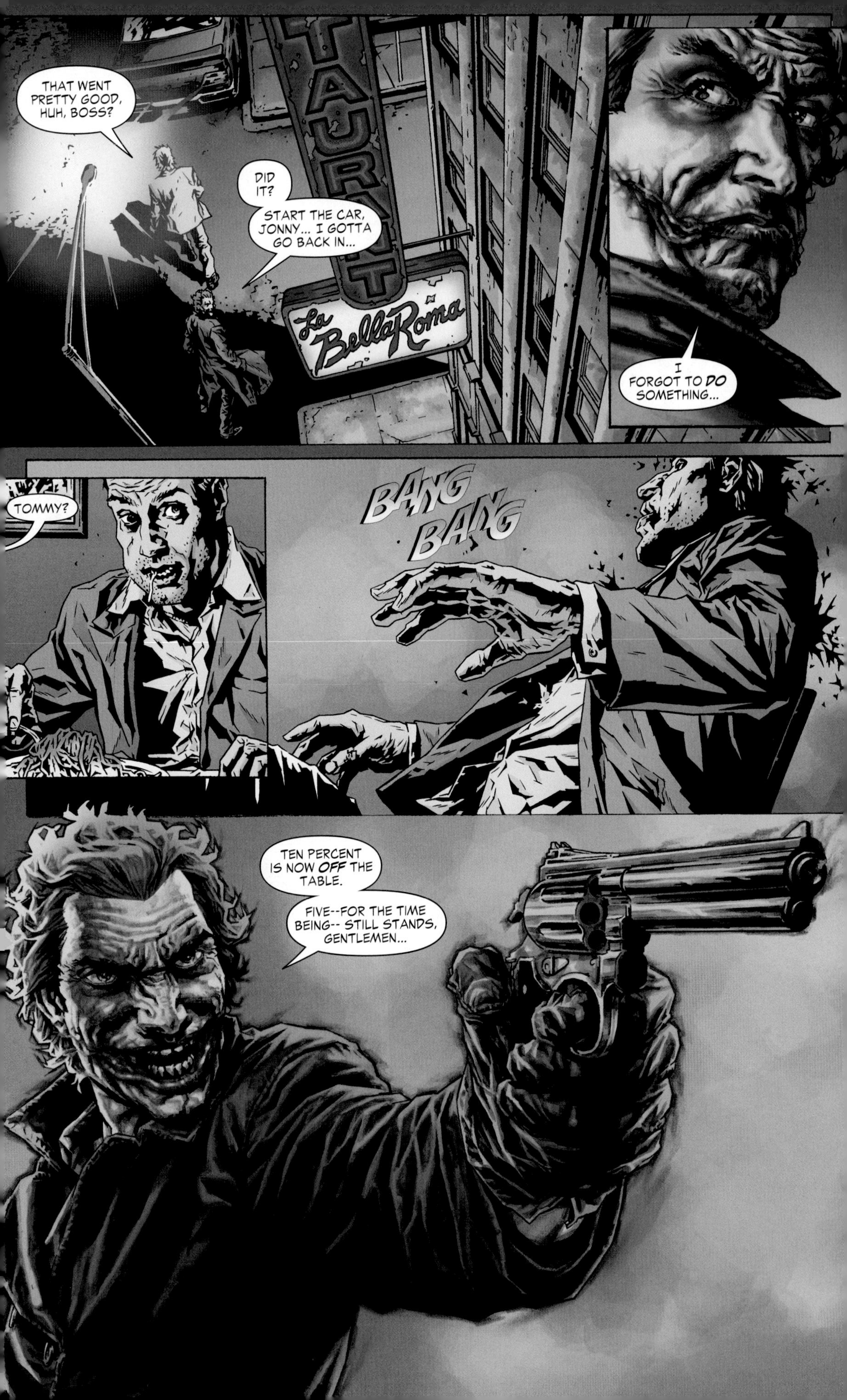
THAT WENT PRETTY GOOD, HUH, BOSS?
DID IT?
START THE CAR, JONNY... I GOTTA GO BACK IN...
La BellaRoma
I FORGOT TO *DO* SOMETHING...
TOMMY?
BANG
BANG
TEN PERCENT IS NOW *OFF* THE TABLE.
FIVE--FOR THE TIME BEING-- STILL STANDS, GENTLEMEN...

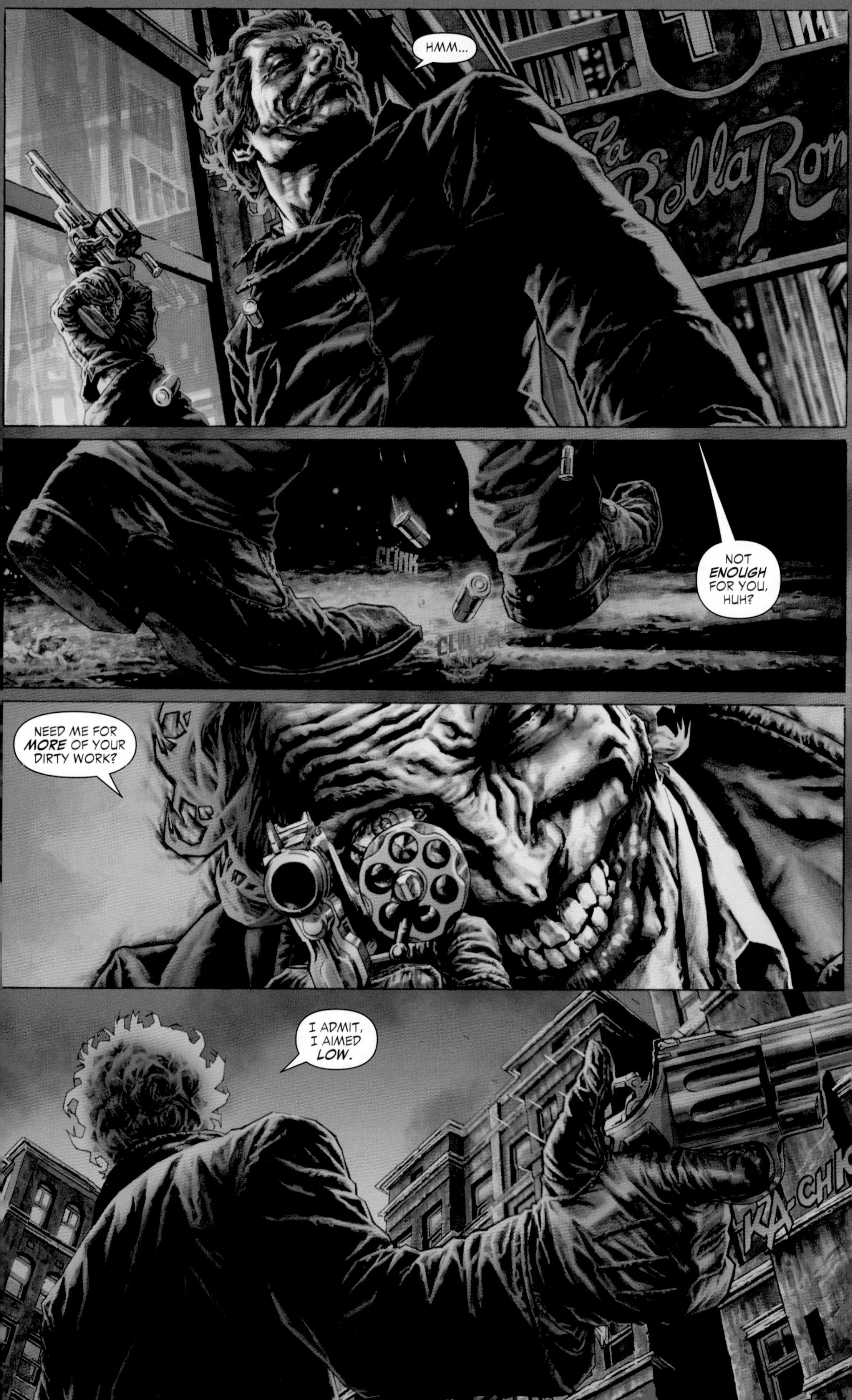
HMM...
La Bella Ron
NOT ENOUGH FOR YOU, HUH?
CLINK
NEED ME FOR MORE OF YOUR DIRTY WORK?
I ADMIT, I AIMED LOW.
KA-CHK

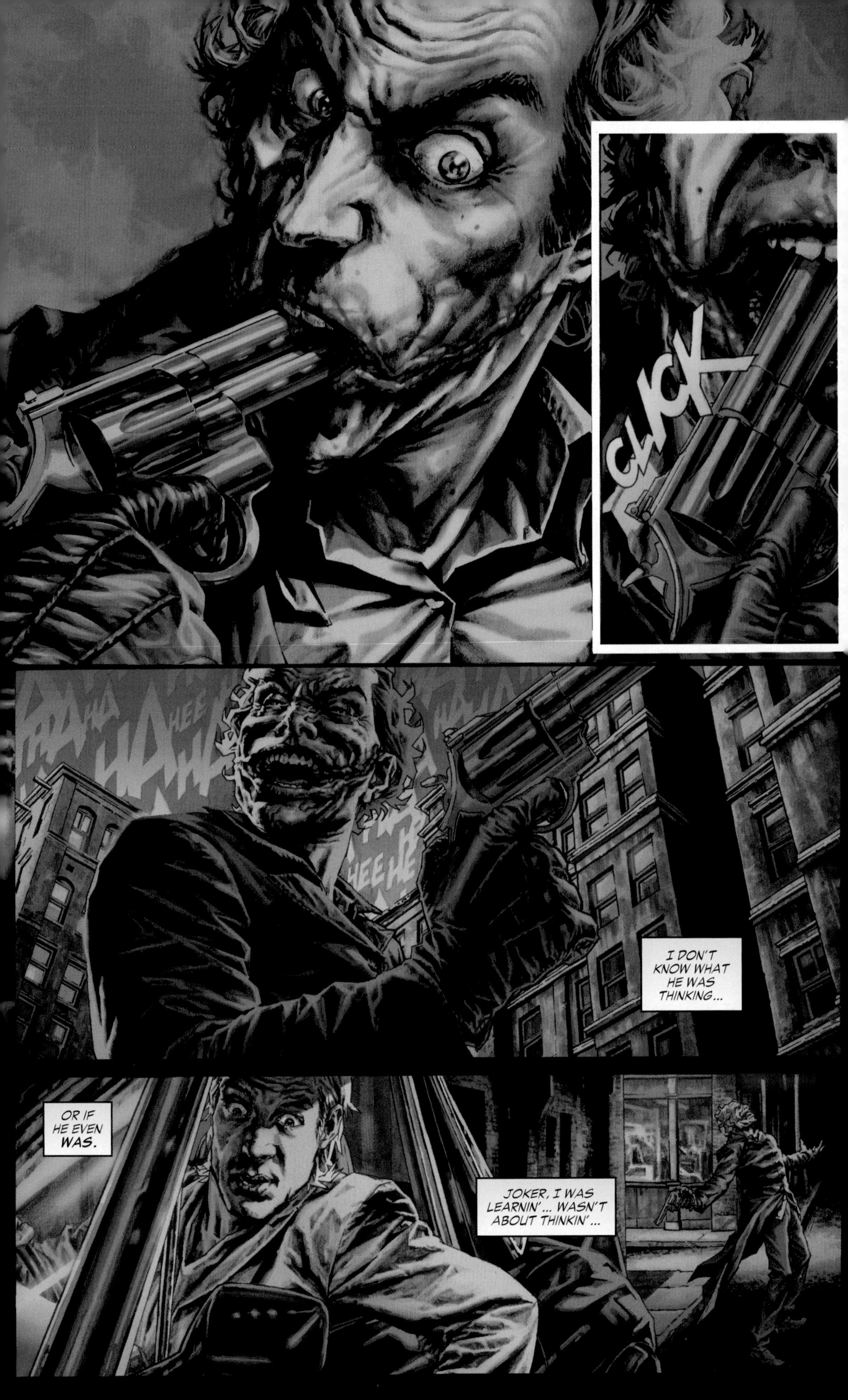
CLICK
HA HA HEE HA HA HA HEE HEE HE
I DON'T KNOW WHAT HE WAS THINKING...
OR IF HE EVEN WAS.
JOKER, I WAS LEARNIN'... WASN'T ABOUT THINKIN'...

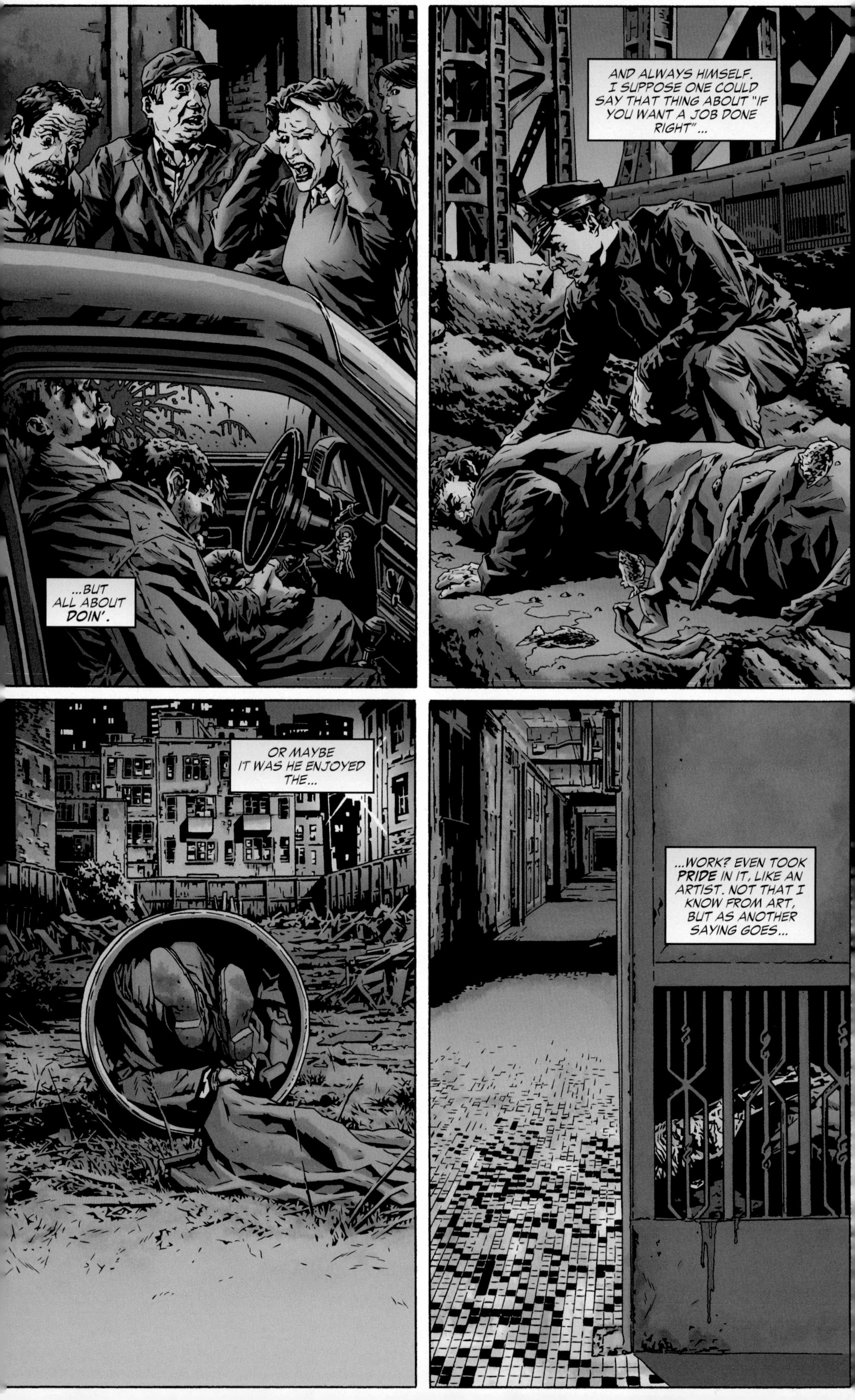
...BUT ALL ABOUT DOIN'.
AND ALWAYS HIMSELF. I SUPPOSE ONE COULD SAY THAT THING ABOUT "IF YOU WANT A JOB DONE RIGHT"...
OR MAYBE IT WAS HE ENJOYED THE...
...WORK? EVEN TOOK PRIDE IN IT, LIKE AN ARTIST. NOT THAT I KNOW FROM ART, BUT AS ANOTHER SAYING GOES...

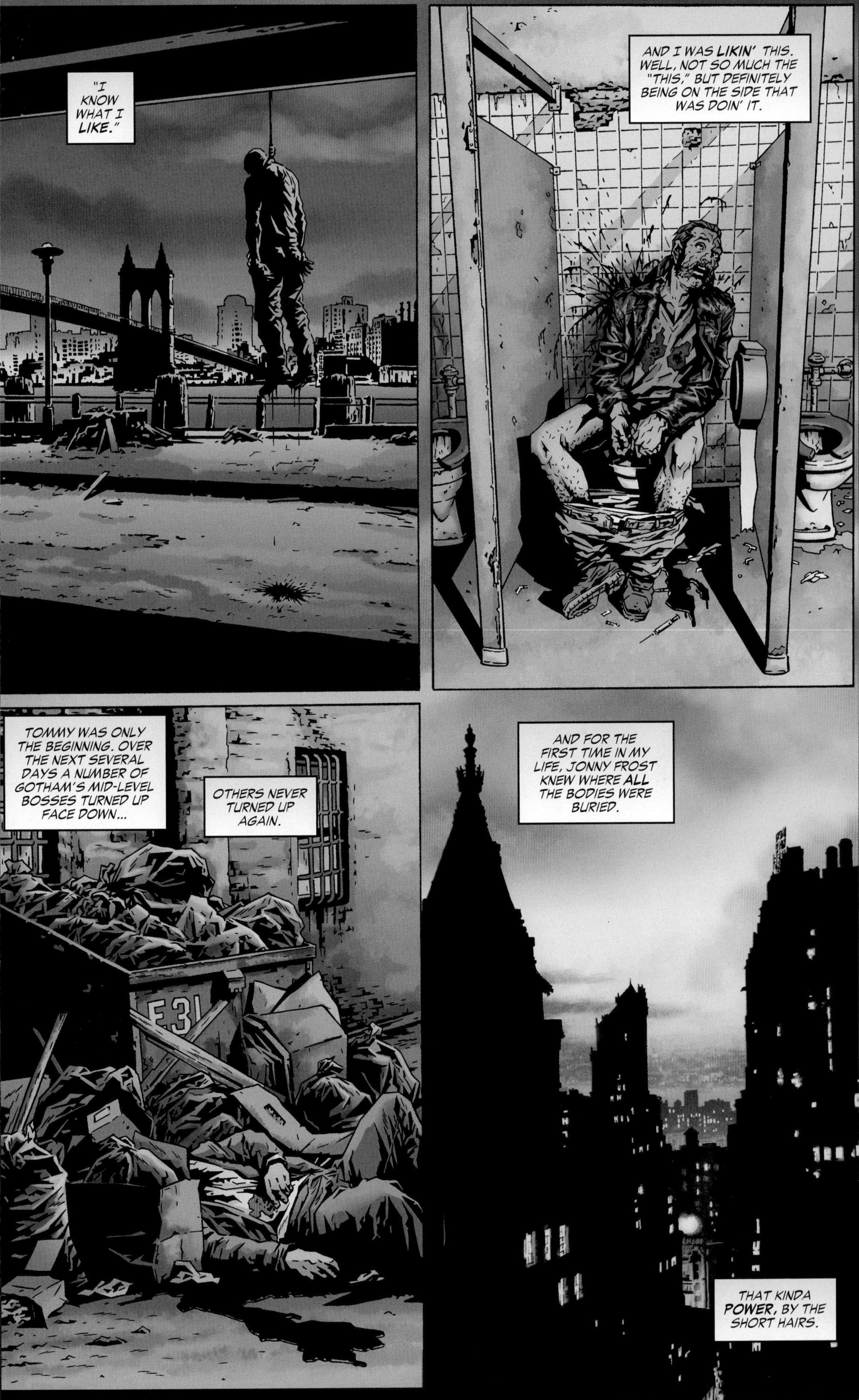
"I KNOW WHAT I LIKE."
AND I WAS LIKIN' THIS. WELL, NOT SO MUCH THE "THIS," BUT DEFINITELY BEING ON THE SIDE THAT WAS DOIN' IT.
TOMMY WAS ONLY THE BEGINNING. OVER THE NEXT SEVERAL DAYS A NUMBER OF GOTHAM'S MID-LEVEL BOSSES TURNED UP FACE DOWN...
OTHERS NEVER TURNED UP AGAIN.
E31
AND FOR THE FIRST TIME IN MY LIFE, JONNY FROST KNEW WHERE ALL THE BODIES WERE BURIED.
THAT KINDA POWER, BY THE SHORT HAIRS.

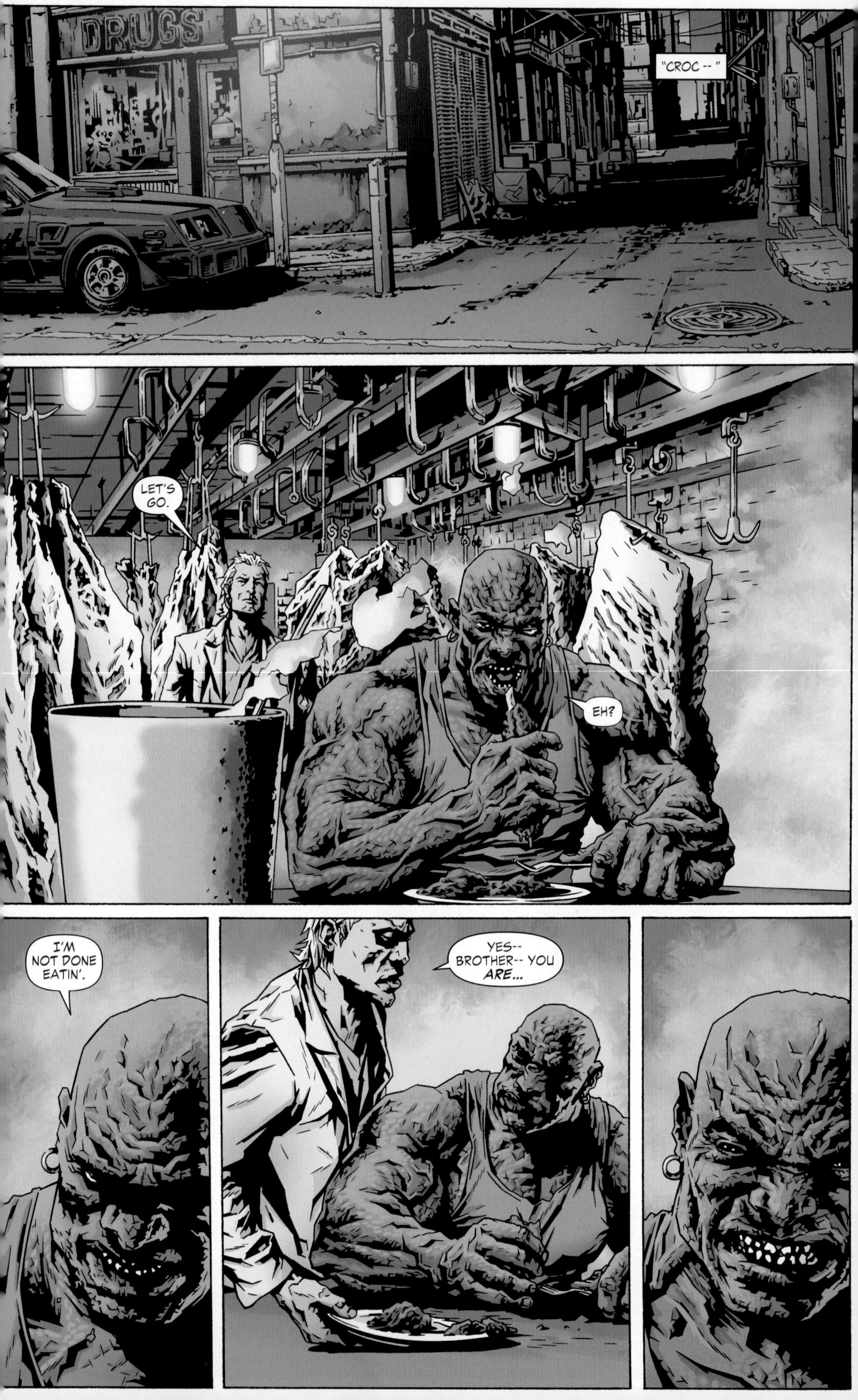
"CROC -- "
LET'S GO.
EH?
I'M NOT DONE EATIN'.
YES-- BROTHER-- YOU ARE...

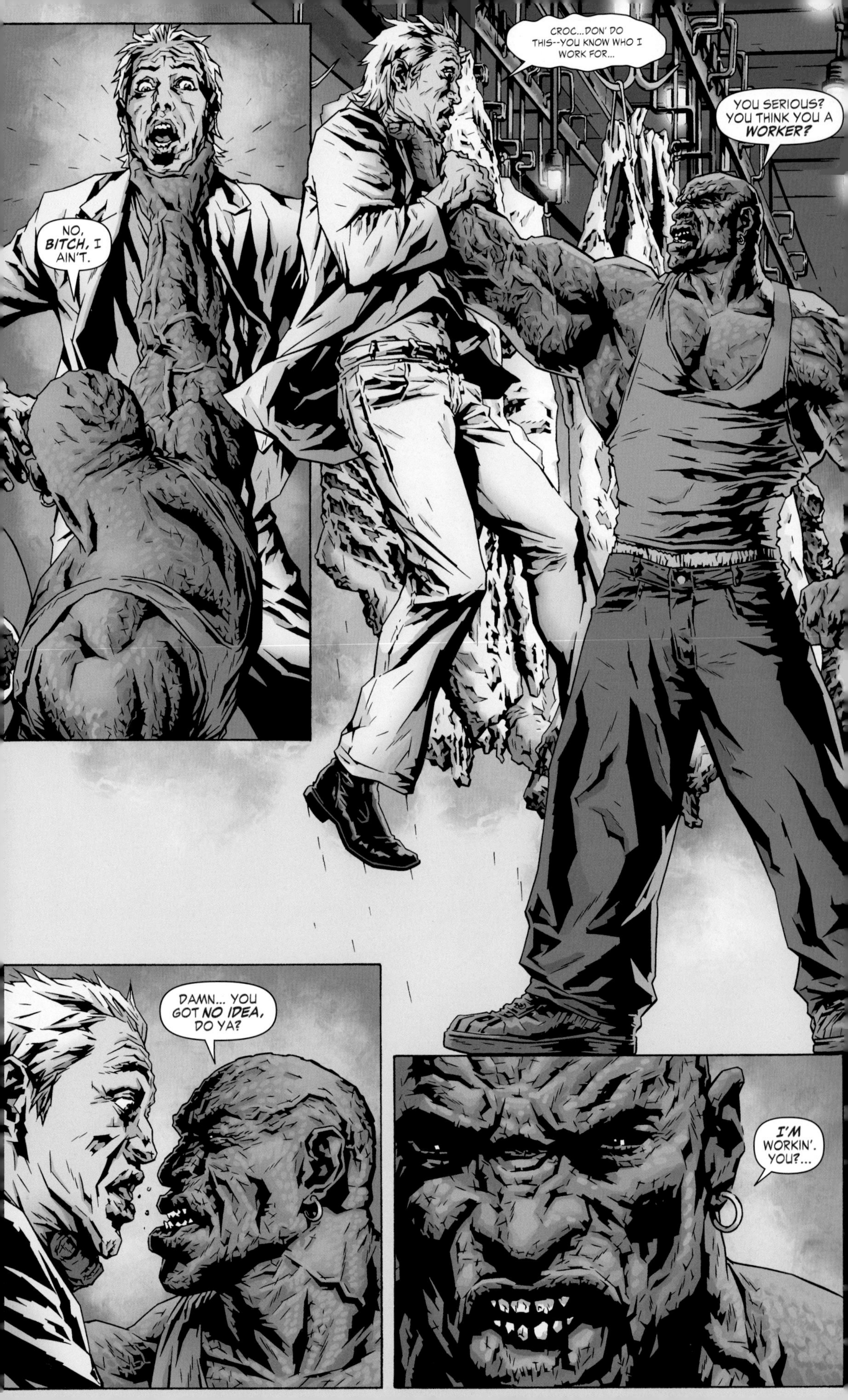

CROC...DON' DO THIS--YOU KNOW WHO I WORK FOR...
YOU SERIOUS? YOU THINK YOU A WORKER?
NO, BITCH, I AIN'T.
DAMN... YOU GOT NO IDEA, DO YA?
I'M WORKIN'. YOU?...

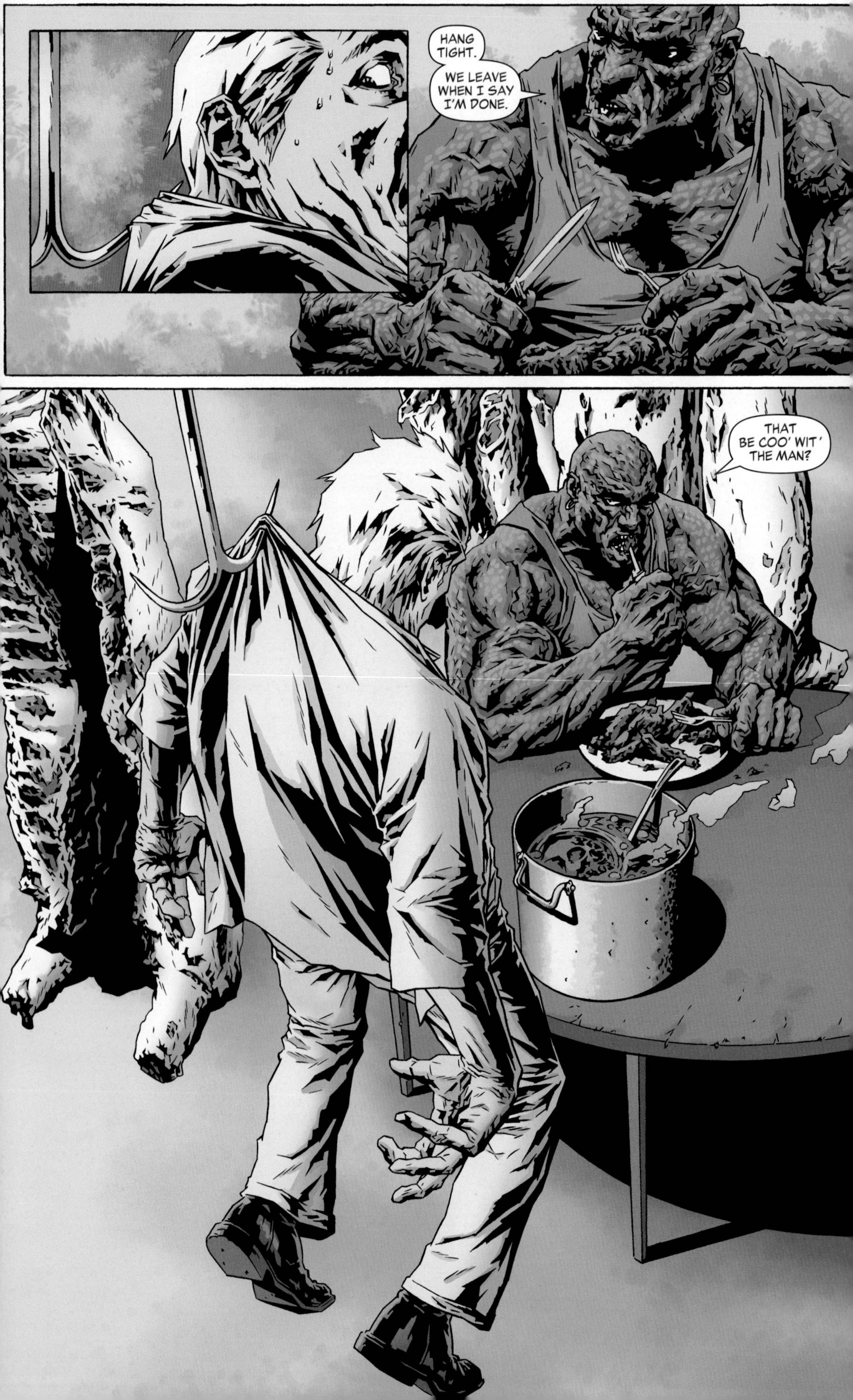
HANG TIGHT.
WE LEAVE WHEN I SAY I'M DONE.
THAT BE COO' WIT' THE MAN?

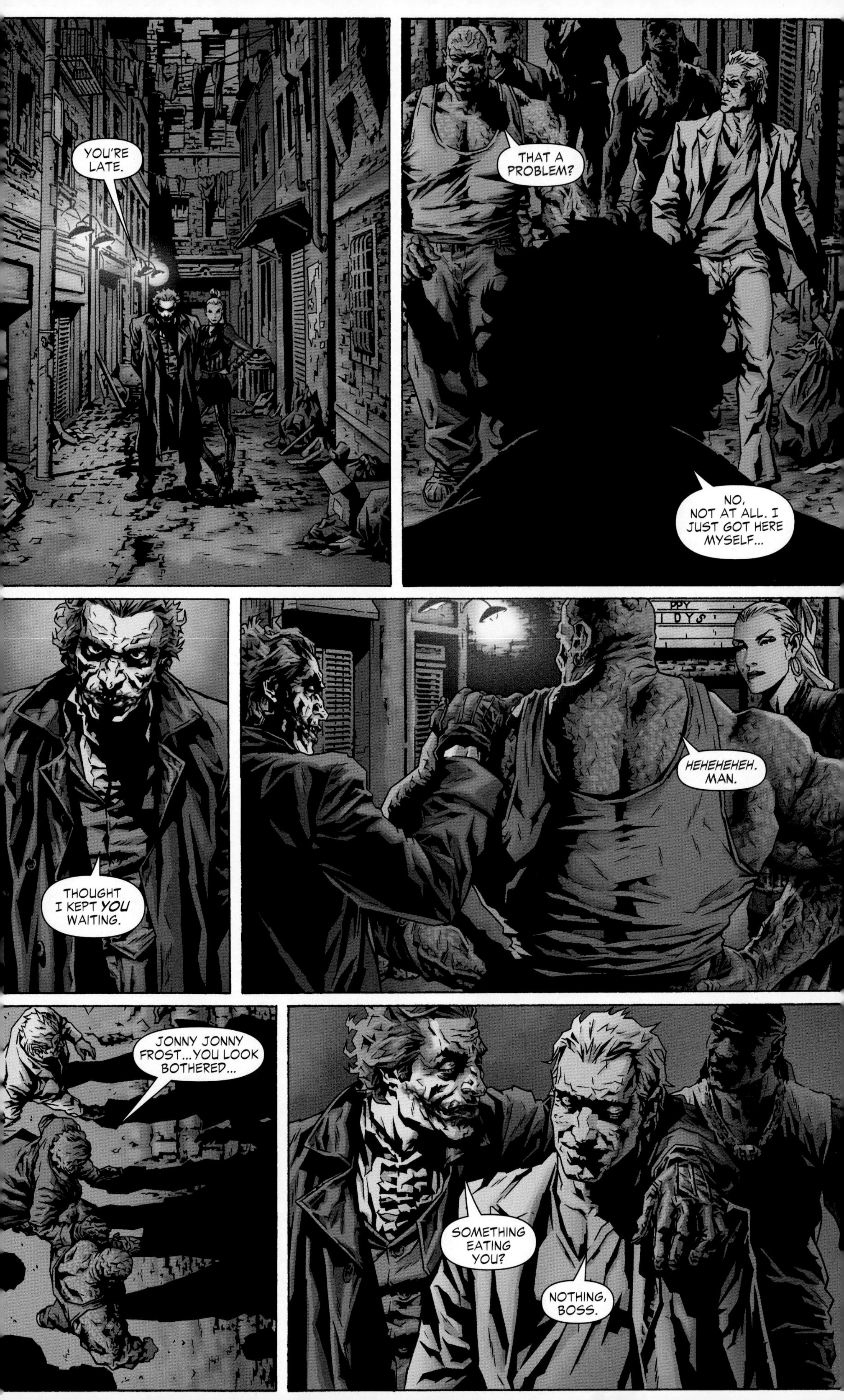
YOU'RE LATE.
THAT A PROBLEM?
NO, NOT AT ALL. I JUST GOT HERE MYSELF...
THOUGHT I KEPT YOU WAITING.
HEHEHEHEH. MAN.
JONNY JONNY FROST...YOU LOOK BOTHERED...
SOMETHING EATING YOU?
NOTHING, BOSS.

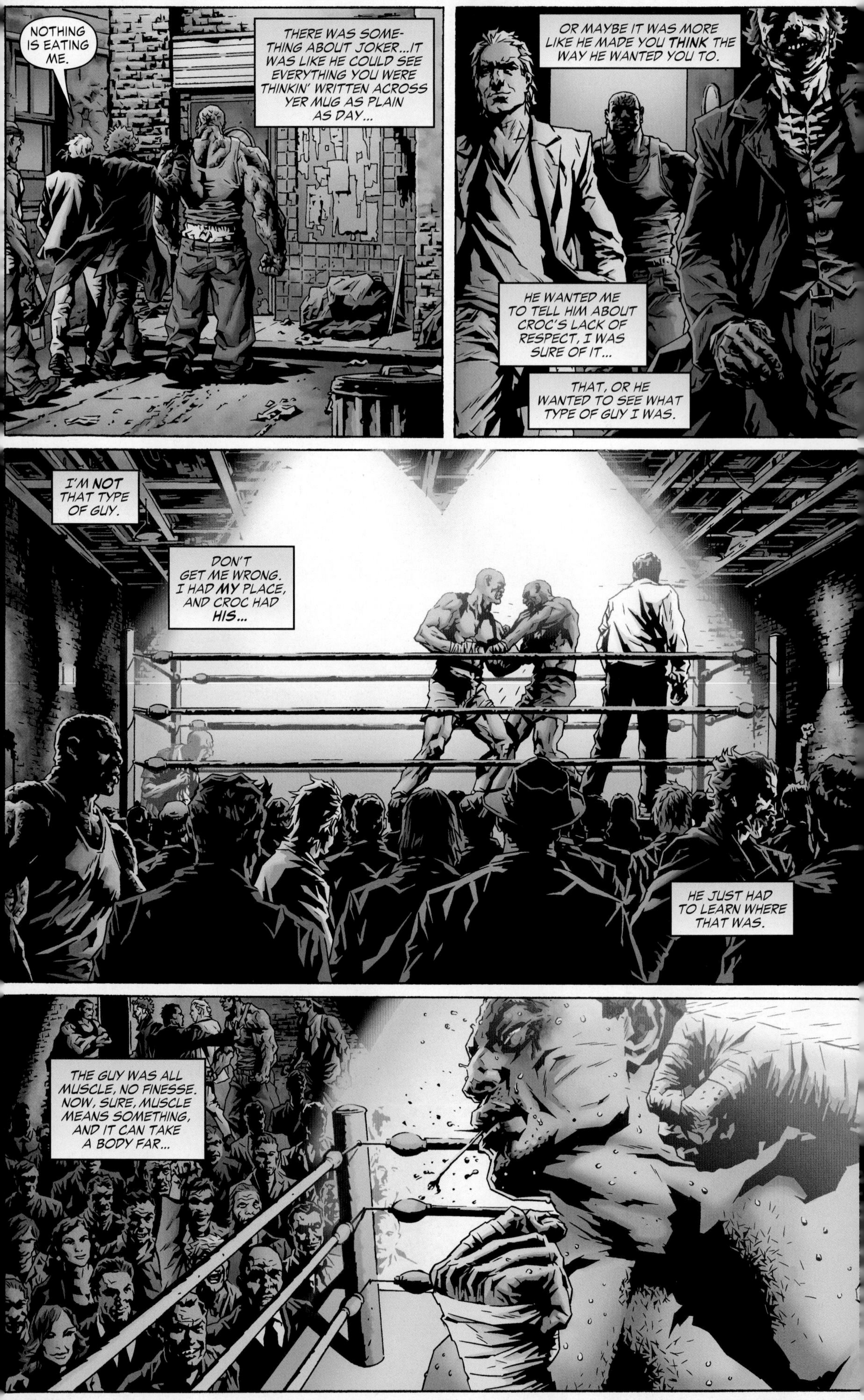

NOTHING IS EATING ME.
THERE WAS SOMETHING ABOUT JOKER...IT WAS LIKE HE COULD SEE EVERYTHING YOU WERE THINKIN' WRITTEN ACROSS YER MUG AS PLAIN AS DAY...
OR MAYBE IT WAS MORE LIKE HE MADE YOU THINK THE WAY HE WANTED YOU TO.
HE WANTED ME TO TELL HIM ABOUT CROC'S LACK OF RESPECT, I WAS SURE OF IT...
THAT, OR HE WANTED TO SEE WHAT TYPE OF GUY I WAS.
I'M NOT THAT TYPE OF GUY.
DON'T GET ME WRONG. I HAD MY PLACE, AND CROC HAD HIS...
HE JUST HAD TO LEARN WHERE THAT WAS.
THE GUY WAS ALL MUSCLE, NO FINESSE. NOW, SURE, MUSCLE MEANS SOMETHING, AND IT CAN TAKE A BODY FAR...

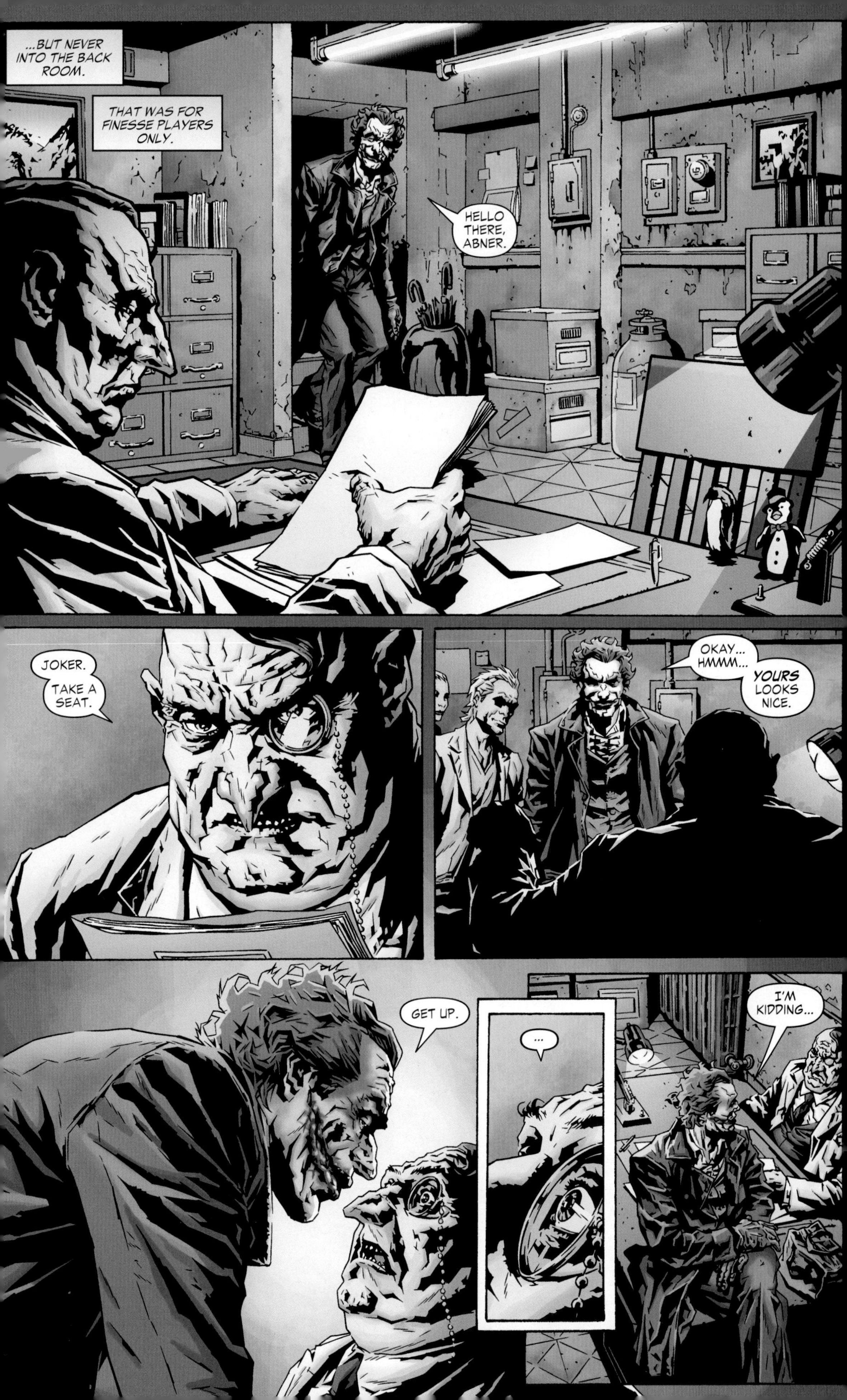
...BUT NEVER INTO THE BACK ROOM.
THAT WAS FOR FINESSE PLAYERS ONLY.
HELLO THERE, ABNER.
JOKER. TAKE A SEAT.
OKAY... HMMM... YOURS LOOKS NICE.
GET UP.
...
I'M KIDDING...

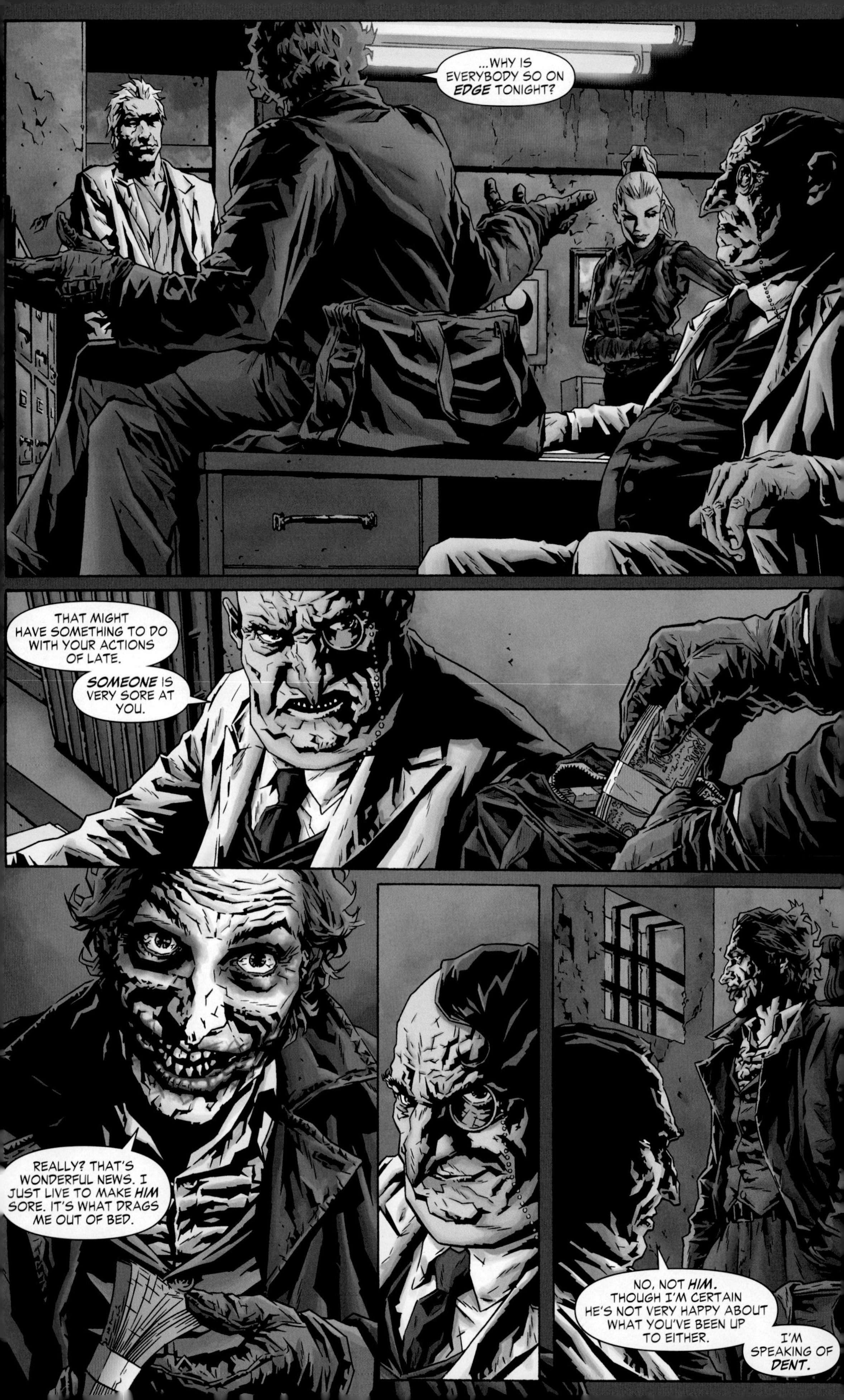
...WHY IS EVERYBODY SO ON *EDGE* TONIGHT?
THAT MIGHT HAVE SOMETHING TO DO WITH YOUR ACTIONS OF LATE.
SOMEONE IS VERY SORE AT YOU.
REALLY? THAT'S WONDERFUL NEWS. I JUST LIVE TO MAKE *HIM* SORE. IT'S WHAT DRAGS ME OUT OF BED.
NO, NOT *HIM*. THOUGH I'M CERTAIN HE'S NOT VERY HAPPY ABOUT WHAT YOU'VE BEEN UP TO EITHER.
I'M SPEAKING OF *DENT*.

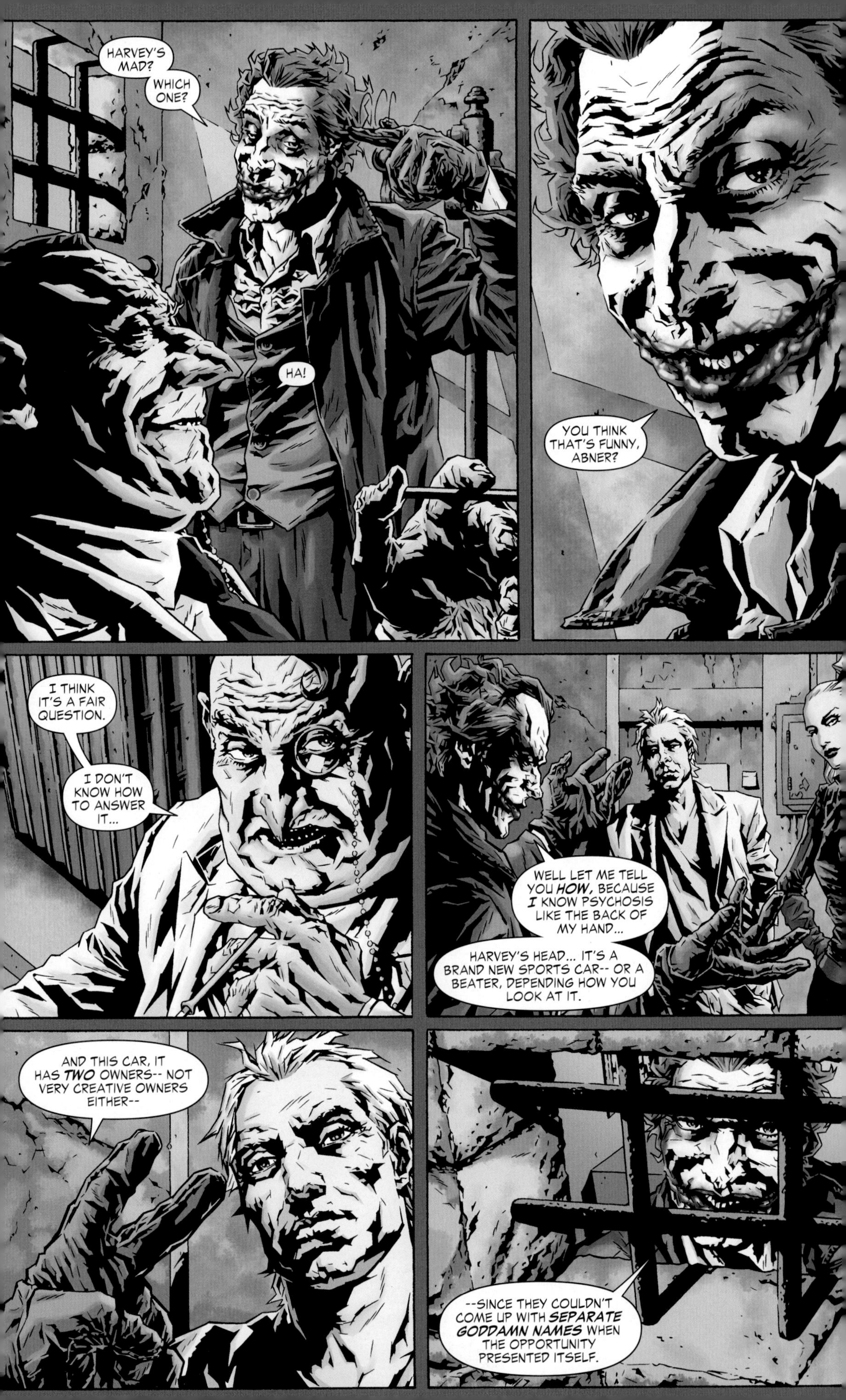
HARVEY'S MAD?
WHICH ONE?
HA!
YOU THINK THAT'S FUNNY, ABNER?
I THINK IT'S A FAIR QUESTION.
I DON'T KNOW HOW TO ANSWER IT...
WELL LET ME TELL YOU HOW, BECAUSE I KNOW PSYCHOSIS LIKE THE BACK OF MY HAND...
HARVEY'S HEAD... IT'S A BRAND NEW SPORTS CAR-- OR A BEATER, DEPENDING HOW YOU LOOK AT IT.
AND THIS CAR, IT HAS TWO OWNERS-- NOT VERY CREATIVE OWNERS EITHER--
--SINCE THEY COULDN'T COME UP WITH SEPARATE GODDAMN NAMES WHEN THE OPPORTUNITY PRESENTED ITSELF.

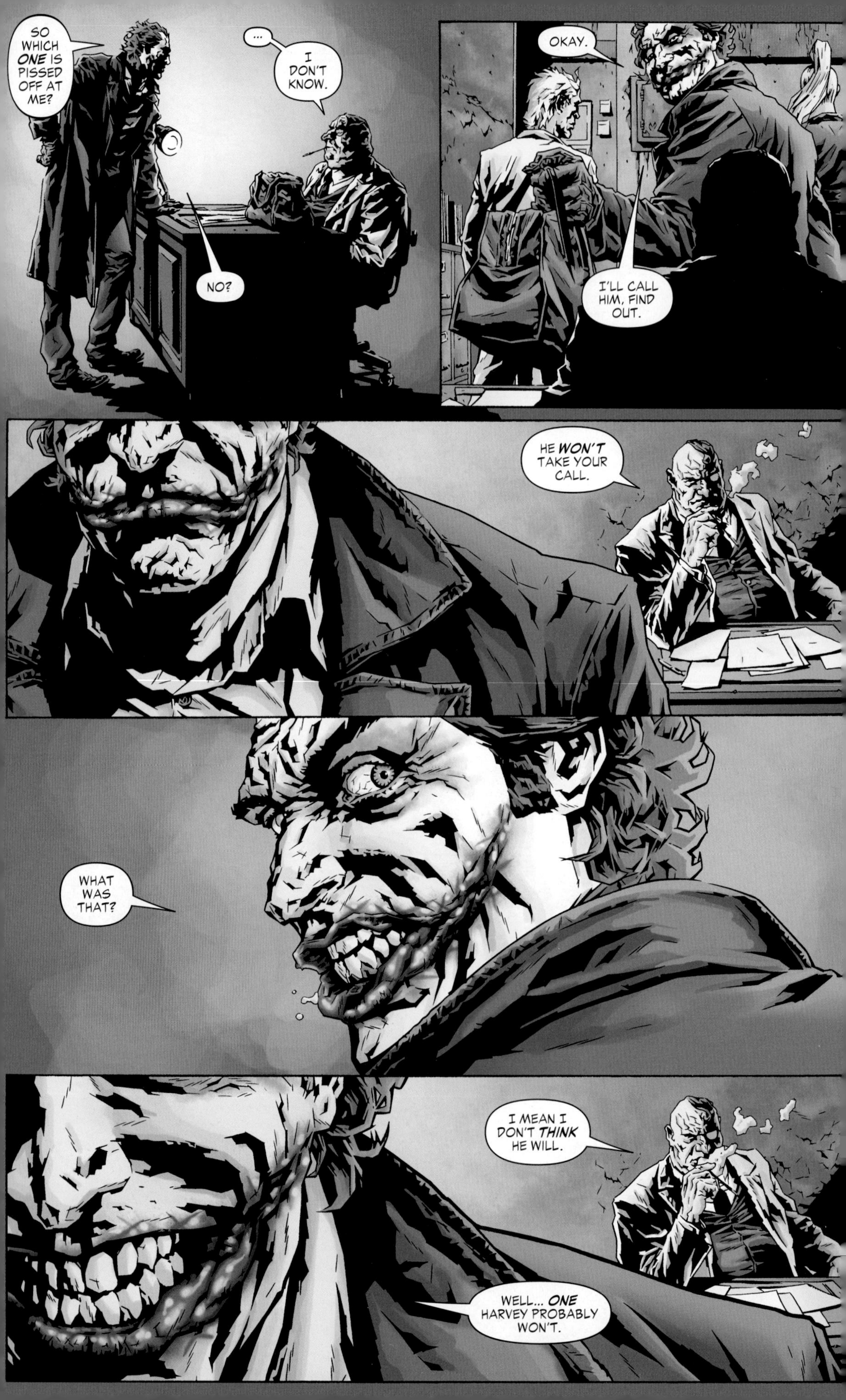
SO WHICH *ONE* IS PISSED OFF AT ME?
...
I DON'T KNOW.
NO?
OKAY.
I'LL CALL HIM, FIND OUT.
HE *WON'T* TAKE YOUR CALL.
WHAT WAS THAT?
I MEAN I DON'T *THINK* HE WILL.
WELL... *ONE* HARVEY PROBABLY WON'T.

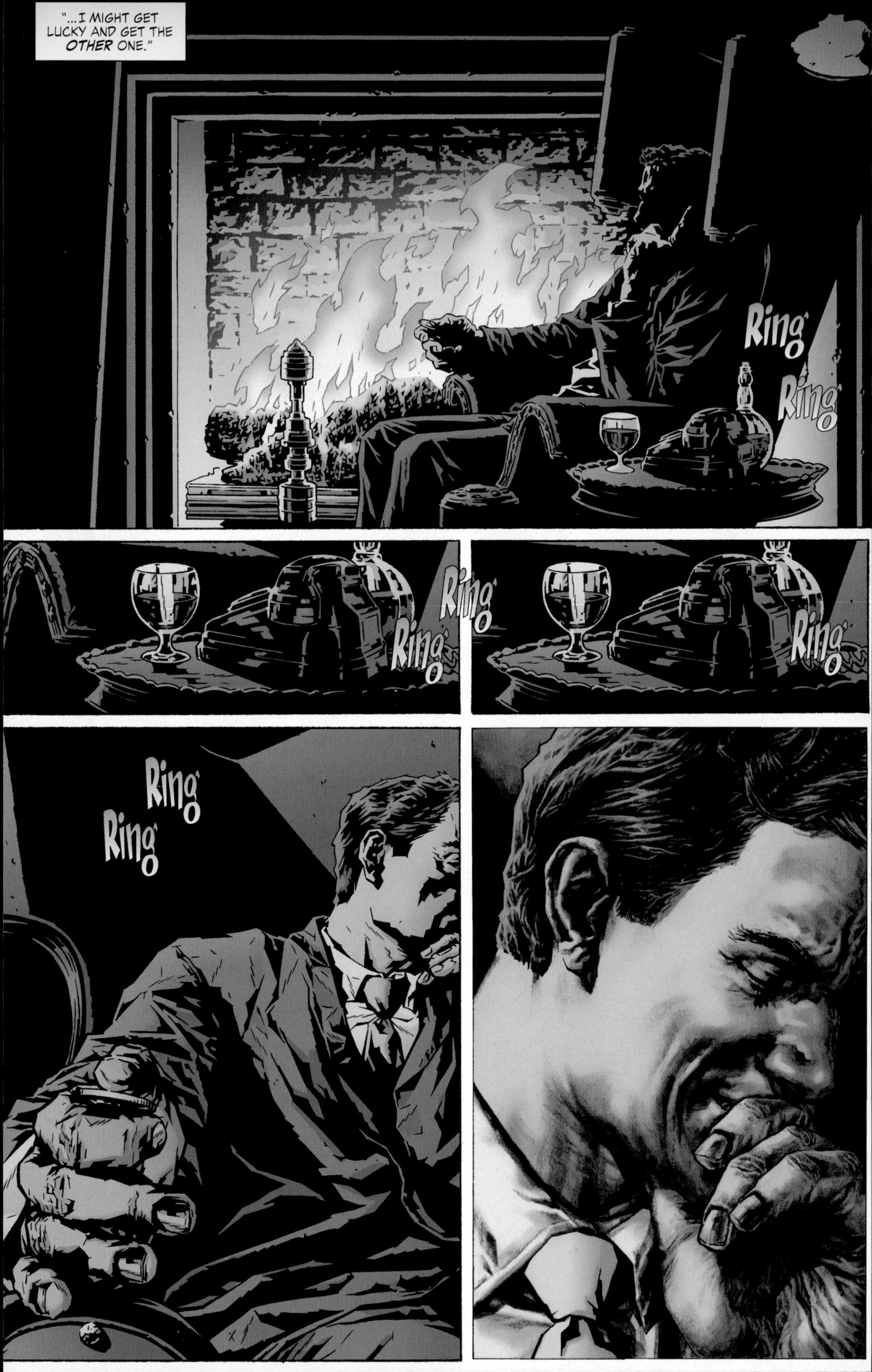
"...I MIGHT GET LUCKY AND GET THE *OTHER* ONE."
Ring
Ring
Ring
Ring
Ring
Ring
Ring

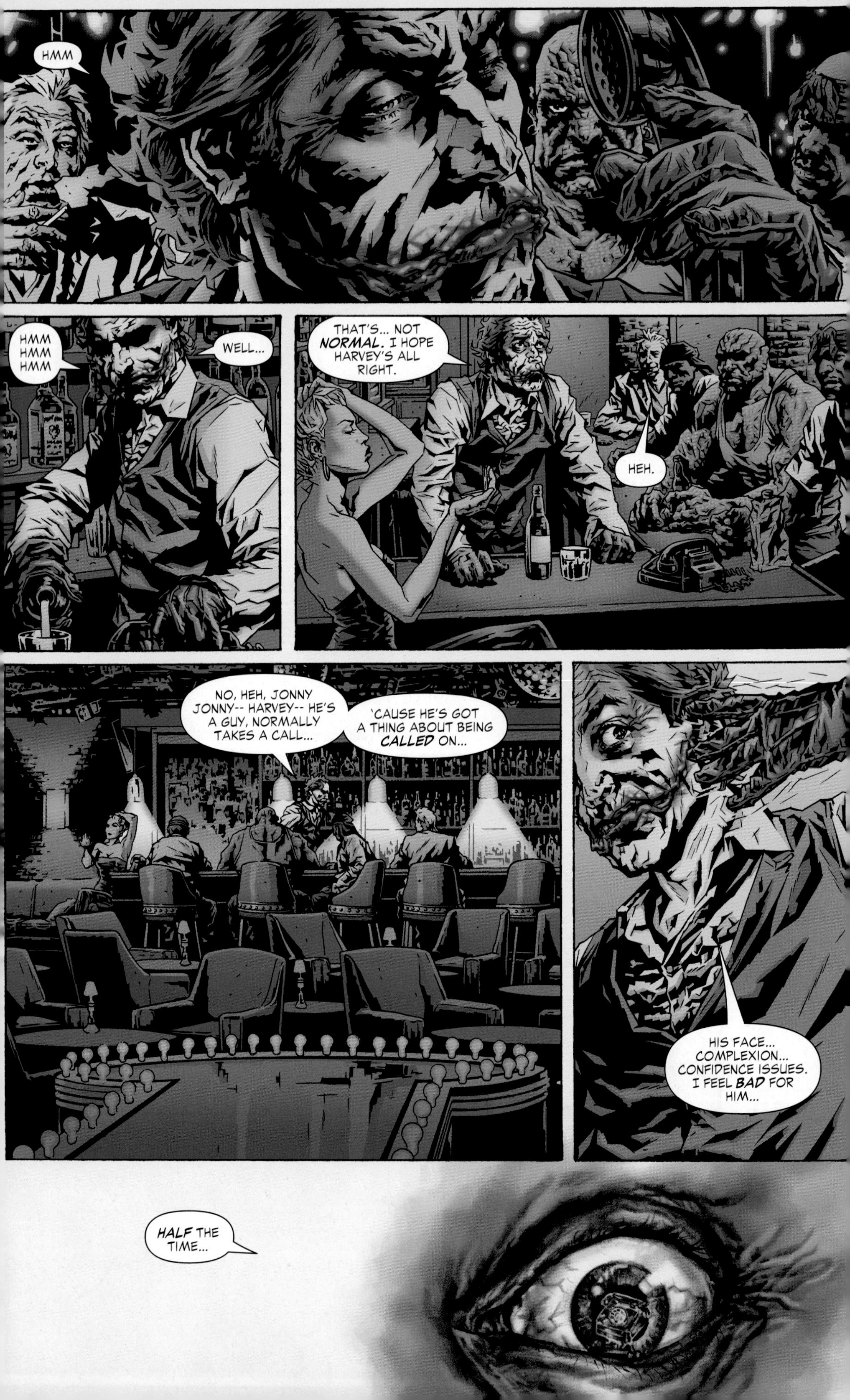
HMM
HMM HMM HMM
WELL...
THAT'S... NOT NORMAL. I HOPE HARVEY'S ALL RIGHT.
HEH.
NO, HEH, JONNY JONNY-- HARVEY-- HE'S A GUY, NORMALLY TAKES A CALL...
'CAUSE HE'S GOT A THING ABOUT BEING CALLED ON...
HIS FACE... COMPLEXION... CONFIDENCE ISSUES. I FEEL BAD FOR HIM...
HALF THE TIME...

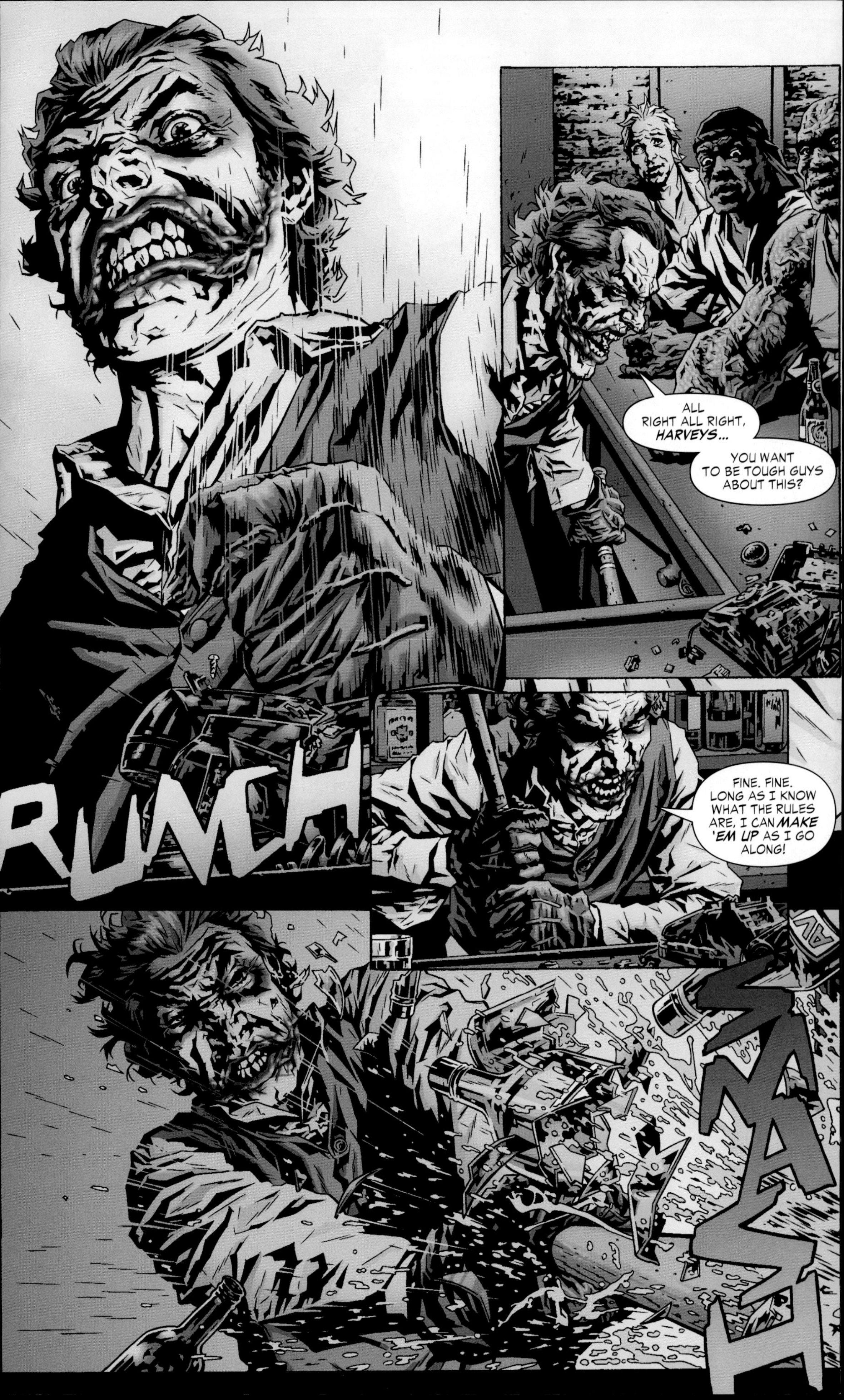
ALL RIGHT ALL RIGHT, *HARVEYS...*
YOU WANT TO BE TOUGH GUYS ABOUT THIS?
RUNCH
FINE. FINE. LONG AS I KNOW WHAT THE RULES ARE, I CAN *MAKE 'EM UP* AS I GO ALONG!

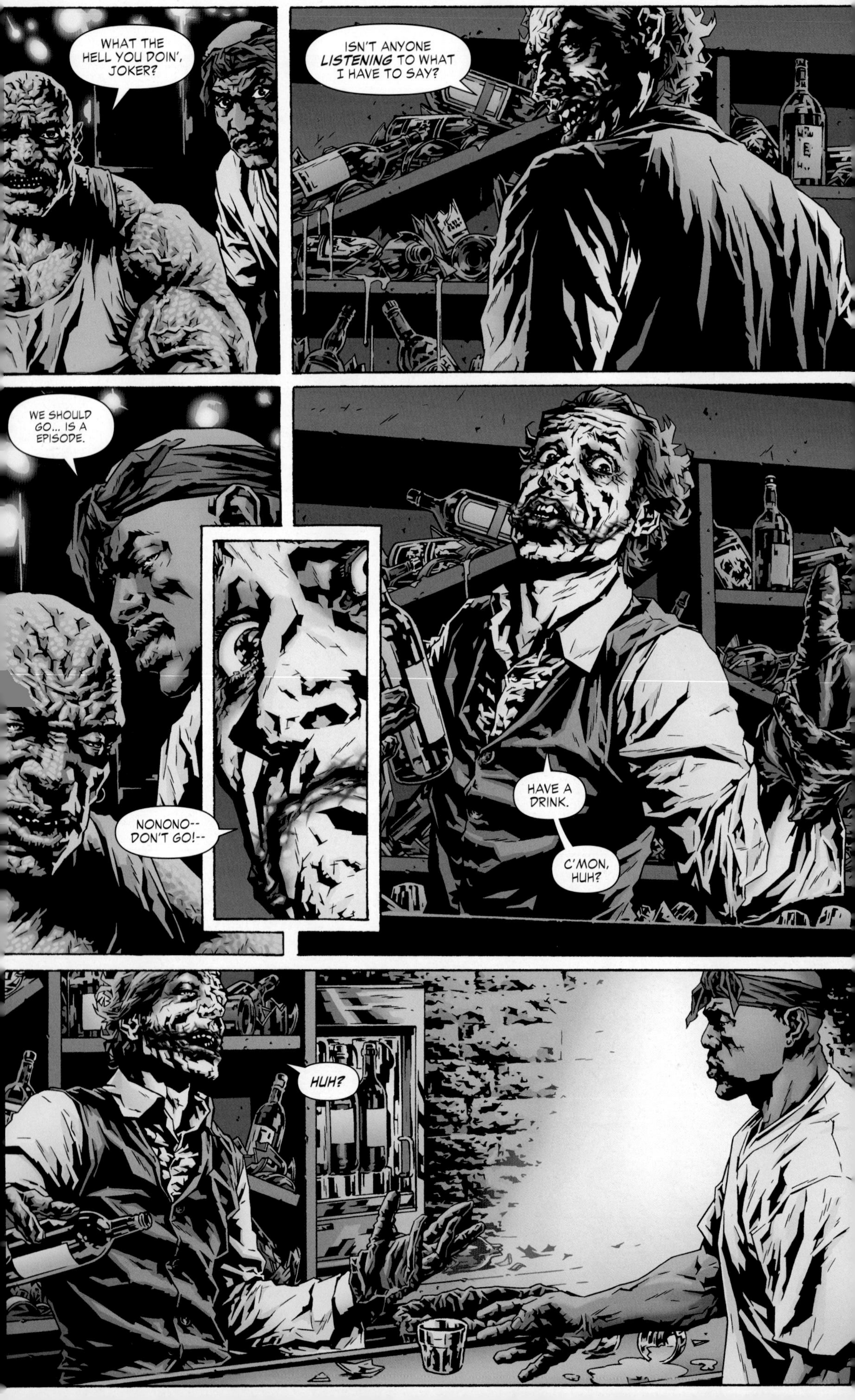
WHAT THE HELL YOU DOIN', JOKER?
ISN'T ANYONE LISTENING TO WHAT I HAVE TO SAY?
WE SHOULD GO... IS A EPISODE.
NONONO-- DON'T GO!--
HAVE A DRINK.
C'MON, HUH?
HUH?

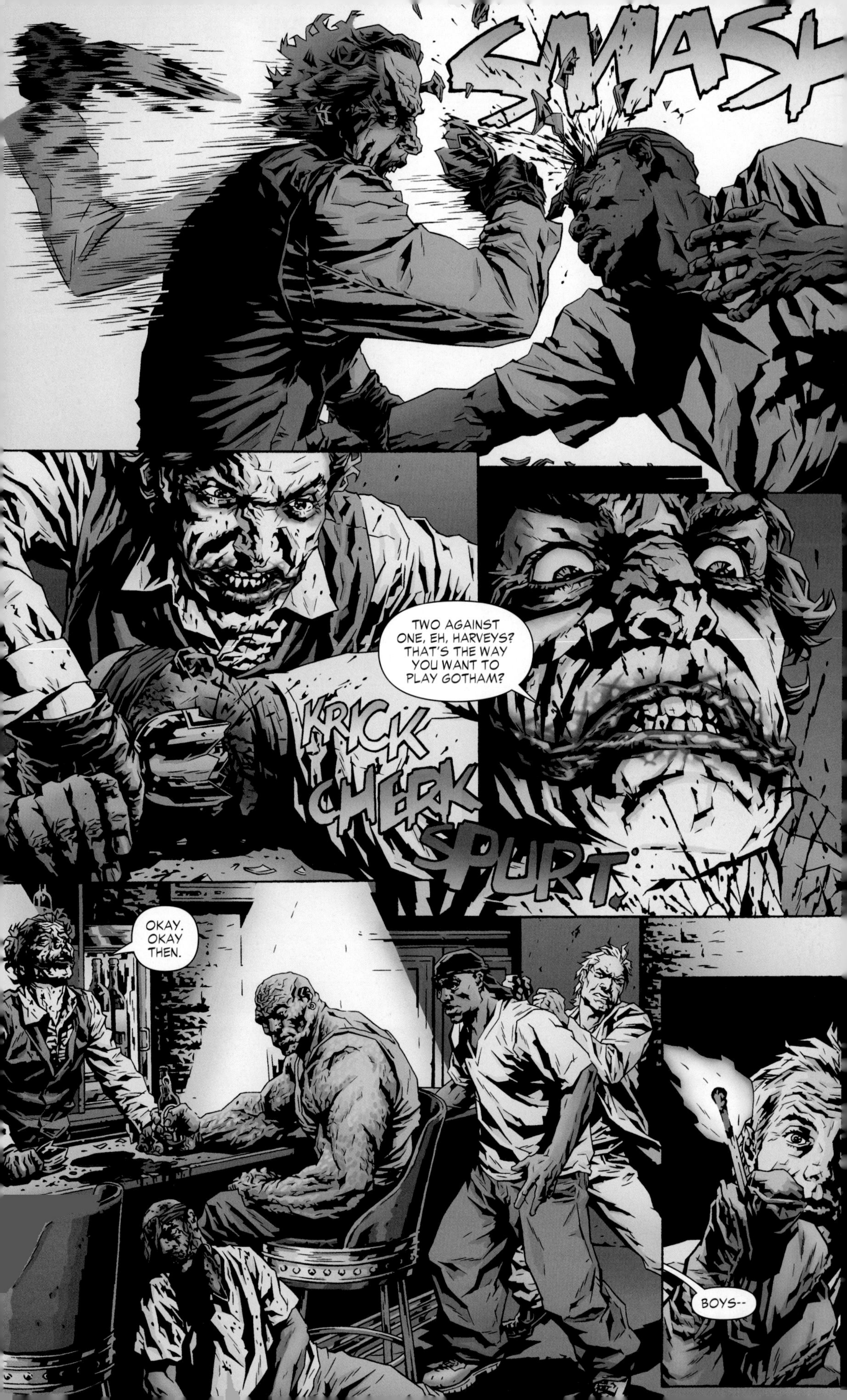
SMASH
TWO AGAINST ONE, EH, HARVEYS? THAT'S THE WAY YOU WANT TO PLAY GOTHAM?
KRICK
CHERK
SPURT
OKAY. OKAY THEN.
BOYS--

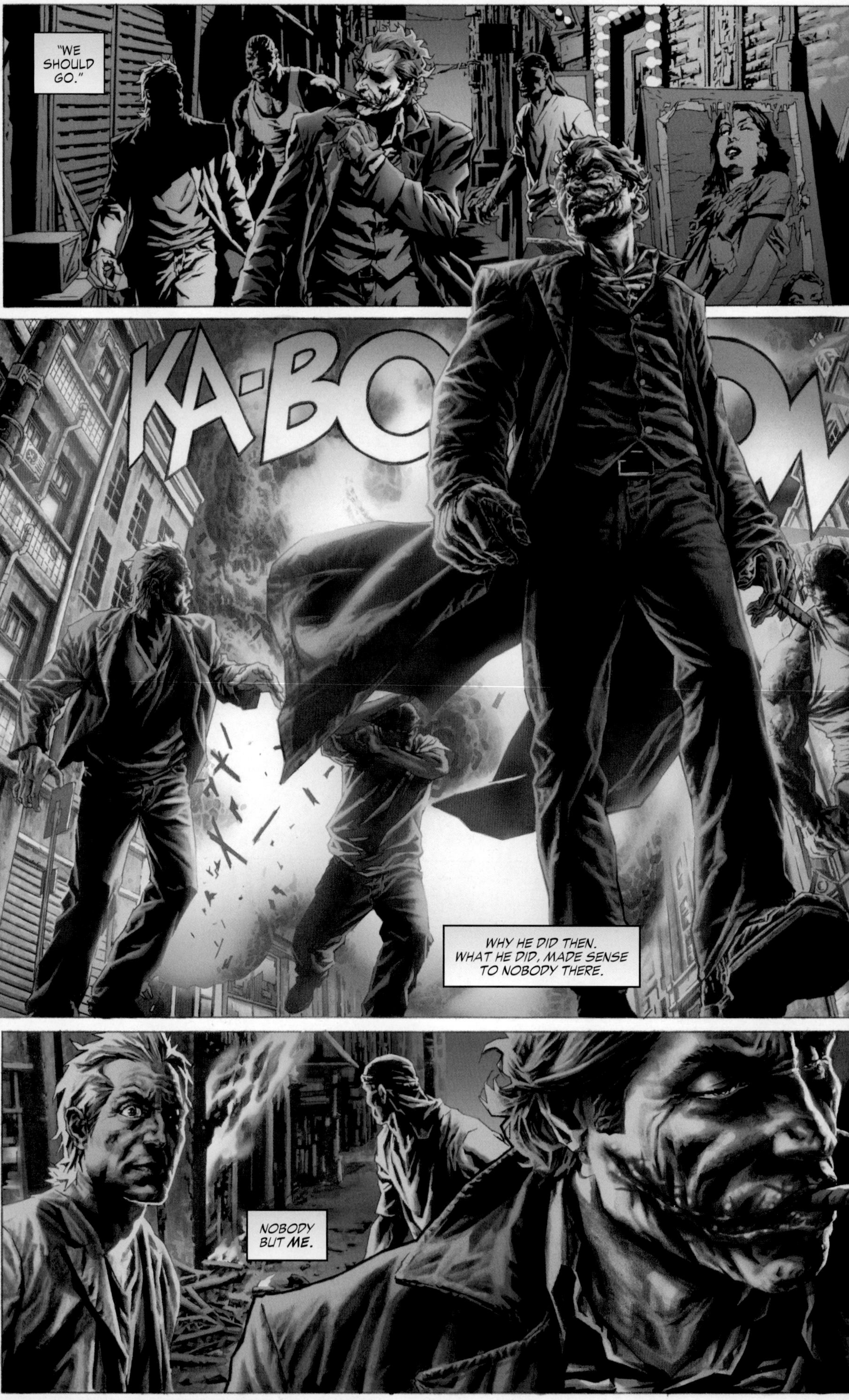
"WE SHOULD GO."
KA-BOOOM
WHY HE DID THEN. WHAT HE DID, MADE SENSE TO NOBODY THERE.
NOBODY BUT ME.

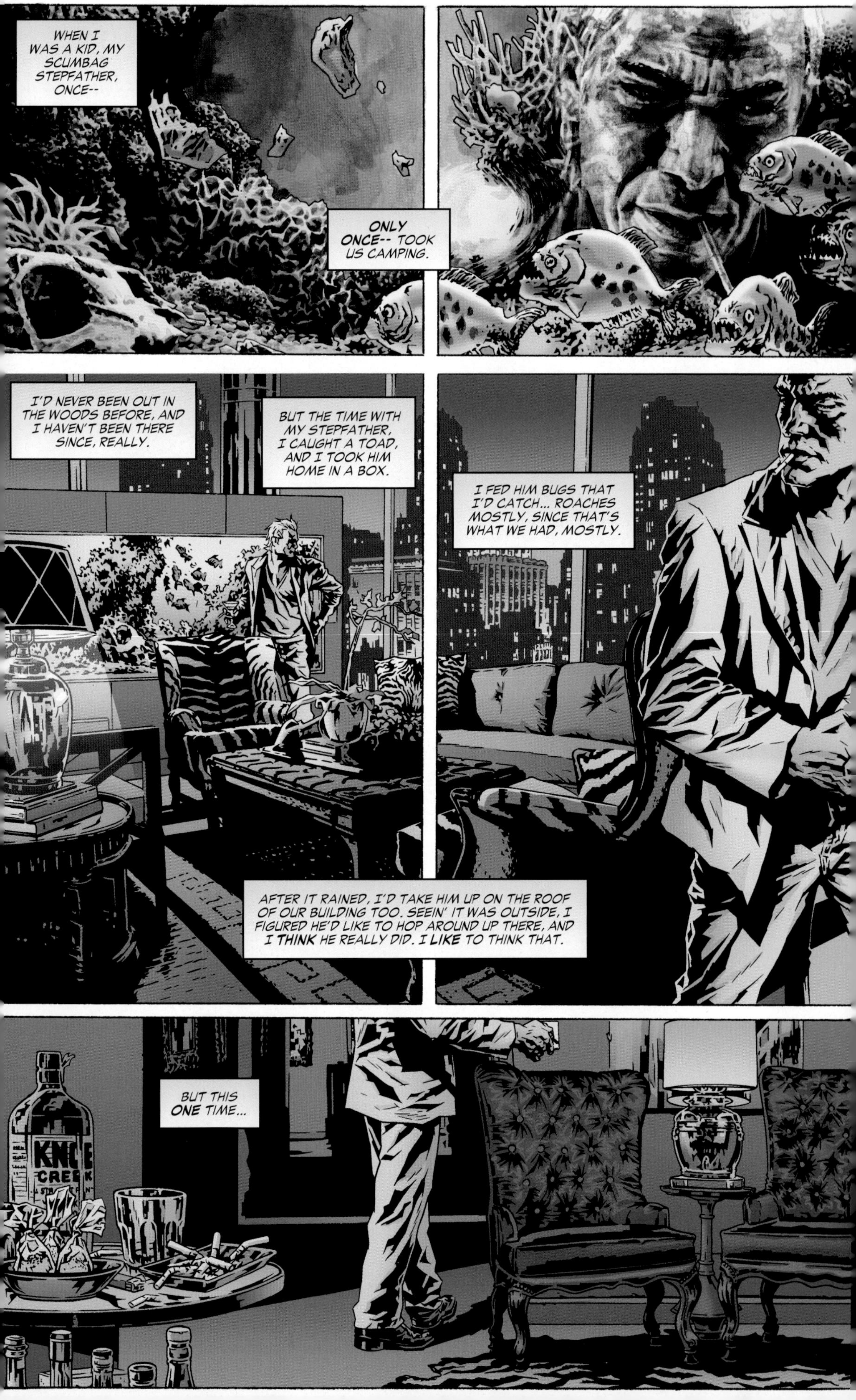
WHEN I WAS A KID, MY SCUMBAG STEPFATHER, ONCE--
ONLY ONCE-- TOOK US CAMPING.
I'D NEVER BEEN OUT IN THE WOODS BEFORE, AND I HAVEN'T BEEN THERE SINCE, REALLY.
BUT THE TIME WITH MY STEPFATHER, I CAUGHT A TOAD, AND I TOOK HIM HOME IN A BOX.
I FED HIM BUGS THAT I'D CATCH... ROACHES MOSTLY, SINCE THAT'S WHAT WE HAD, MOSTLY.
AFTER IT RAINED, I'D TAKE HIM UP ON THE ROOF OF OUR BUILDING TOO. SEEIN' IT WAS OUTSIDE, I FIGURED HE'D LIKE TO HOP AROUND UP THERE, AND I THINK HE REALLY DID. I LIKE TO THINK THAT.
BUT THIS ONE TIME...

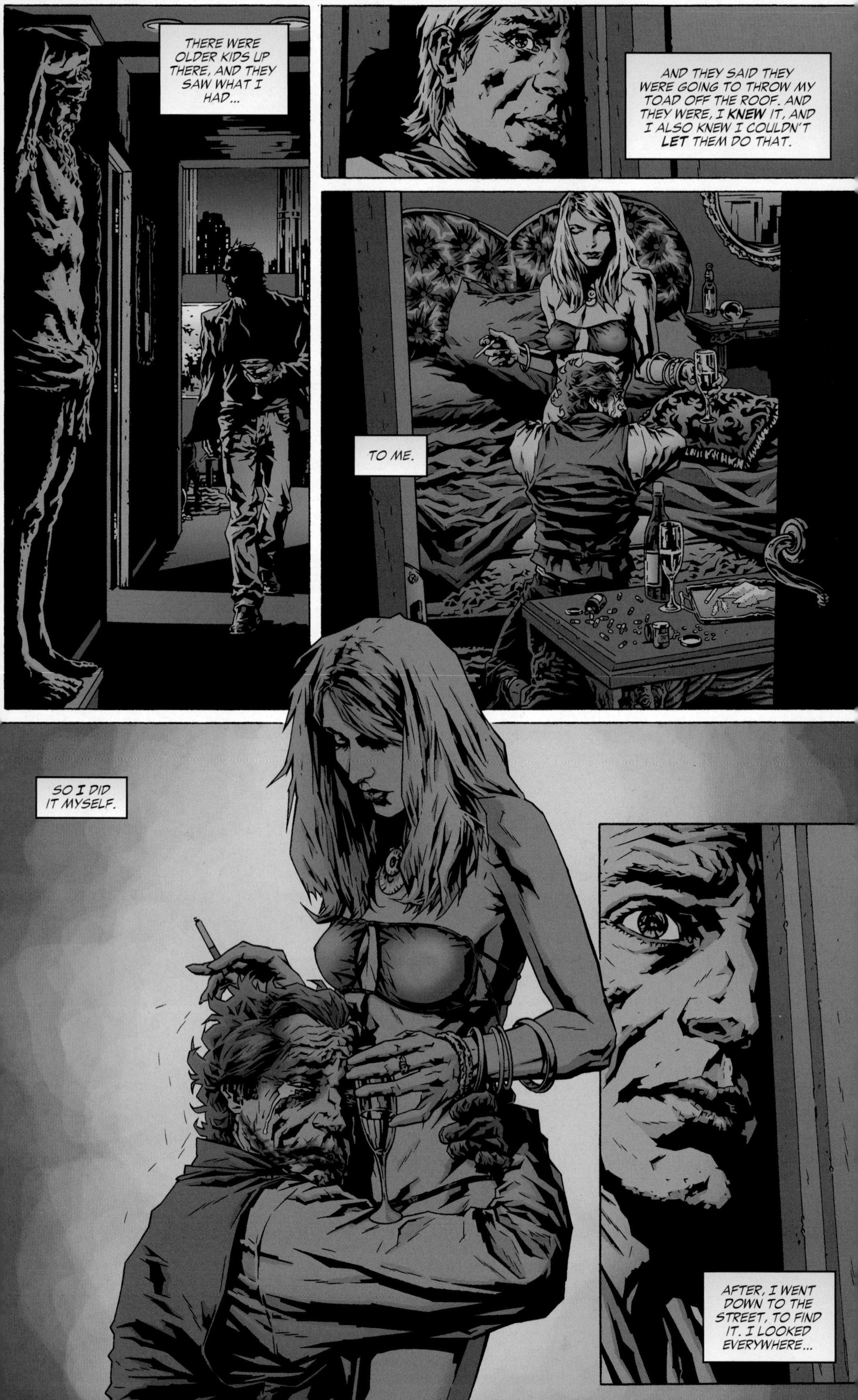
THERE WERE OLDER KIDS UP THERE, AND THEY SAW WHAT I HAD...
AND THEY SAID THEY WERE GOING TO THROW MY TOAD OFF THE ROOF. AND THEY WERE, I KNEW IT, AND I ALSO KNEW I COULDN'T LET THEM DO THAT.
TO ME.
SO I DID IT MYSELF.
AFTER, I WENT DOWN TO THE STREET, TO FIND IT. I LOOKED EVERYWHERE...

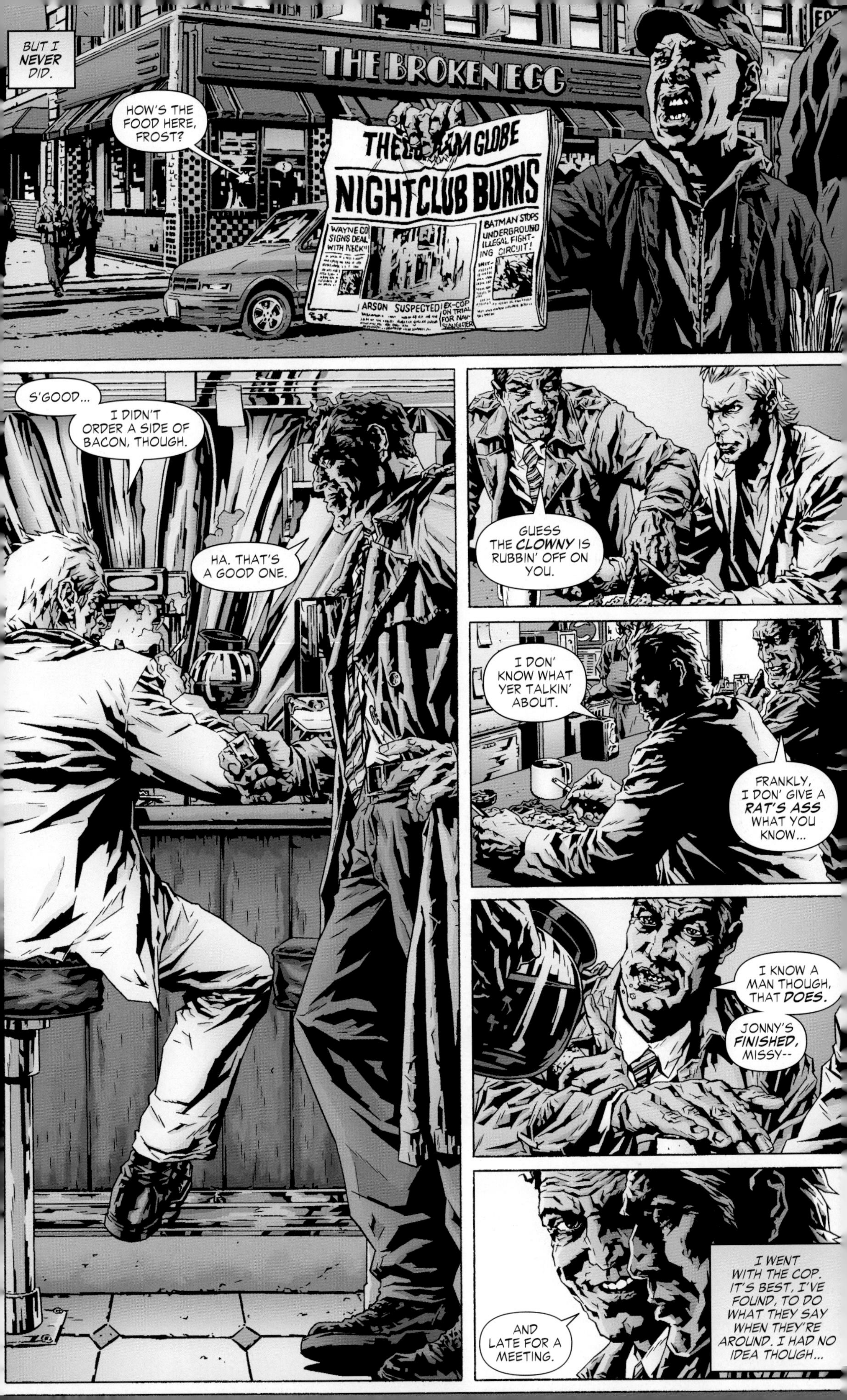
BUT I NEVER DID.
THE BROKEN EGG
HOW'S THE FOOD HERE, FROST?
NIGHTCLUB BURNS
WAYNE CO. SIGNS DEAL WITH RECK!!
BATMAN STOPS UNDERGROUND ILLEGAL FIGHTING CIRCUIT!
ARSON SUSPECTED
EX-COP ON TRIAL FOR MAN-SLAUGHTER
S'GOOD...
I DIDN'T ORDER A SIDE OF BACON, THOUGH.
HA. THAT'S A GOOD ONE.
GUESS THE CLOWNY IS RUBBIN' OFF ON YOU.
I DON' KNOW WHAT YER TALKIN' ABOUT.
FRANKLY, I DON' GIVE A RAT'S ASS WHAT YOU KNOW...
I KNOW A MAN THOUGH, THAT DOES.
JONNY'S FINISHED, MISSY--
AND LATE FOR A MEETING.
I WENT WITH THE COP. IT'S BEST, I'VE FOUND, TO DO WHAT THEY SAY WHEN THEY'RE AROUND. I HAD NO IDEA THOUGH...

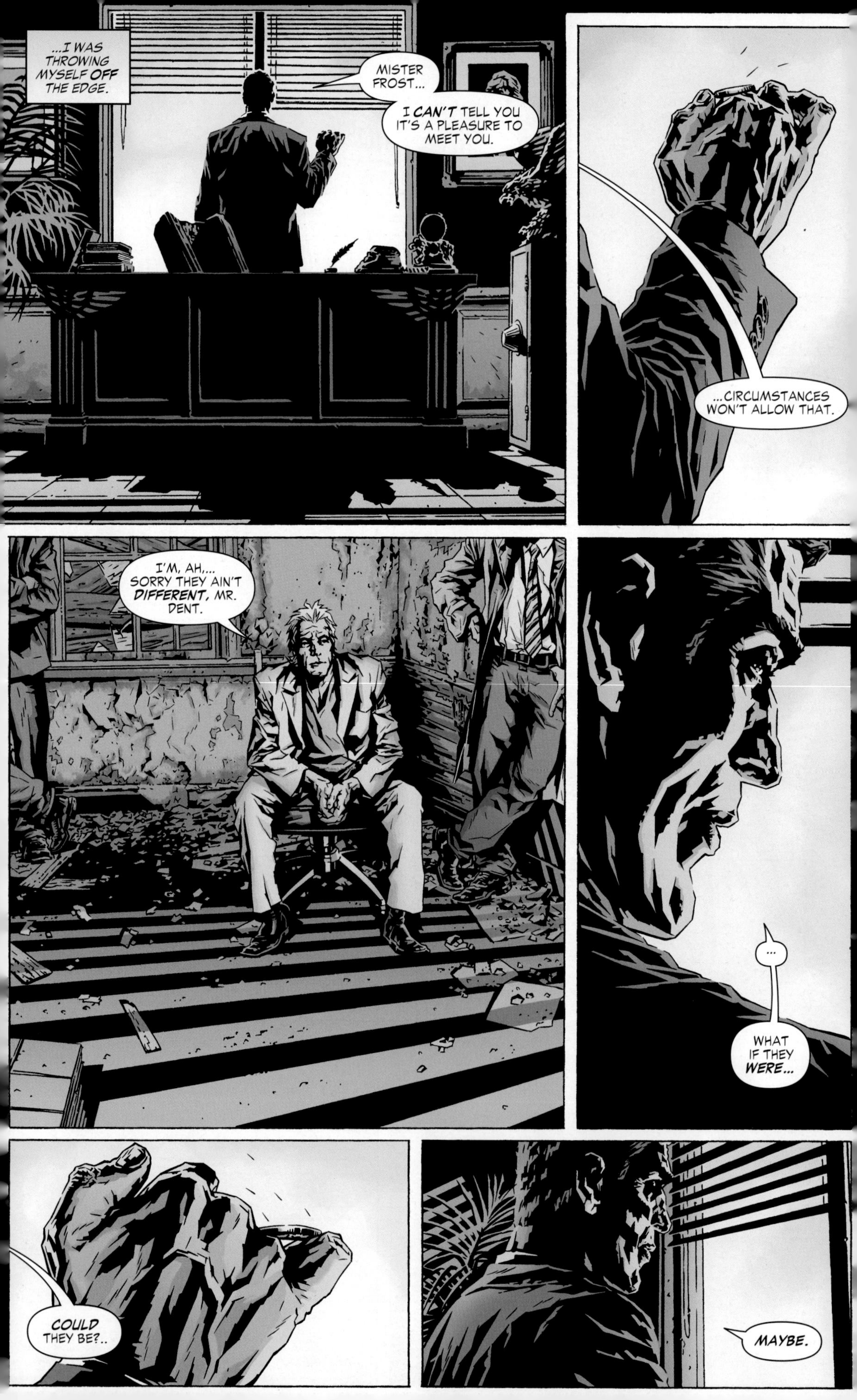
...I WAS THROWING MYSELF OFF THE EDGE.
MISTER FROST...
I CAN'T TELL YOU IT'S A PLEASURE TO MEET YOU.
...CIRCUMSTANCES WON'T ALLOW THAT.
I'M, AH,... SORRY THEY AIN'T DIFFERENT, MR. DENT.
...
WHAT IF THEY WERE...
COULD THEY BE?..
MAYBE.

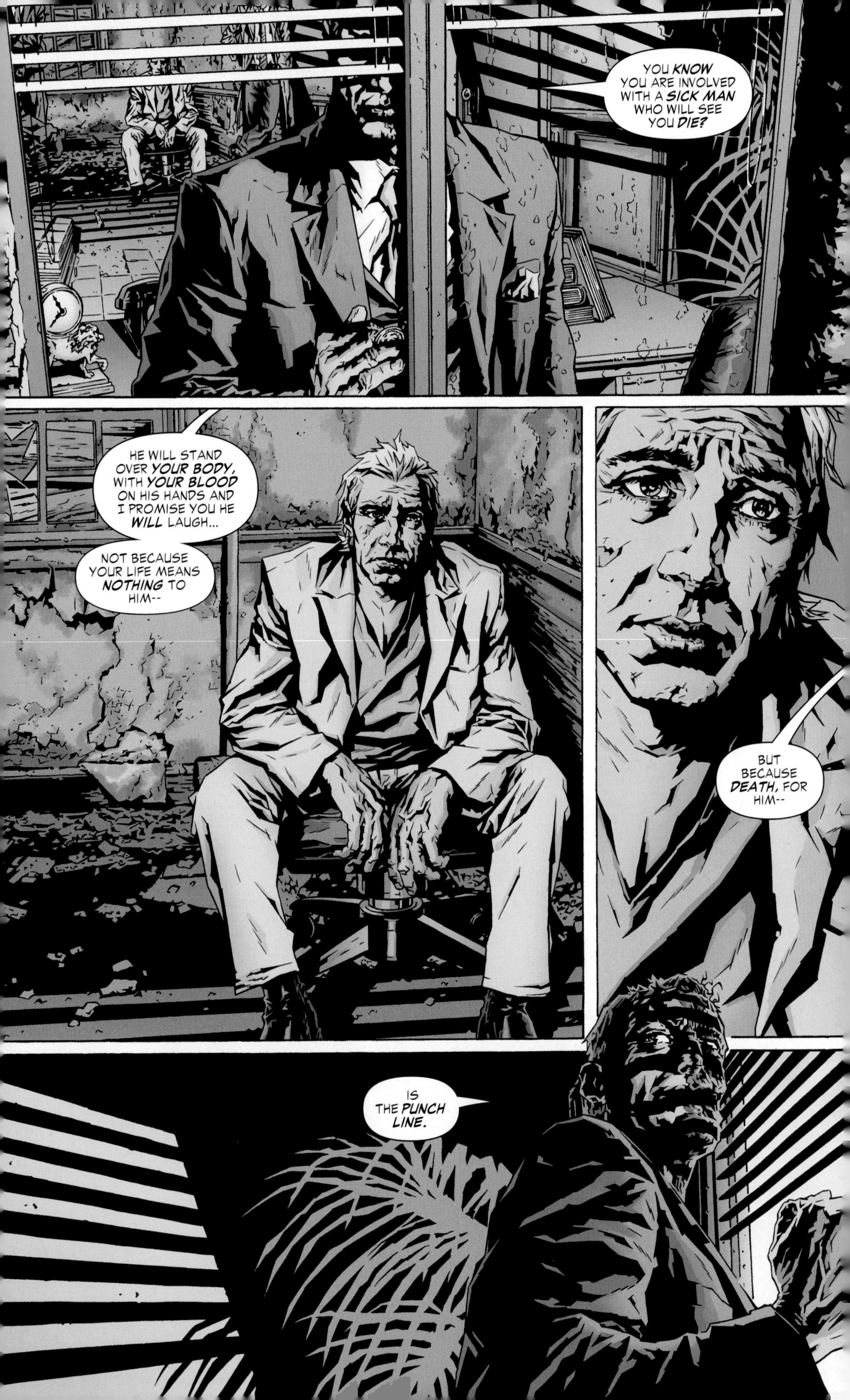
YOU KNOW YOU ARE INVOLVED WITH A SICK MAN WHO WILL SEE YOU DIE?
HE WILL STAND OVER YOUR BODY, WITH YOUR BLOOD ON HIS HANDS AND I PROMISE YOU HE WILL LAUGH...
NOT BECAUSE YOUR LIFE MEANS NOTHING TO HIM--
BUT BECAUSE DEATH, FOR HIM--
IS THE PUNCH LINE.

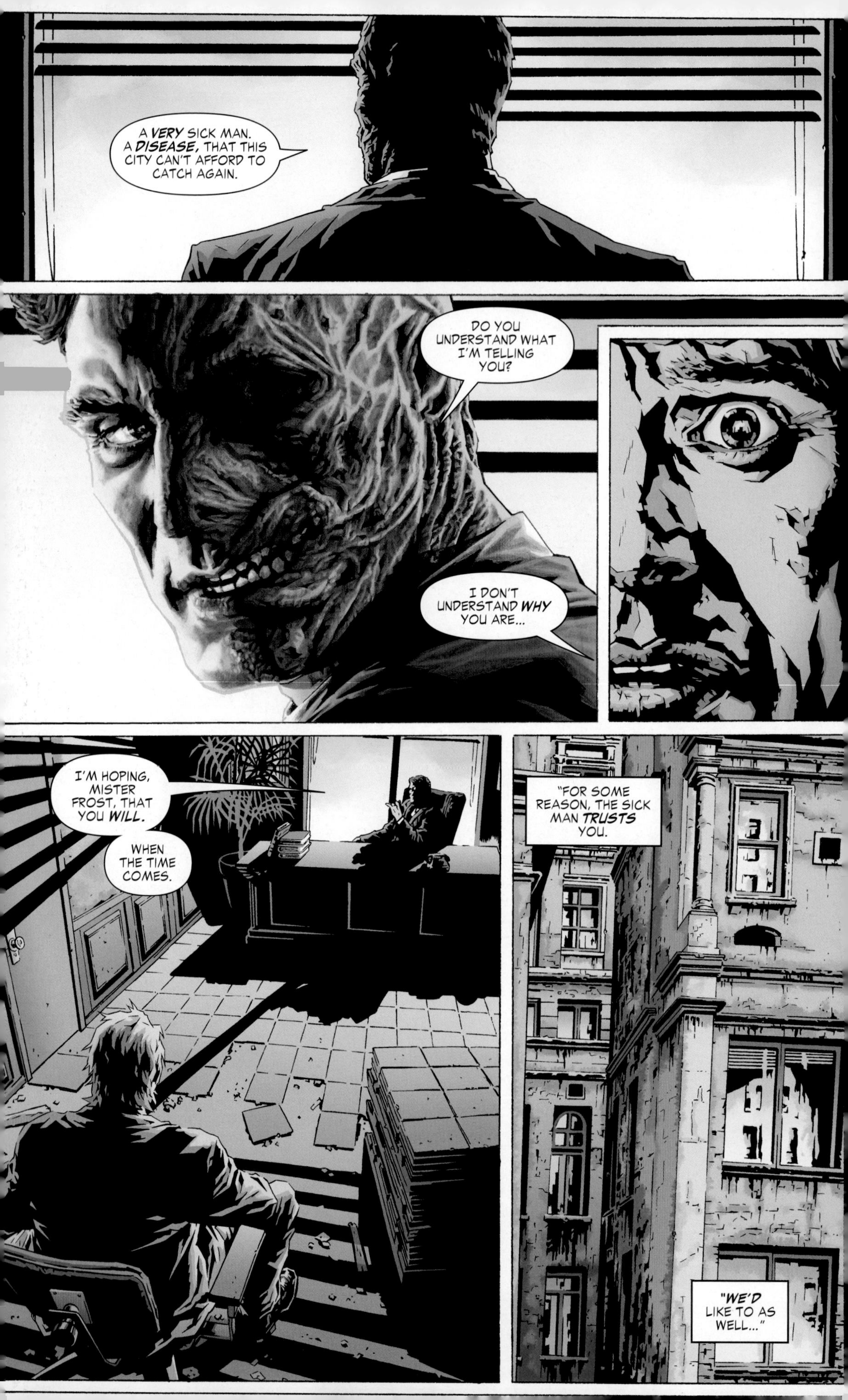
A VERY SICK MAN. A DISEASE, THAT THIS CITY CAN'T AFFORD TO CATCH AGAIN.
DO YOU UNDERSTAND WHAT I'M TELLING YOU?
I DON'T UNDERSTAND WHY YOU ARE...
I'M HOPING, MISTER FROST, THAT YOU WILL.
WHEN THE TIME COMES.
"FOR SOME REASON, THE SICK MAN TRUSTS YOU.
"WE'D LIKE TO AS WELL..."

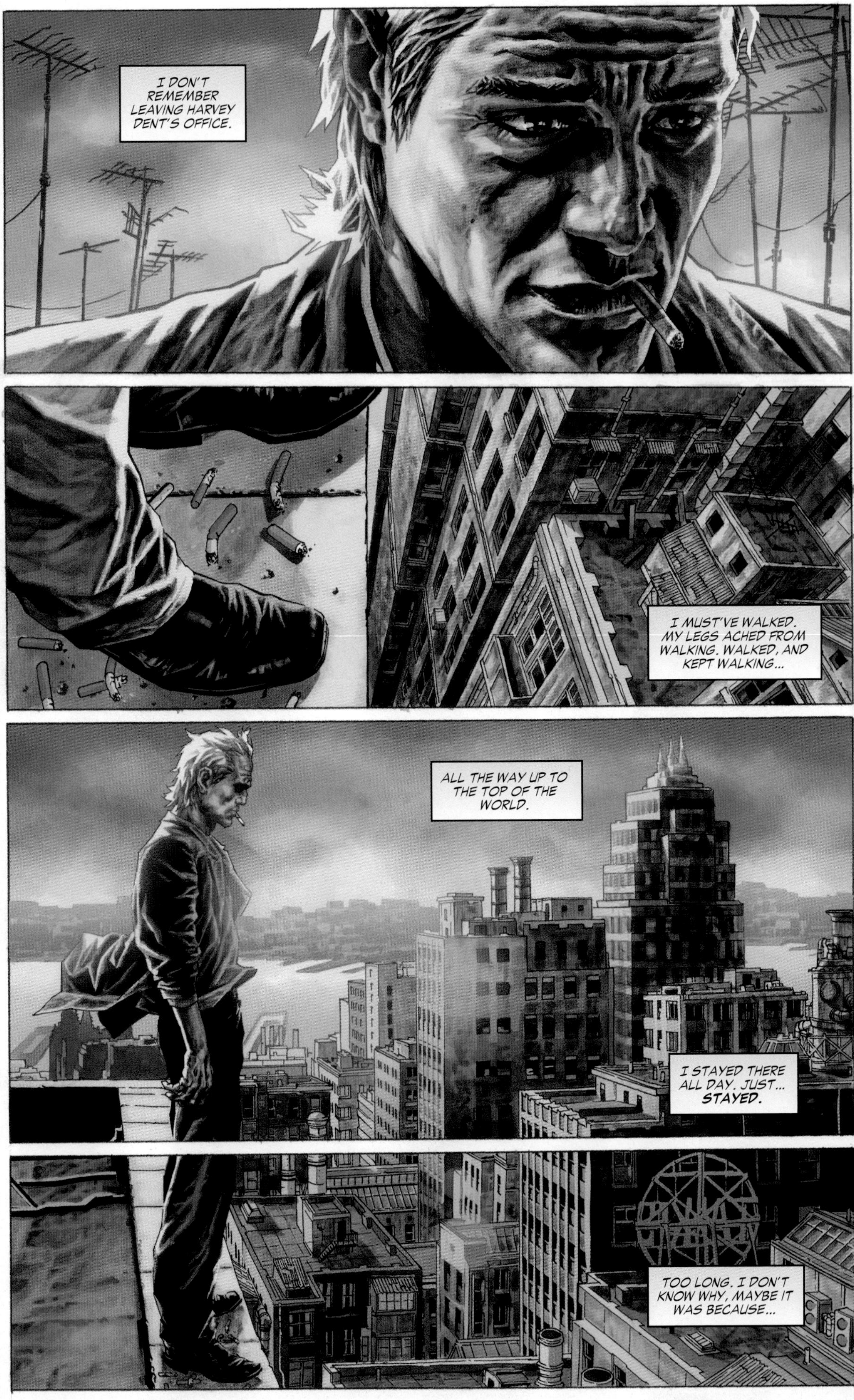
I DON'T REMEMBER LEAVING HARVEY DENT'S OFFICE.
I MUST'VE WALKED. MY LEGS ACHED FROM WALKING. WALKED, AND KEPT WALKING...
ALL THE WAY UP TO THE TOP OF THE WORLD.
I STAYED THERE ALL DAY. JUST... **STAYED.**
TOO LONG. I DON'T KNOW WHY, MAYBE IT WAS BECAUSE...

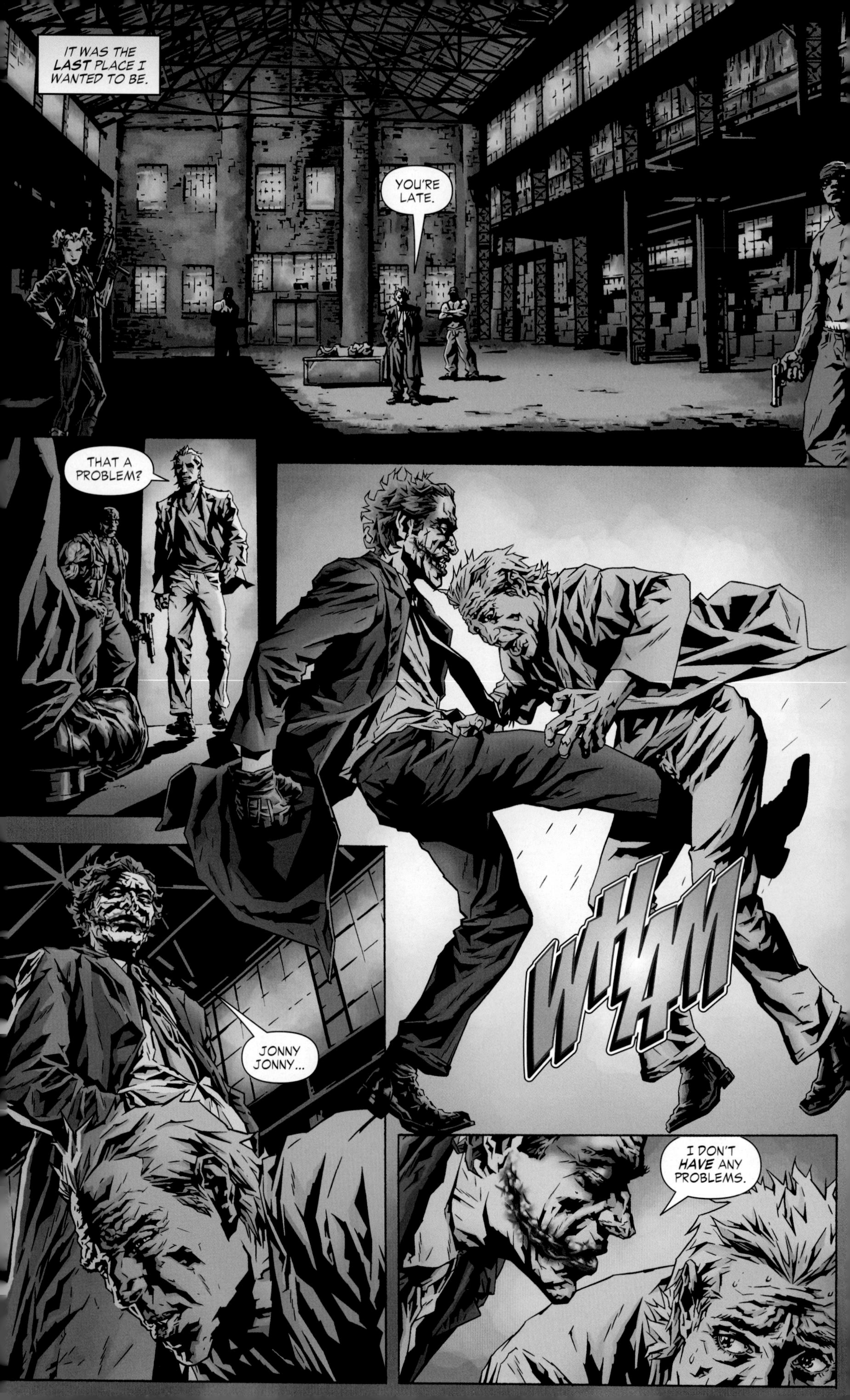
IT WAS THE LAST PLACE I WANTED TO BE.
YOU'RE LATE.
THAT A PROBLEM?
WHAM
JONNY JONNY...
I DON'T HAVE ANY PROBLEMS.

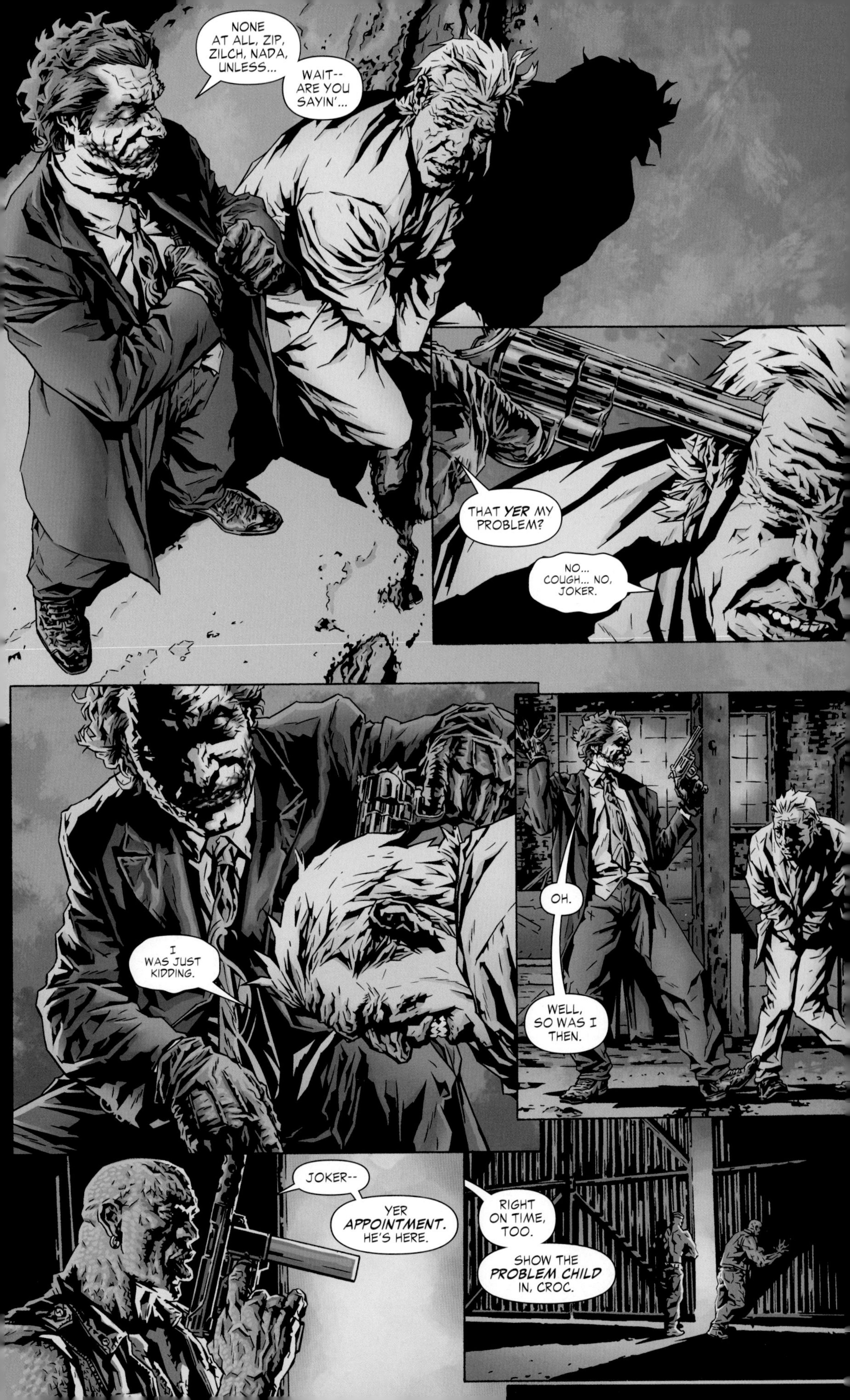
NONE AT ALL, ZIP, ZILCH, NADA, UNLESS...
WAIT-- ARE YOU SAYIN'...
THAT YER MY PROBLEM?
NO... COUGH... NO, JOKER.
I WAS JUST KIDDING.
OH.
WELL, SO WAS I THEN.
JOKER--
YER APPOINTMENT. HE'S HERE.
RIGHT ON TIME, TOO.
SHOW THE PROBLEM CHILD IN, CROC.

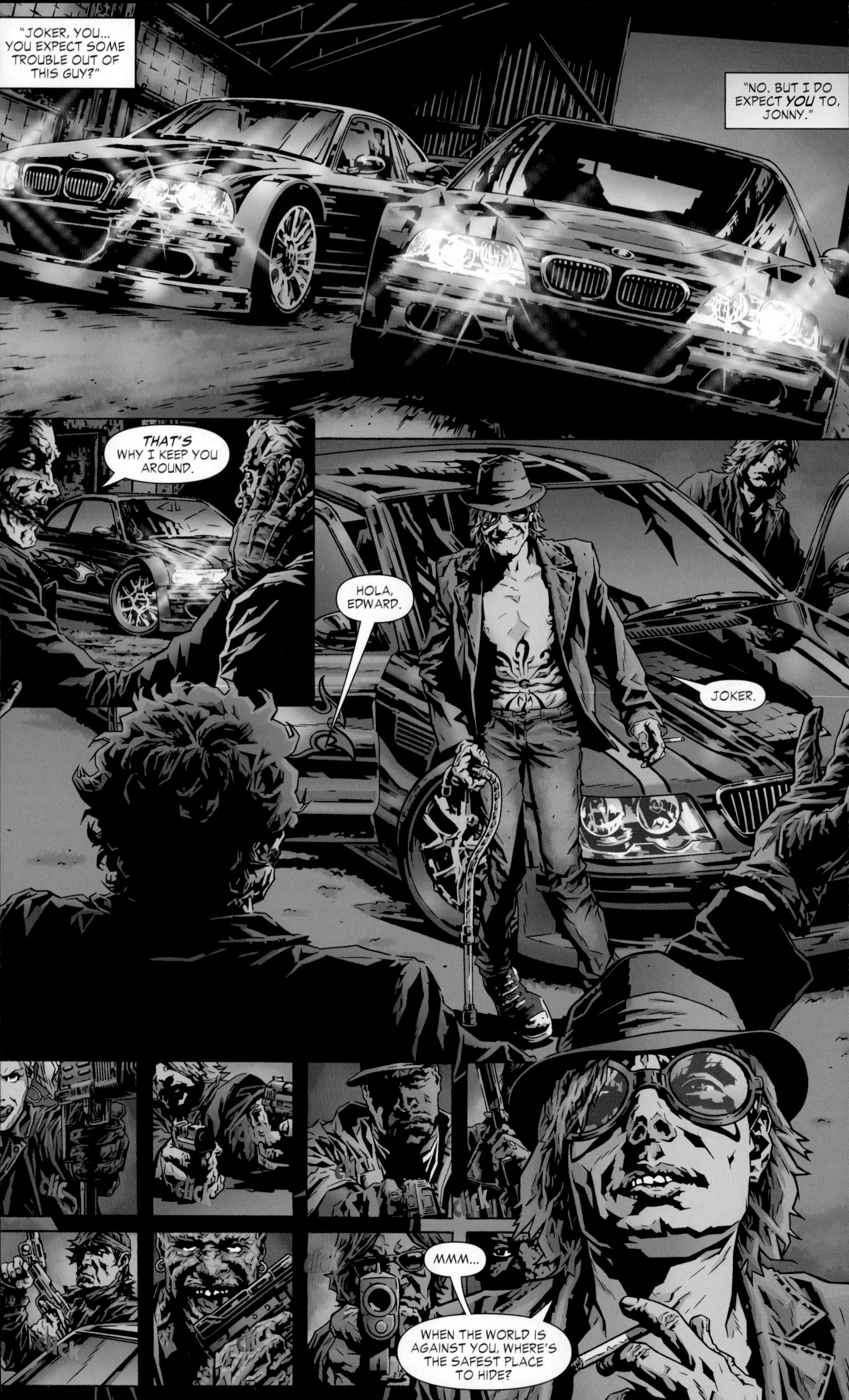
"JOKER, YOU... YOU EXPECT SOME TROUBLE OUT OF THIS GUY?"
"NO. BUT I DO EXPECT *YOU* TO, JONNY."
THAT'S WHY I KEEP YOU AROUND.
HOLA, EDWARD.
JOKER.
MMM...
WHEN THE WORLD IS AGAINST YOU, WHERE'S THE SAFEST PLACE TO HIDE?

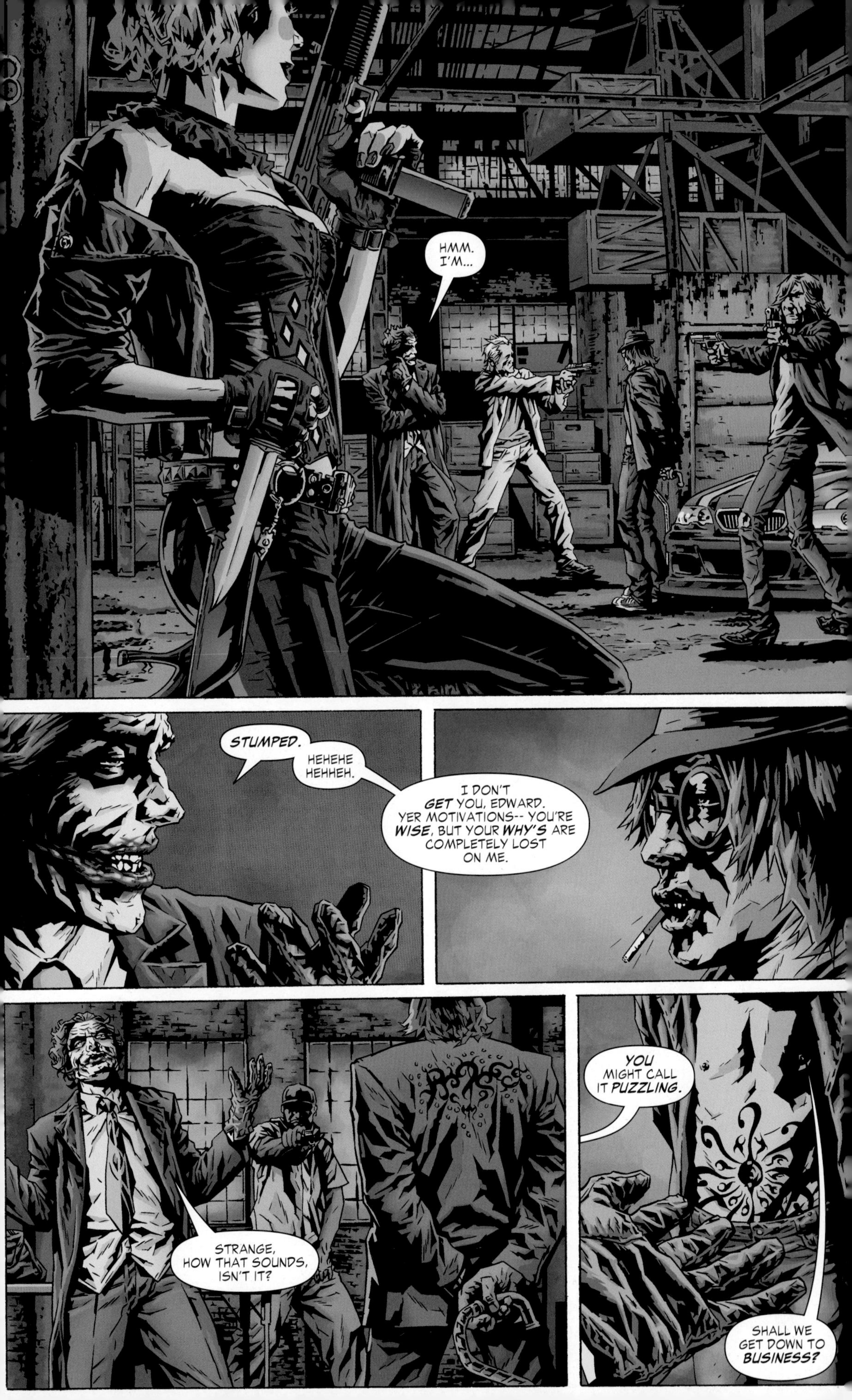
HMM. I'M...
STUMPED.
HEHEHE HEHHEH.
I DON'T GET YOU, EDWARD. YER MOTIVATIONS-- YOU'RE WISE, BUT YOUR WHY'S ARE COMPLETELY LOST ON ME.
STRANGE, HOW THAT SOUNDS, ISN'T IT?
YOU MIGHT CALL IT PUZZLING.
SHALL WE GET DOWN TO BUSINESS?

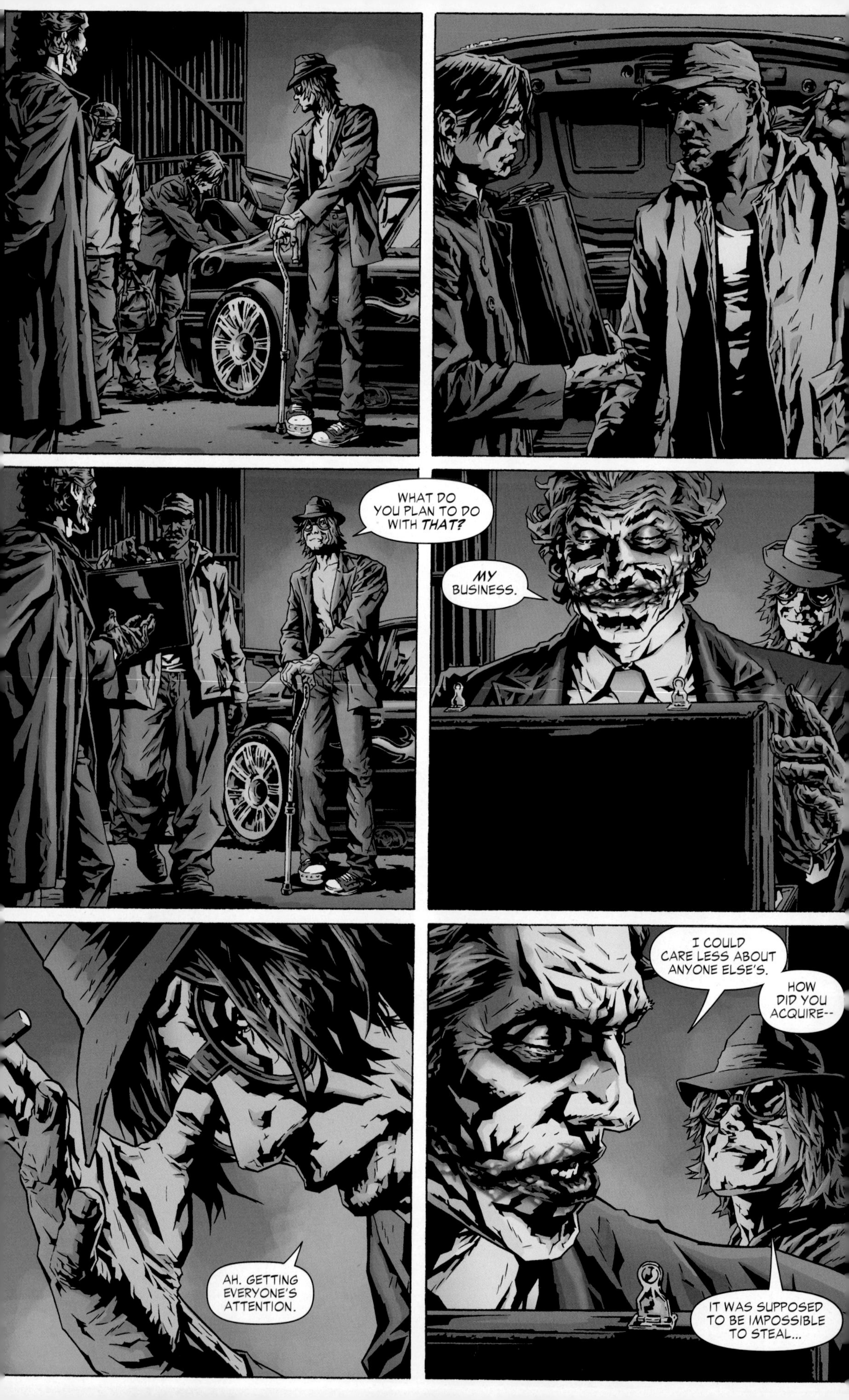
WHAT DO YOU PLAN TO DO WITH *THAT?*
MY BUSINESS.
AH. GETTING EVERYONE'S ATTENTION.
I COULD CARE LESS ABOUT ANYONE ELSE'S.
HOW DID YOU ACQUIRE--
IT WAS SUPPOSED TO BE IMPOSSIBLE TO STEAL...

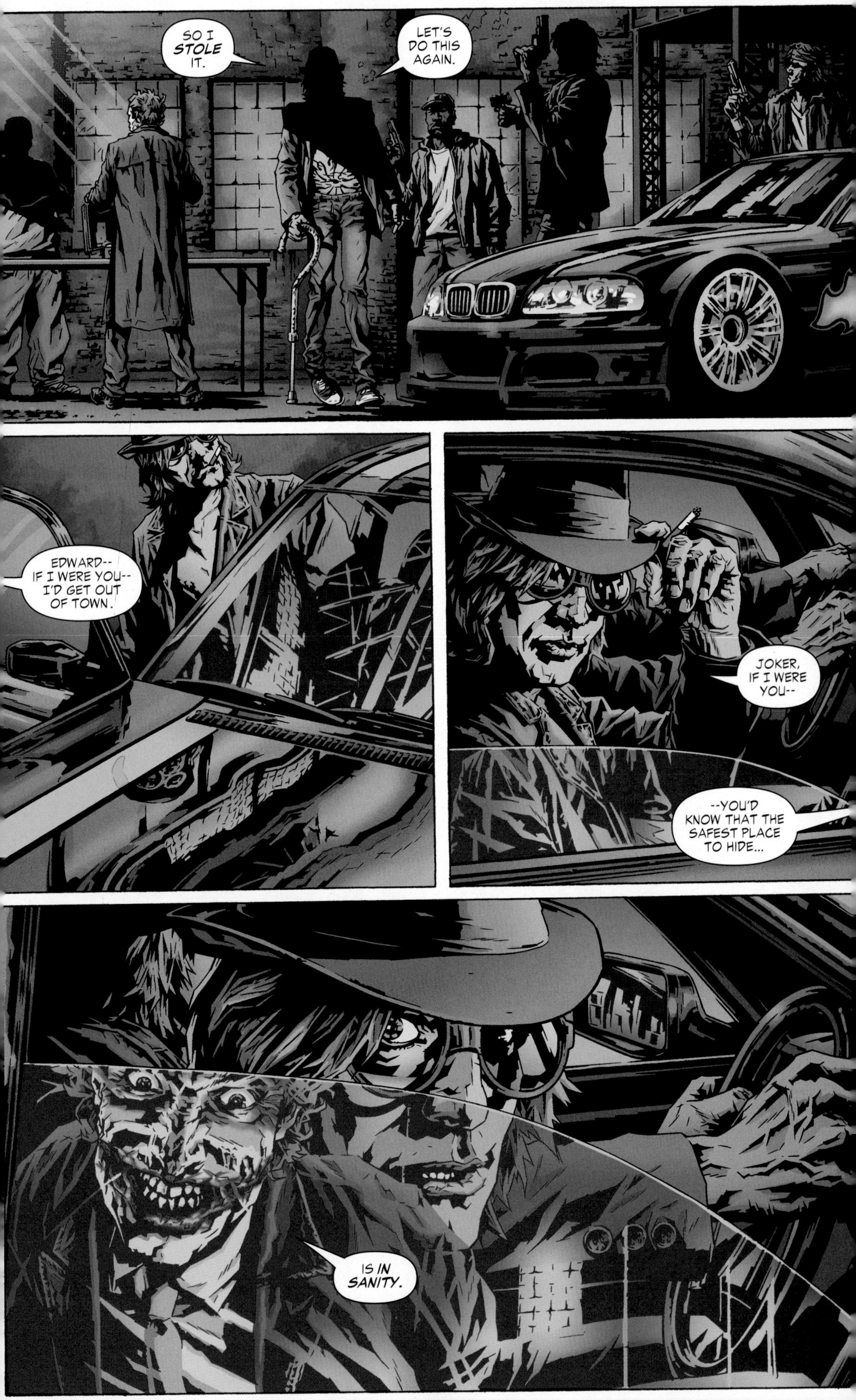
SO I STOLE IT.
LET'S DO THIS AGAIN.
EDWARD-- IF I WERE YOU-- I'D GET OUT OF TOWN.
JOKER, IF I WERE YOU--
--YOU'D KNOW THAT THE SAFEST PLACE TO HIDE...
IS IN SANITY.

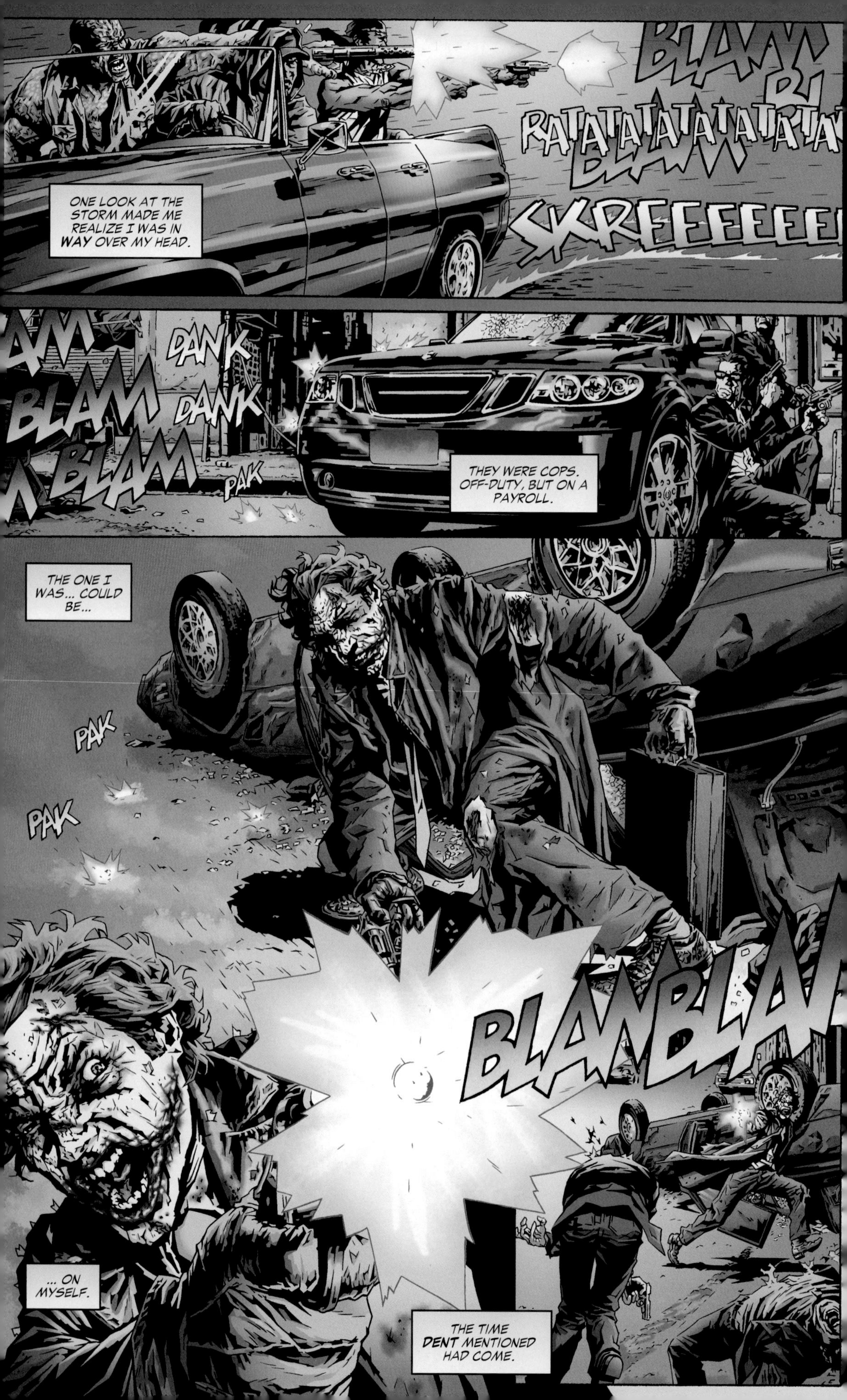

BLAMM BLAMM
RATATATATATATATATAT
SKREEEEEEE
ONE LOOK AT THE STORM MADE ME REALIZE I WAS IN WAY OVER MY HEAD.
BLAM BLAM BLAM
DANK DANK
PAK
THEY WERE COPS. OFF-DUTY, BUT ON A PAYROLL.
THE ONE I WAS... COULD BE...
PAK
PAK
BLAMBLAM
... ON MYSELF.
THE TIME DENT MENTIONED HAD COME.

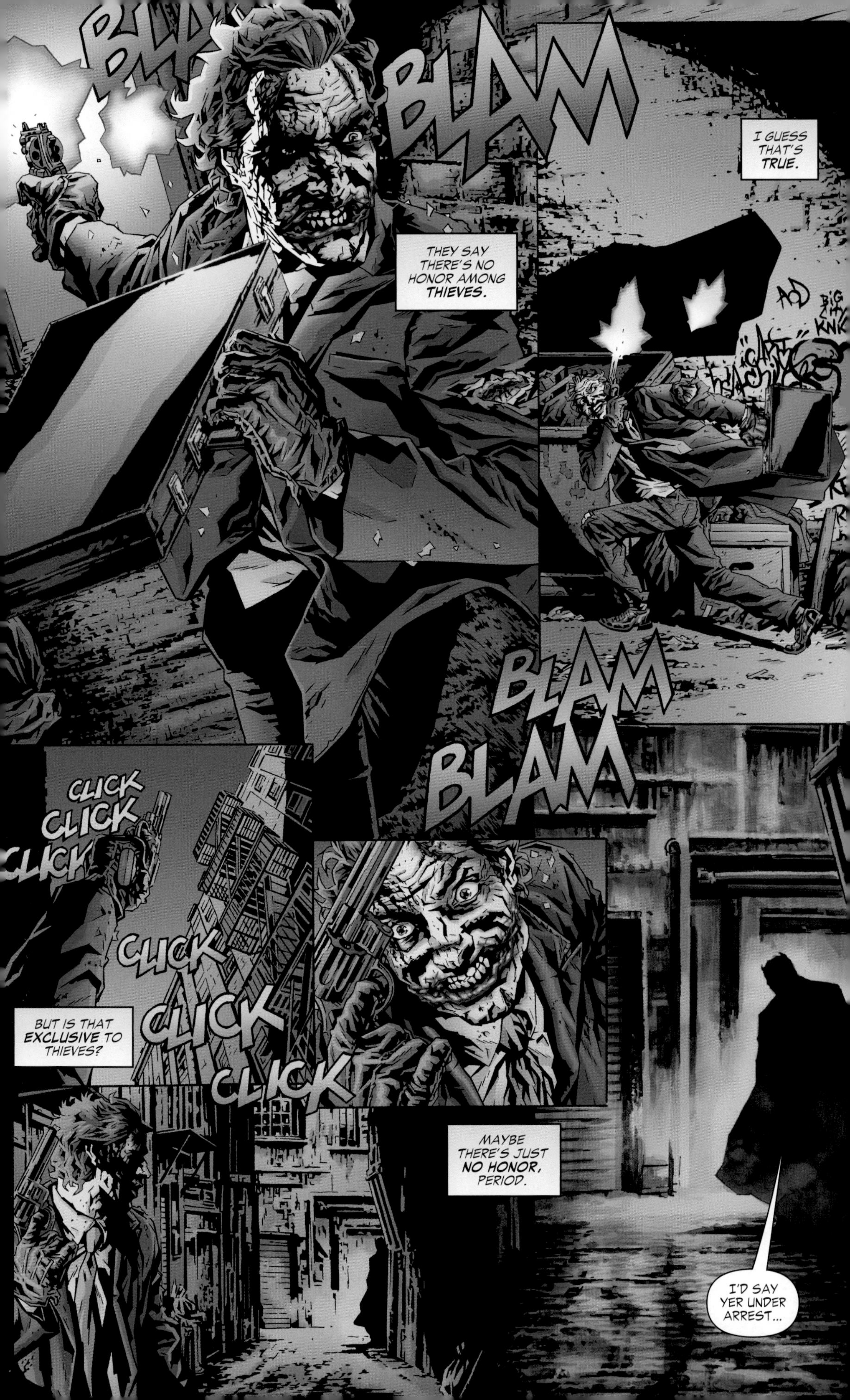
BLAM
BLAM
THEY SAY THERE'S NO HONOR AMONG THIEVES.
I GUESS THAT'S TRUE.
BLAM
BLAM
CLICK
CLICK
CLICK
CLICK
CLICK
CLICK
BUT IS THAT EXCLUSIVE TO THIEVES?
MAYBE THERE'S JUST NO HONOR, PERIOD.
I'D SAY YER UNDER ARREST...

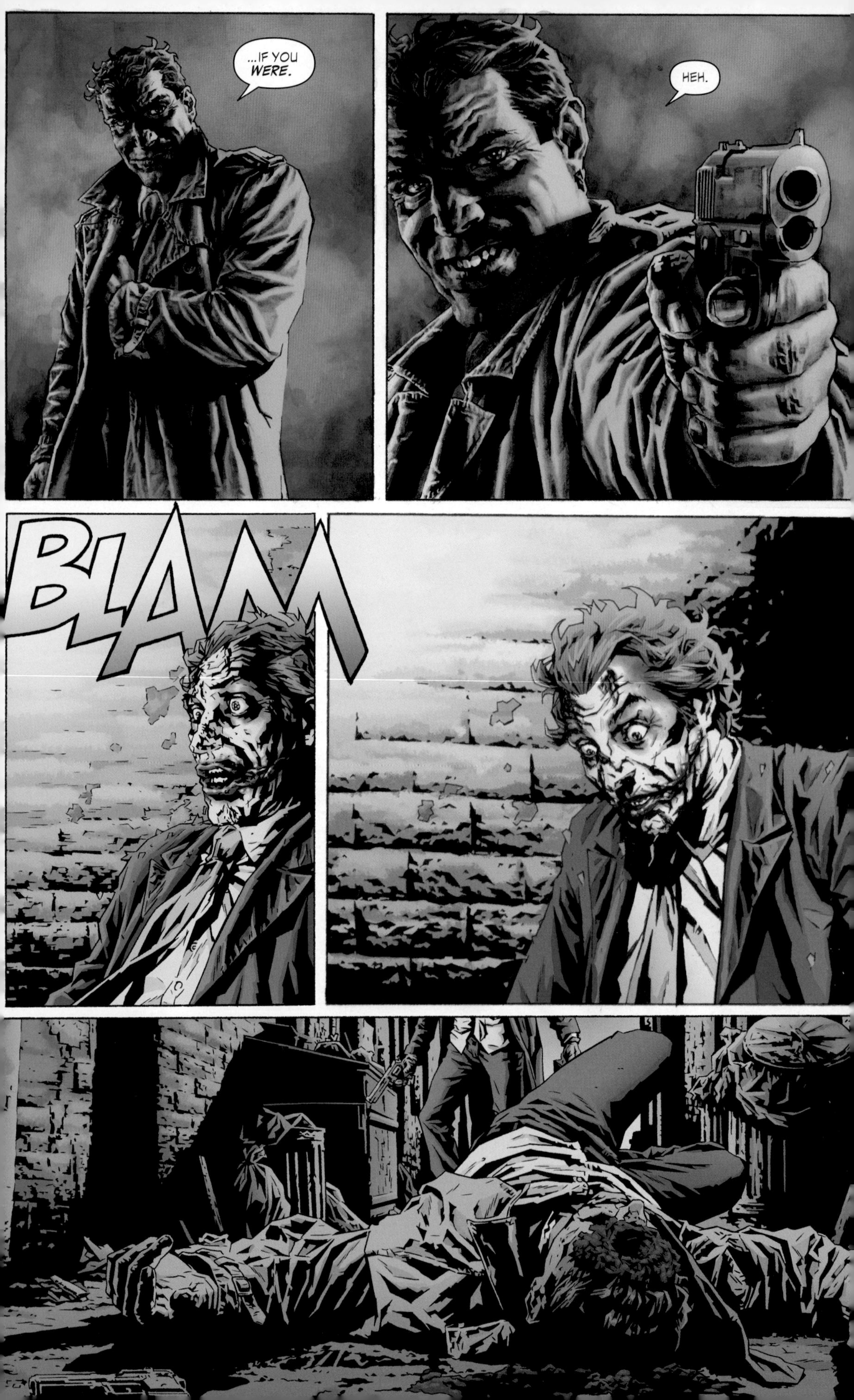
...IF YOU WERE.
HEH.
BLAM

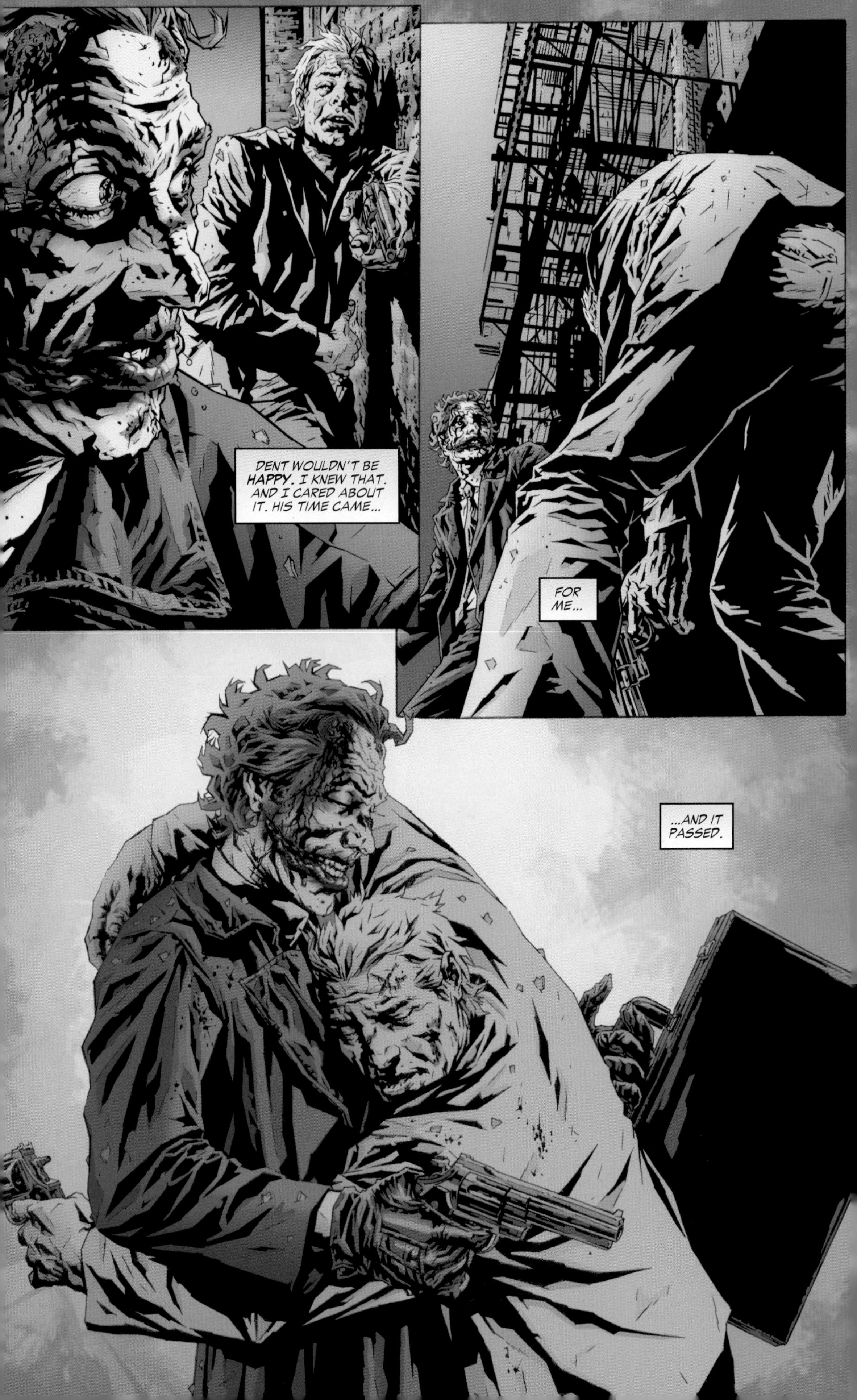
DENT WOULDN'T BE HAPPY. I KNEW THAT. AND I CARED ABOUT IT. HIS TIME CAME...
FOR ME...
...AND IT PASSED.

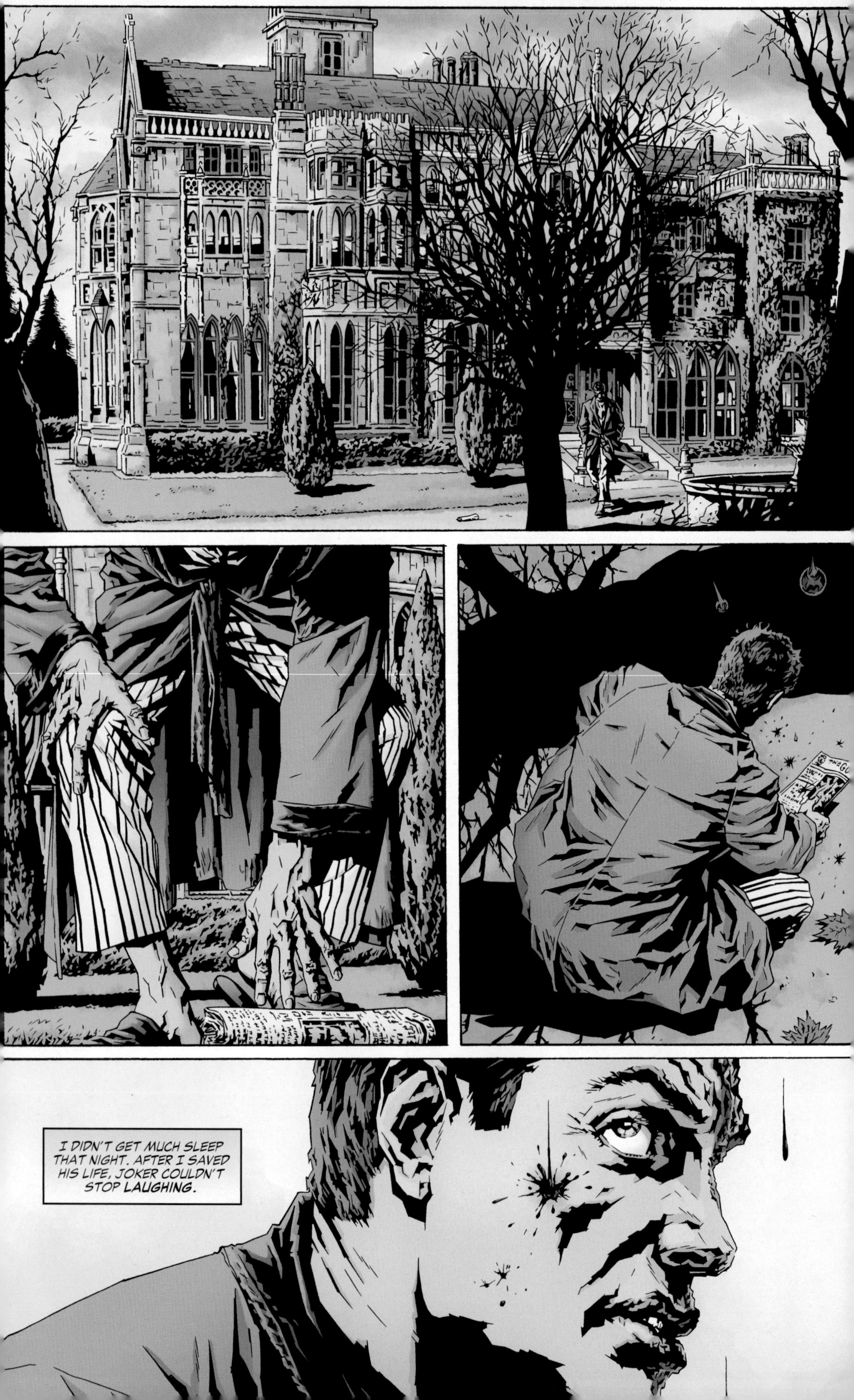
I DIDN'T GET MUCH SLEEP THAT NIGHT. AFTER I SAVED HIS LIFE, JOKER COULDN'T STOP LAUGHING.

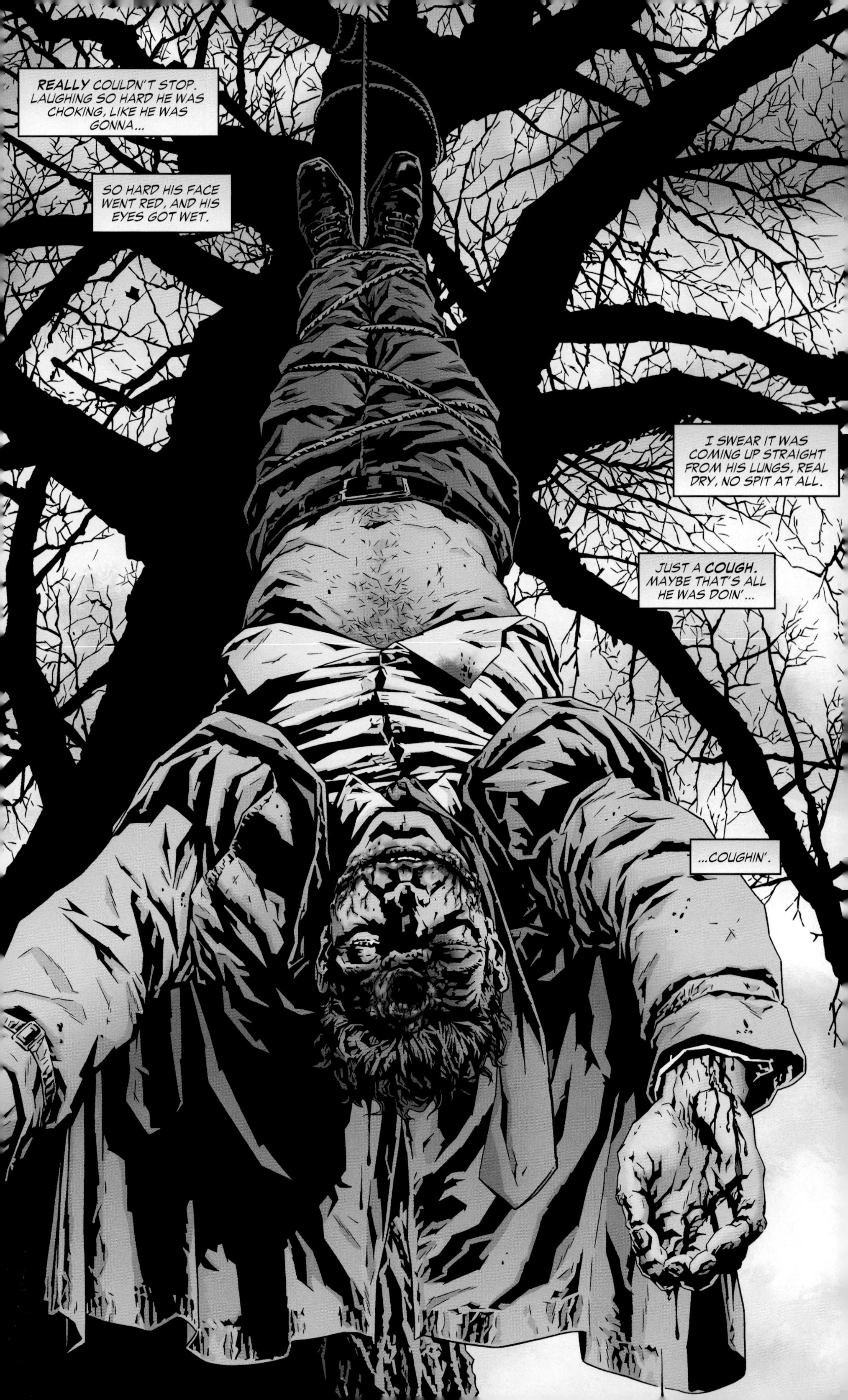
REALLY COULDN'T STOP. LAUGHING SO HARD HE WAS CHOKING, LIKE HE WAS GONNA...
SO HARD HIS FACE WENT RED, AND HIS EYES GOT WET.
I SWEAR IT WAS COMING UP STRAIGHT FROM HIS LUNGS, REAL DRY, NO SPIT AT ALL.
JUST A COUGH. MAYBE THAT'S ALL HE WAS DOIN'...
...COUGHIN'.

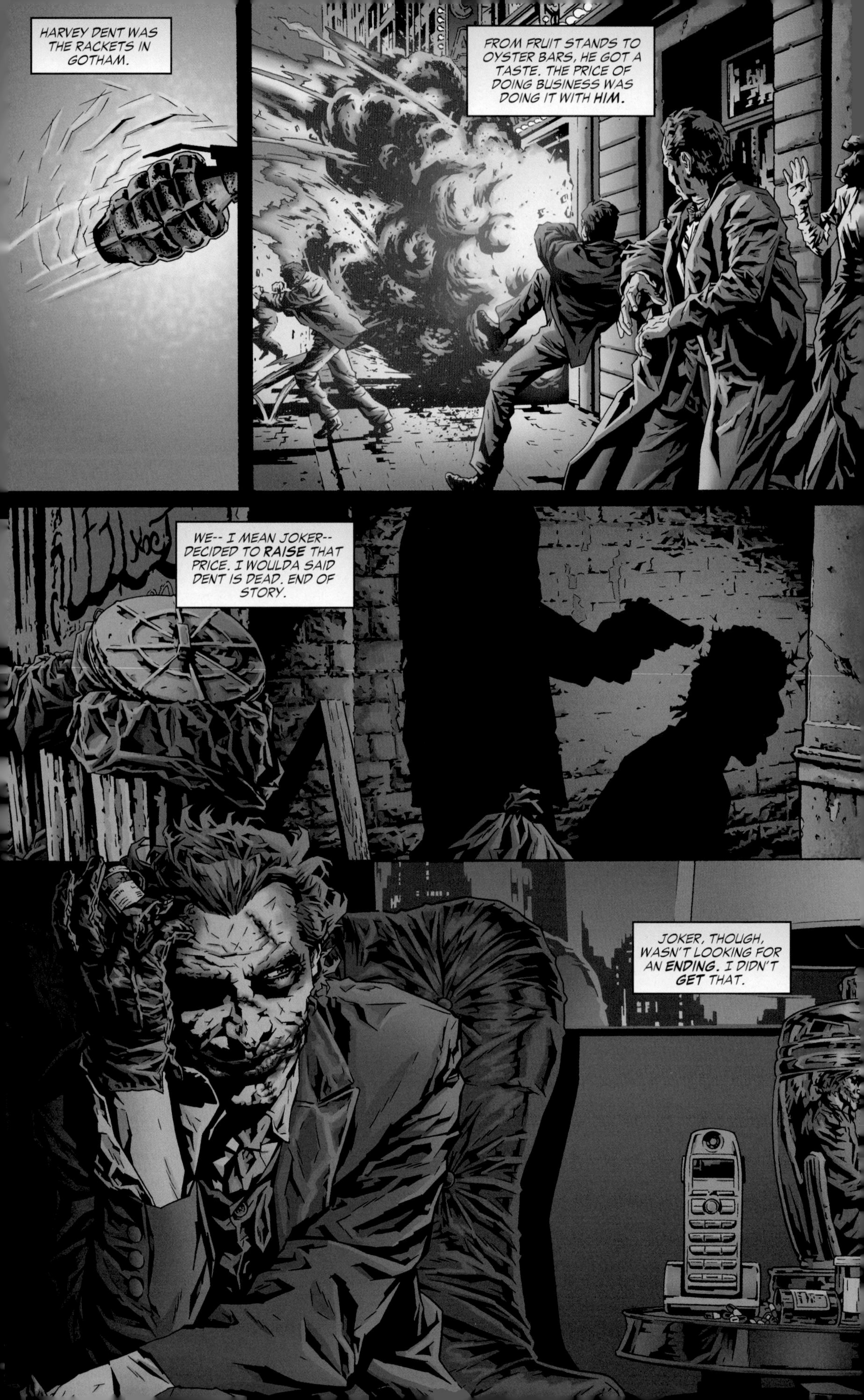
HARVEY DENT WAS THE RACKETS IN GOTHAM.
FROM FRUIT STANDS TO OYSTER BARS, HE GOT A TASTE. THE PRICE OF DOING BUSINESS WAS DOING IT WITH HIM.
WE-- I MEAN JOKER-- DECIDED TO RAISE THAT PRICE. I WOULDA SAID DENT IS DEAD. END OF STORY.
JOKER, THOUGH, WASN'T LOOKING FOR AN ENDING. I DIDN'T GET THAT.

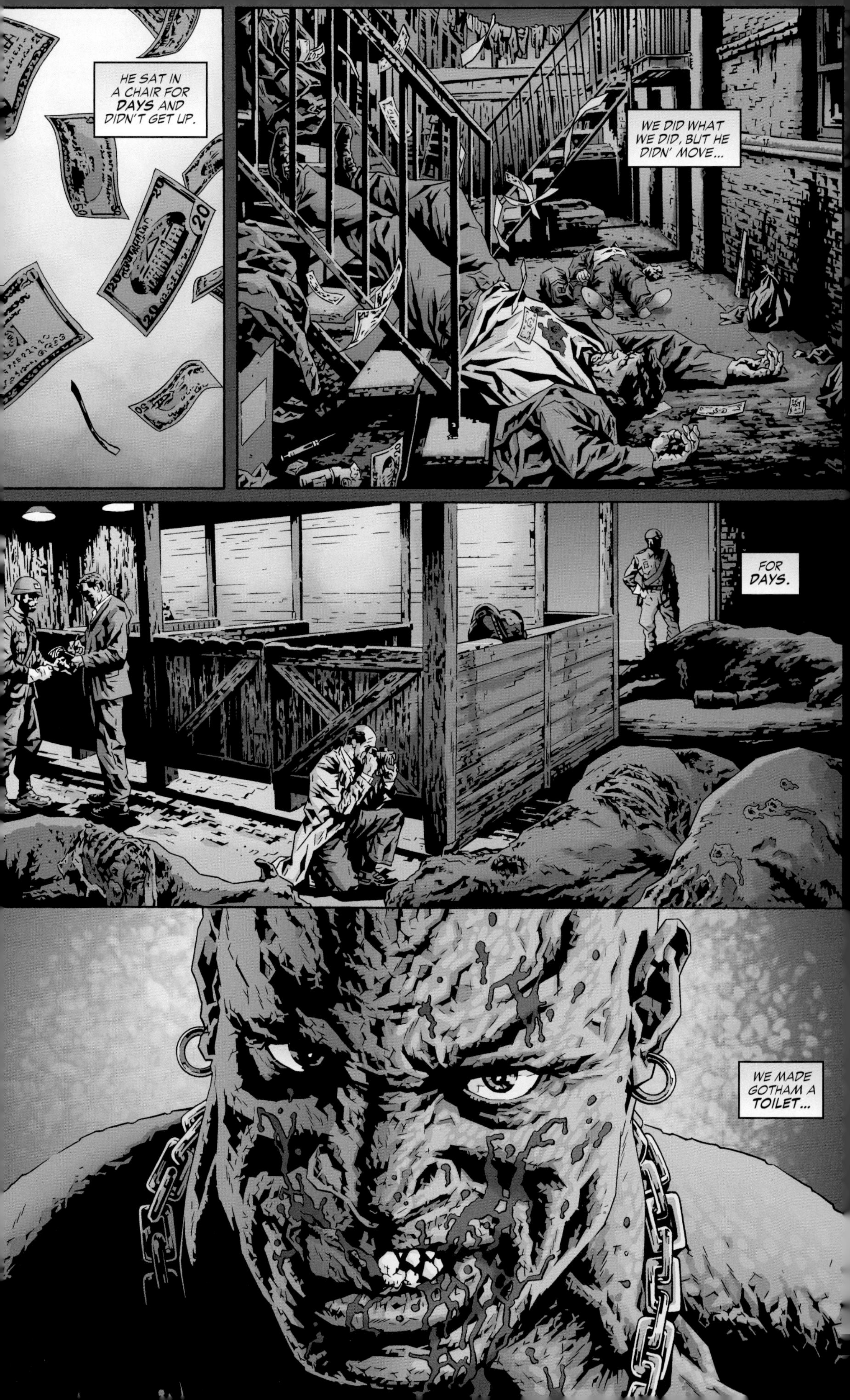
HE SAT IN A CHAIR FOR DAYS AND DIDN'T GET UP.
WE DID WHAT WE DID, BUT HE DIDN' MOVE...
FOR DAYS.
WE MADE GOTHAM A TOILET...

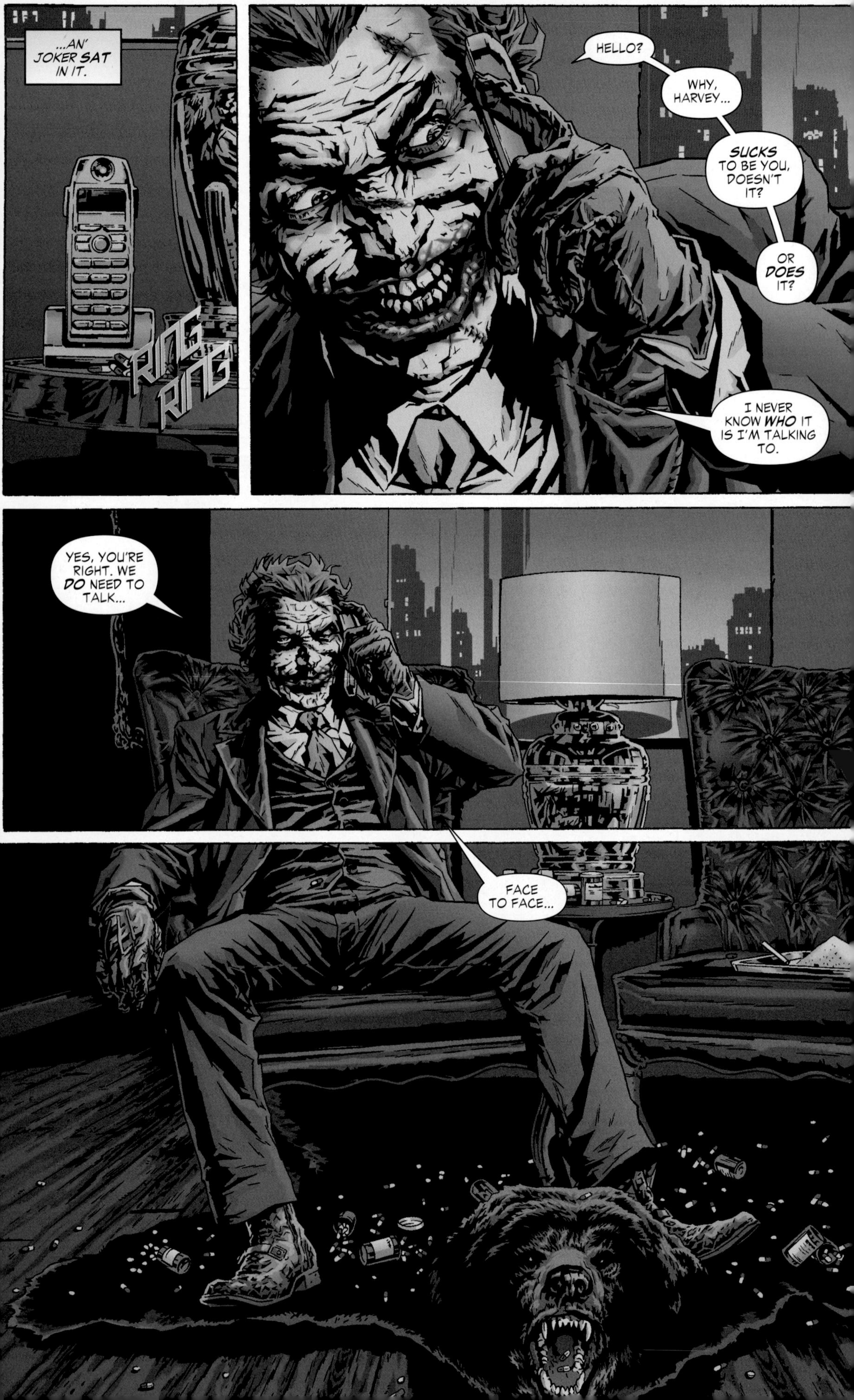
...AN' JOKER SAT IN IT.
RING RING
HELLO?
WHY, HARVEY...
SUCKS TO BE YOU, DOESN'T IT?
OR DOES IT?
I NEVER KNOW WHO IT IS I'M TALKING TO.
YES, YOU'RE RIGHT. WE DO NEED TO TALK...
FACE TO FACE...

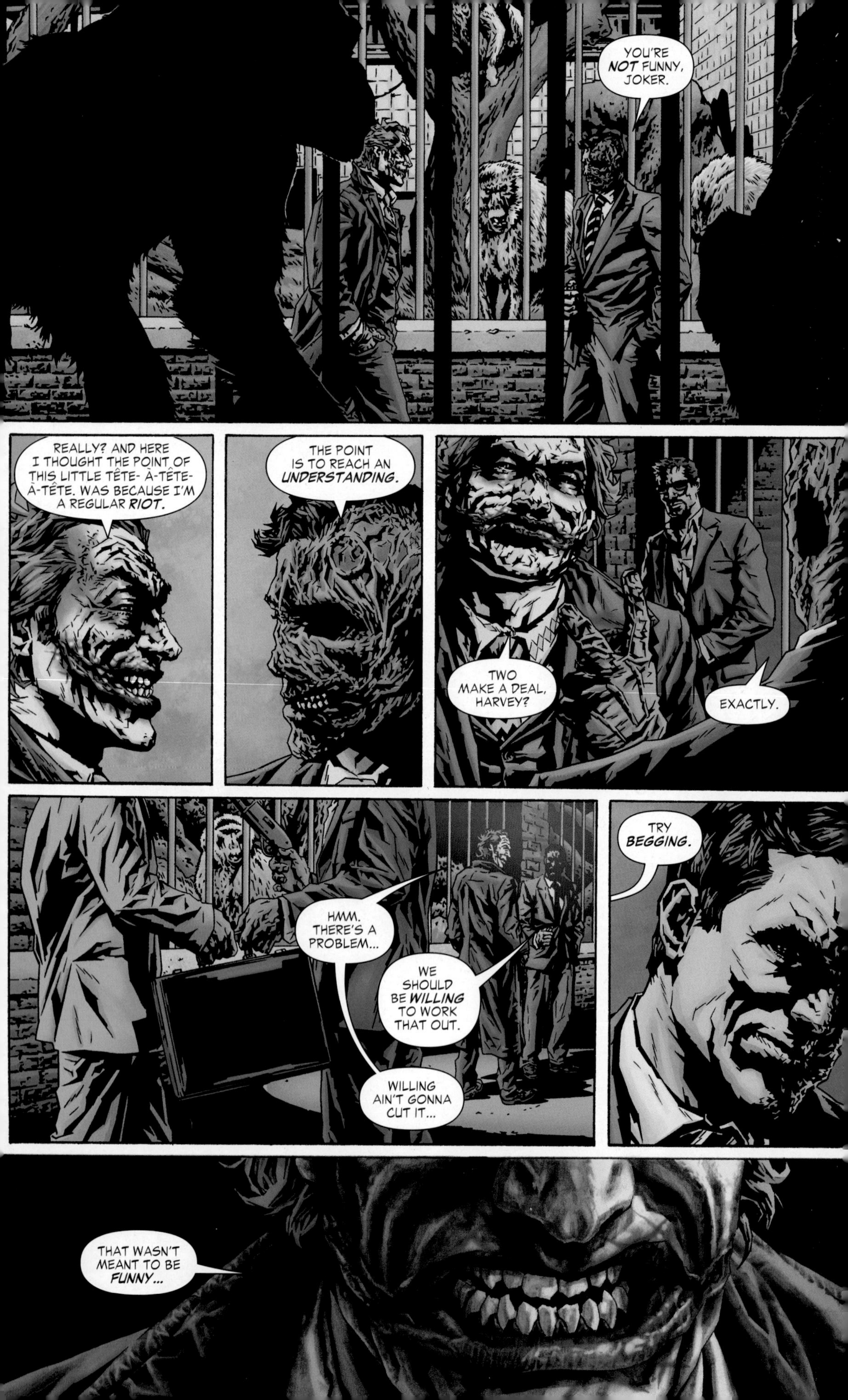
YOU'RE NOT FUNNY, JOKER.
REALLY? AND HERE I THOUGHT THE POINT OF THIS LITTLE TÊTE- À-TÊTE-À-TÊTE. WAS BECAUSE I'M A REGULAR RIOT.
THE POINT IS TO REACH AN UNDERSTANDING.
TWO MAKE A DEAL, HARVEY?
EXACTLY.
HMM. THERE'S A PROBLEM...
WE SHOULD BE WILLING TO WORK THAT OUT.
WILLING AIN'T GONNA CUT IT...
TRY BEGGING.
THAT WASN'T MEANT TO BE FUNNY...

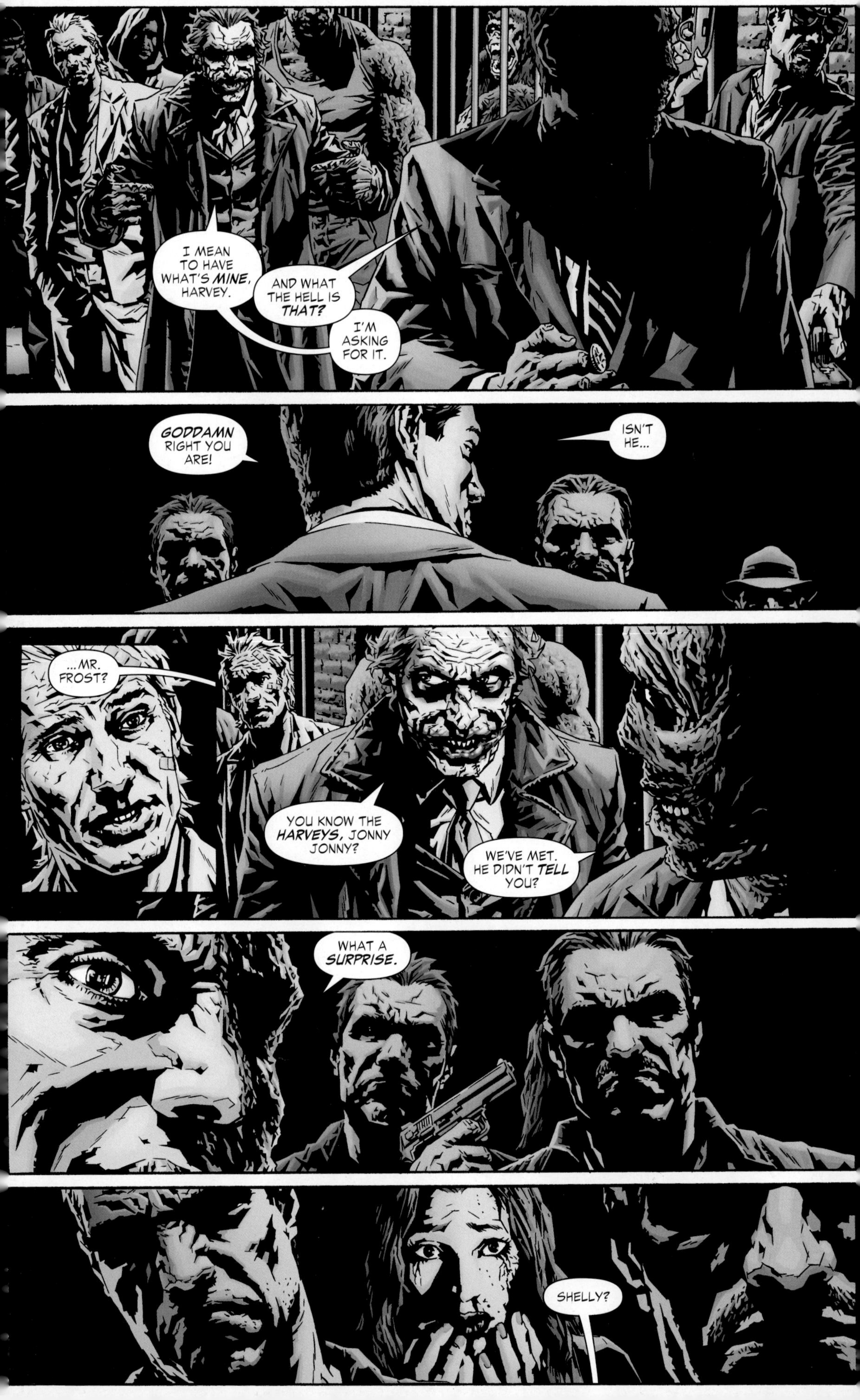
I MEAN TO HAVE WHAT'S *MINE,* HARVEY.
AND WHAT THE HELL IS *THAT?*
I'M ASKING FOR IT.
GODDAMN RIGHT YOU ARE!
ISN'T HE...
...MR. FROST?
YOU KNOW THE *HARVEYS,* JONNY JONNY?
WE'VE MET. HE DIDN'T *TELL* YOU?
WHAT A *SURPRISE.*
SHELLY?

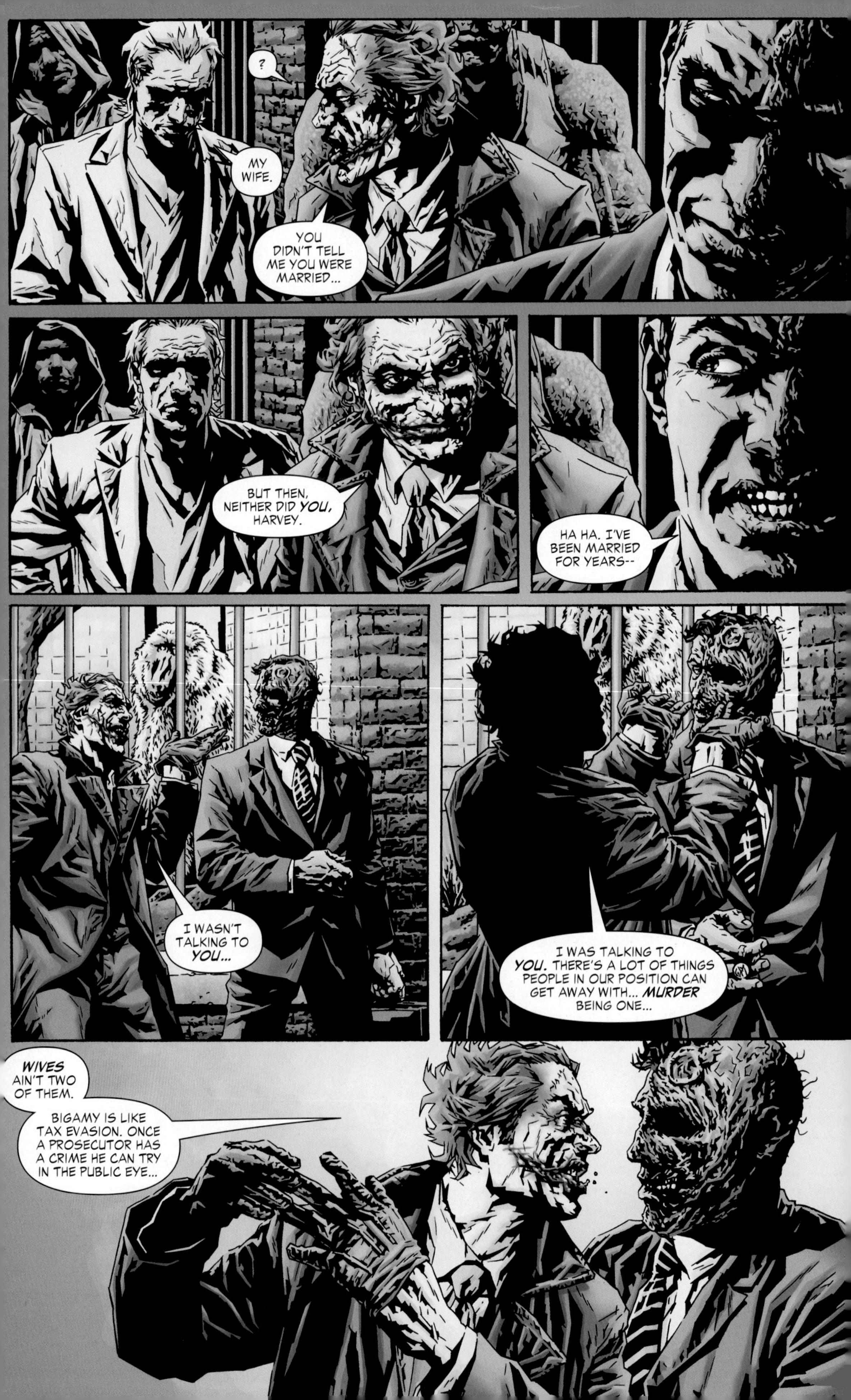

?
MY WIFE.
YOU DIDN'T TELL ME YOU WERE MARRIED...
BUT THEN, NEITHER DID *YOU,* HARVEY.
HA HA. I'VE BEEN MARRIED FOR YEARS--
I WASN'T TALKING TO *YOU...*
I WAS TALKING TO *YOU.* THERE'S A LOT OF THINGS PEOPLE IN OUR POSITION CAN GET AWAY WITH... *MURDER* BEING ONE...
WIVES AIN'T TWO OF THEM.
BIGAMY IS LIKE TAX EVASION. ONCE A PROSECUTOR HAS A CRIME HE CAN TRY IN THE PUBLIC EYE...

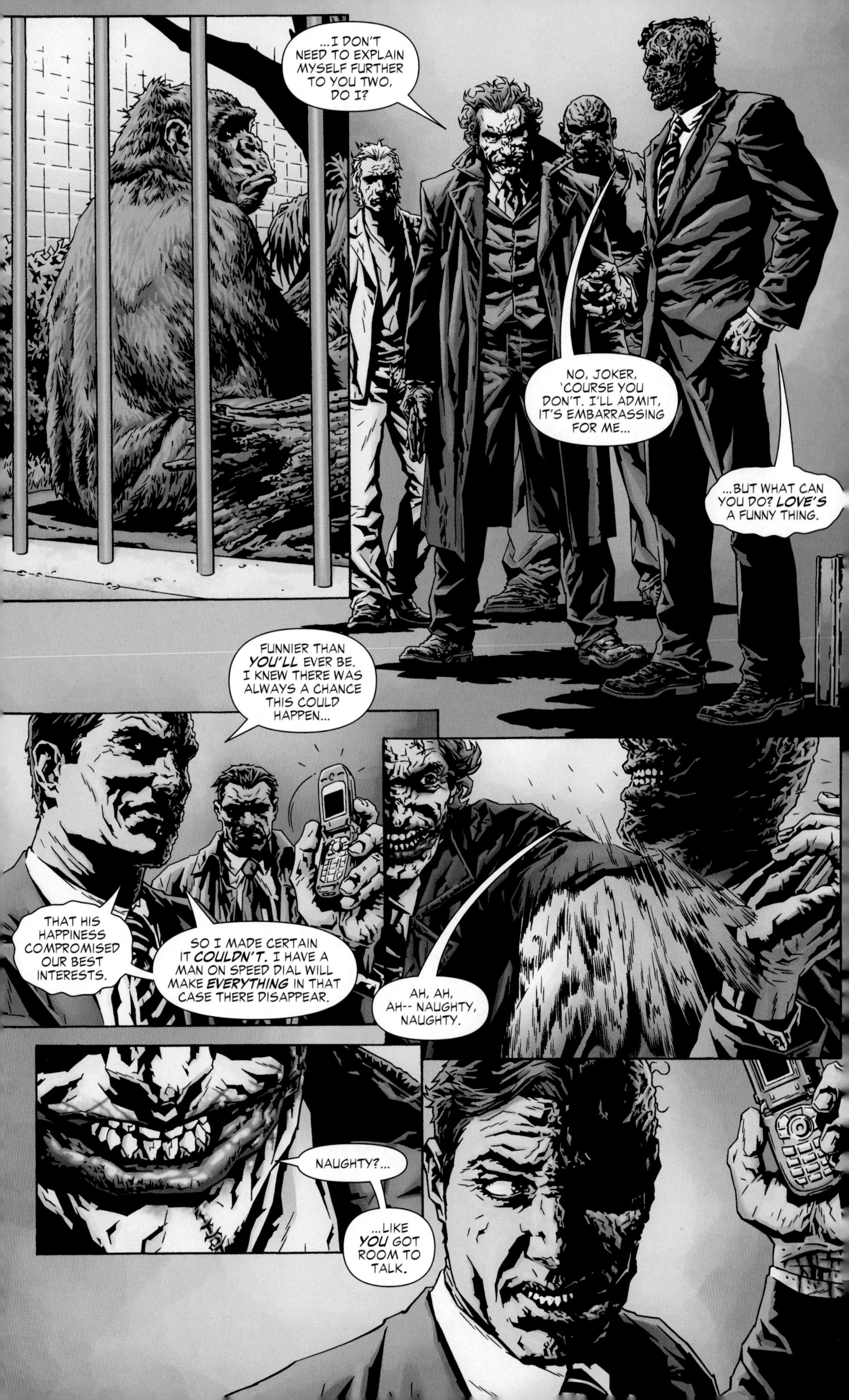
...I DON'T NEED TO EXPLAIN MYSELF FURTHER TO YOU TWO, DO I?
NO, JOKER, 'COURSE YOU DON'T. I'LL ADMIT, IT'S EMBARRASSING FOR ME...
...BUT WHAT CAN YOU DO? LOVE'S A FUNNY THING.
FUNNIER THAN YOU'LL EVER BE. I KNEW THERE WAS ALWAYS A CHANCE THIS COULD HAPPEN...
THAT HIS HAPPINESS COMPROMISED OUR BEST INTERESTS.
SO I MADE CERTAIN IT COULDN'T. I HAVE A MAN ON SPEED DIAL WILL MAKE EVERYTHING IN THAT CASE THERE DISAPPEAR.
AH, AH, AH-- NAUGHTY, NAUGHTY.
NAUGHTY?...
...LIKE YOU GOT ROOM TO TALK.

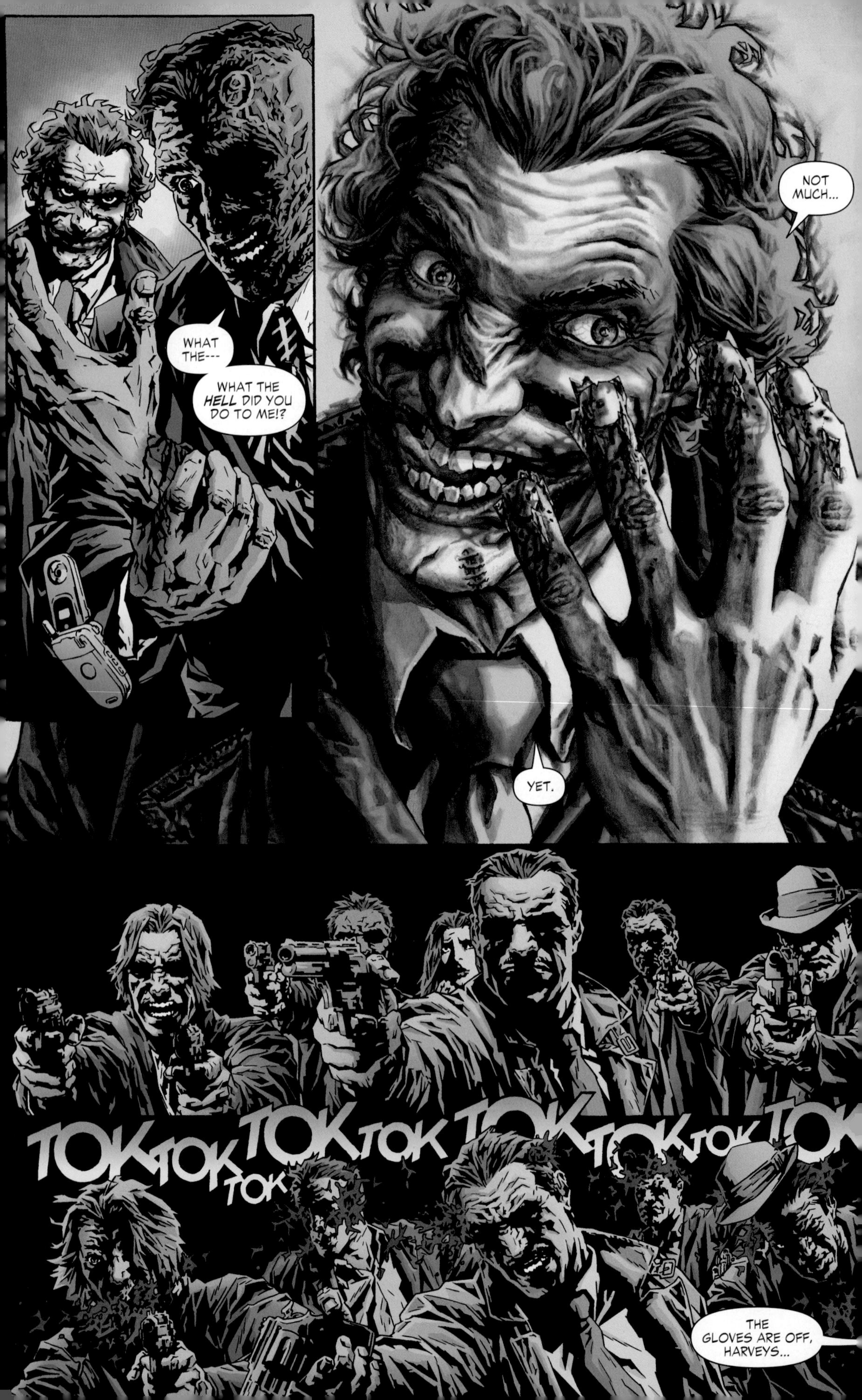
WHAT THE---
WHAT THE HELL DID YOU DO TO ME!?
NOT MUCH...
YET.
TOK TOK TOK TOK TOK TOK TOK TOK TOK
THE GLOVES ARE OFF, HARVEYS...

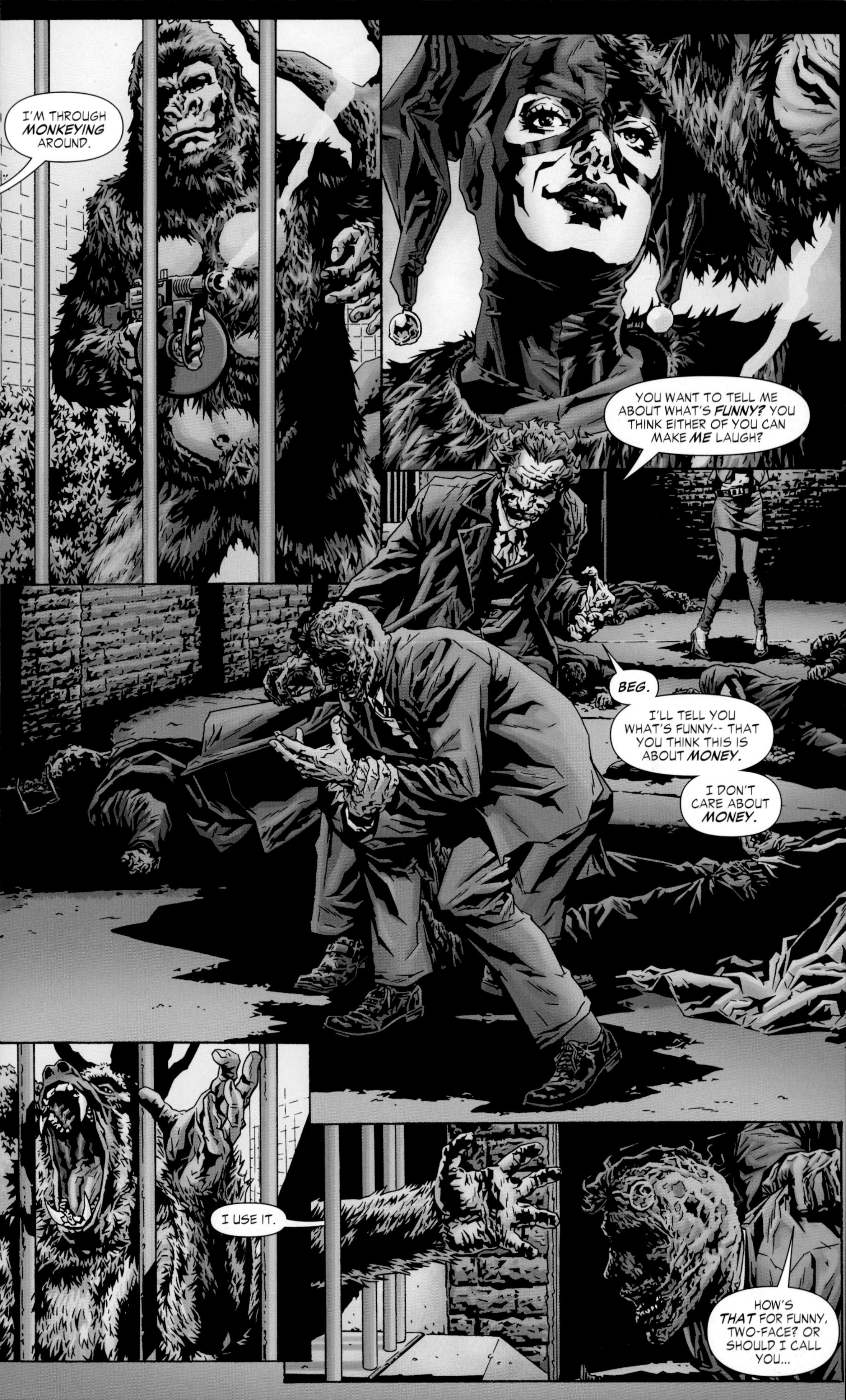

I'M THROUGH MONKEYING AROUND.
YOU WANT TO TELL ME ABOUT WHAT'S FUNNY? YOU THINK EITHER OF YOU CAN MAKE ME LAUGH?
BEG.
I'LL TELL YOU WHAT'S FUNNY-- THAT YOU THINK THIS IS ABOUT MONEY.
I DON'T CARE ABOUT MONEY.
I USE IT.
HOW'S THAT FOR FUNNY, TWO-FACE? OR SHOULD I CALL YOU...

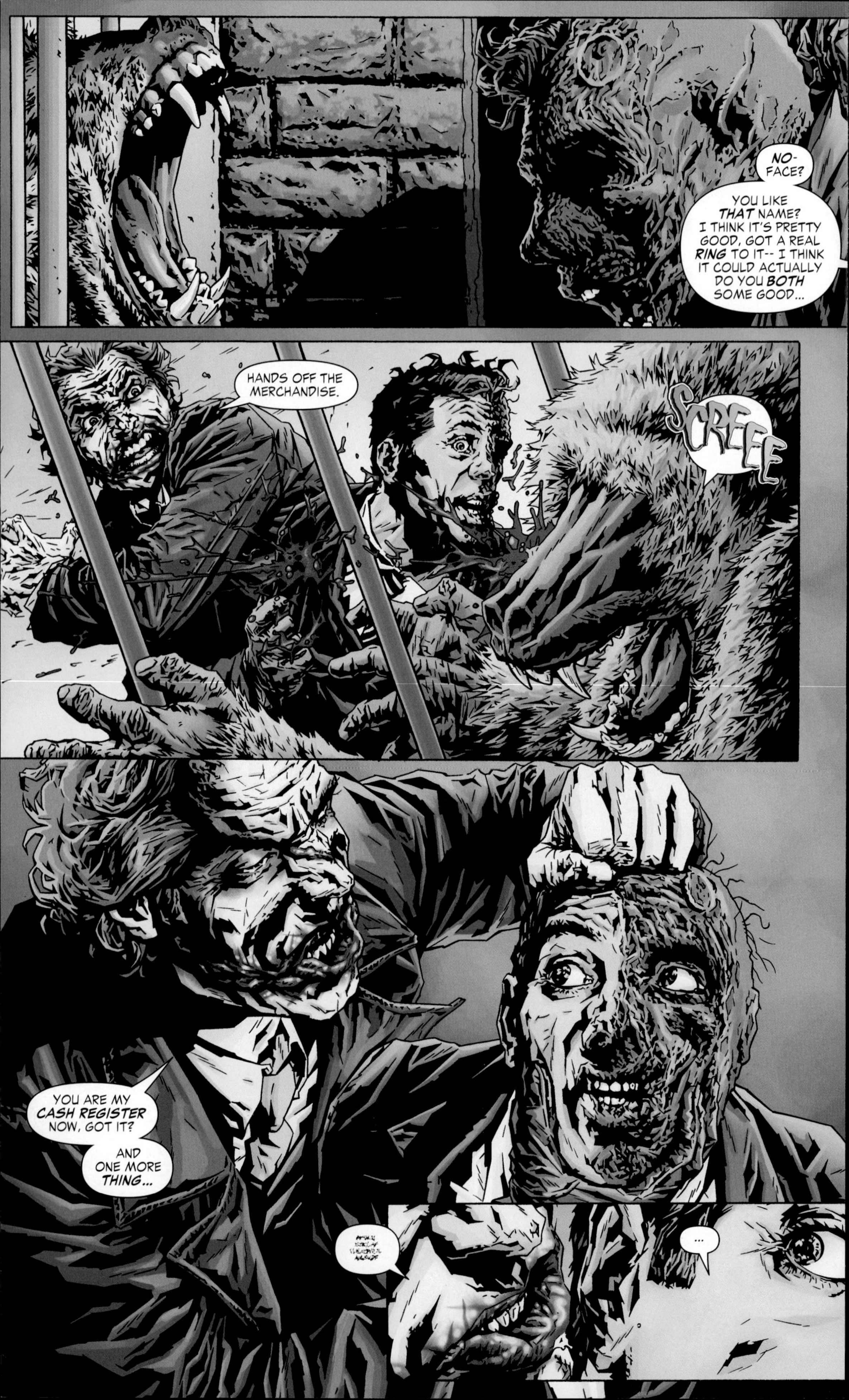

NO-FACE?
YOU LIKE THAT NAME? I THINK IT'S PRETTY GOOD, GOT A REAL RING TO IT-- I THINK IT COULD ACTUALLY DO YOU BOTH SOME GOOD...
HANDS OFF THE MERCHANDISE.
SCREEE
YOU ARE MY CASH REGISTER NOW, GOT IT?
AND ONE MORE THING...
...

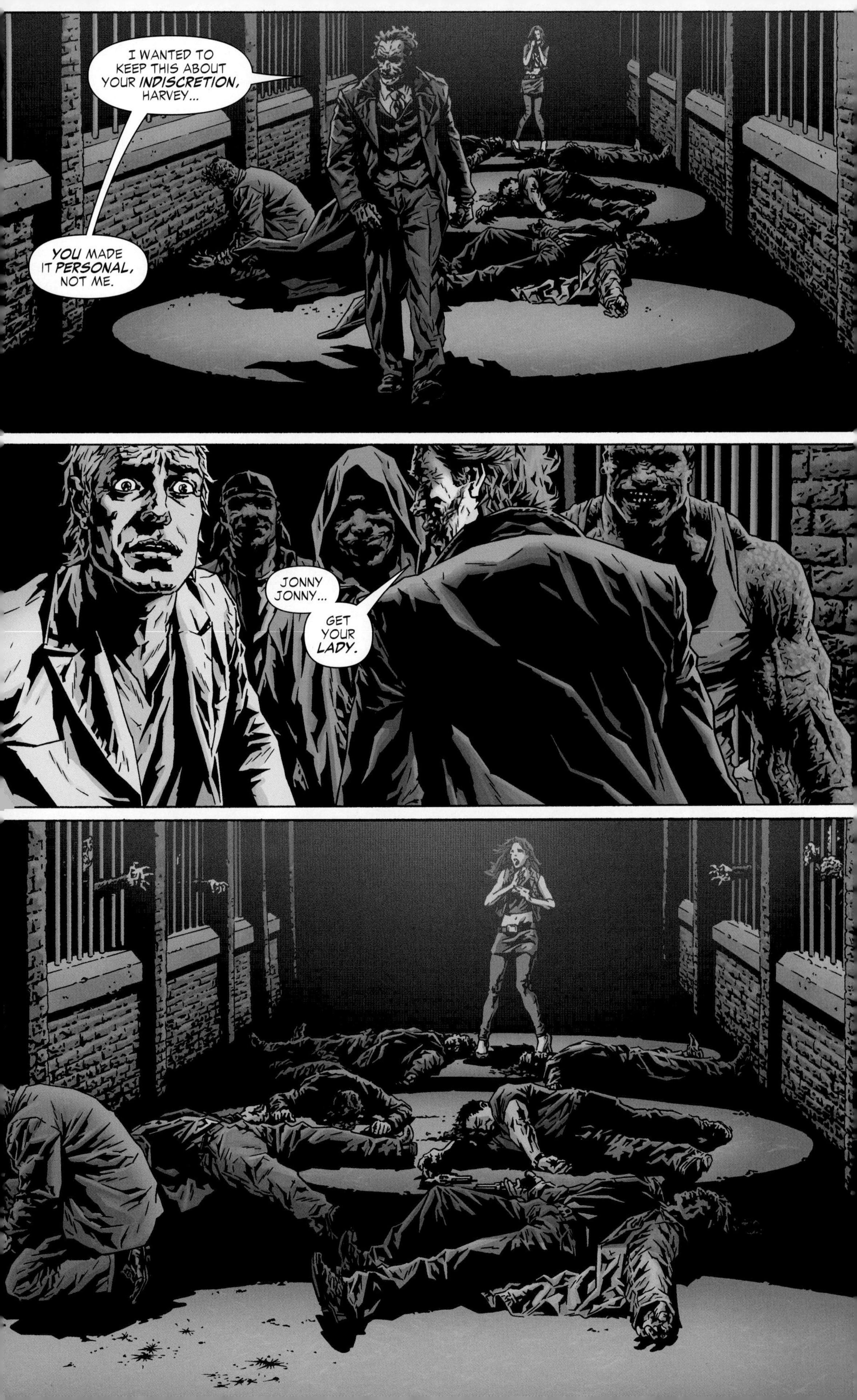

I WANTED TO KEEP THIS ABOUT YOUR INDISCRETION, HARVEY...
YOU MADE IT PERSONAL, NOT ME.
JONNY JONNY...
GET YOUR LADY.

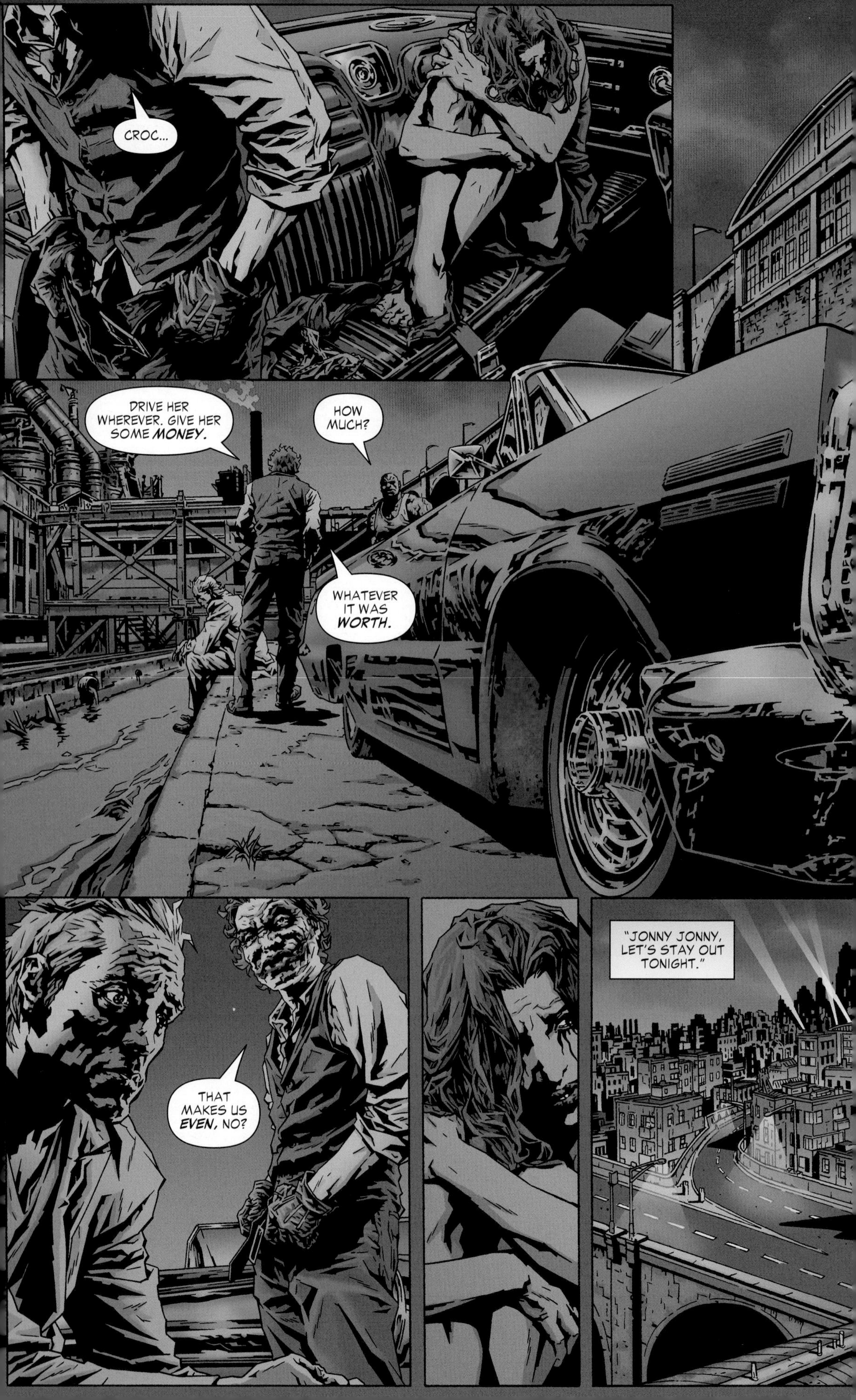
CROC...
DRIVE HER WHEREVER. GIVE HER SOME MONEY.
HOW MUCH?
WHATEVER IT WAS WORTH.
THAT MAKES US EVEN, NO?
"JONNY JONNY, LET'S STAY OUT TONIGHT."

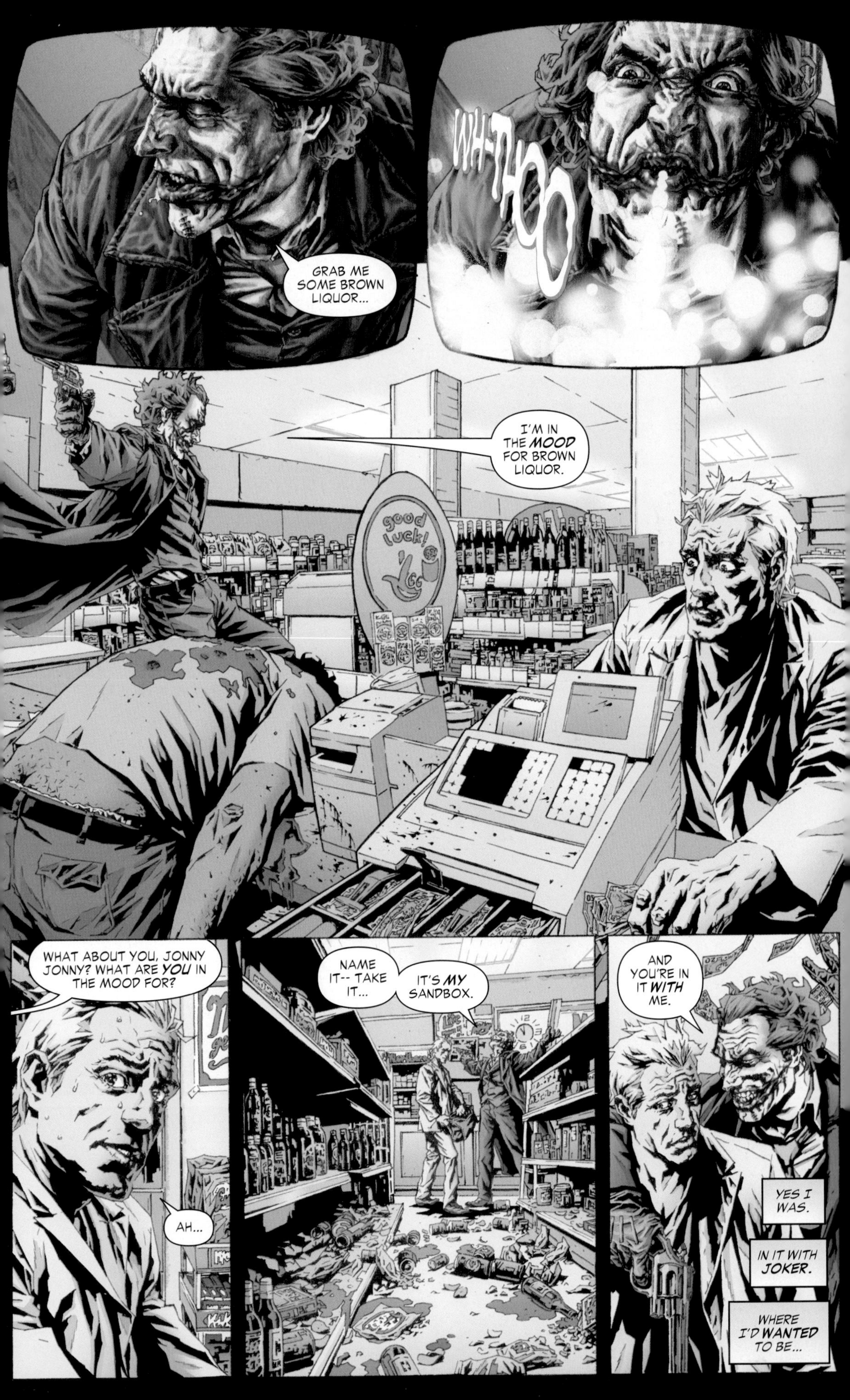
GRAB ME SOME BROWN LIQUOR...
WH-THOO
I'M IN THE MOOD FOR BROWN LIQUOR.
good luck!
WHAT ABOUT YOU, JONNY JONNY? WHAT ARE YOU IN THE MOOD FOR?
AH...
NAME IT-- TAKE IT...
IT'S MY SANDBOX.
AND YOU'RE IN IT WITH ME.
YES I WAS.
IN IT WITH JOKER.
WHERE I'D WANTED TO BE...

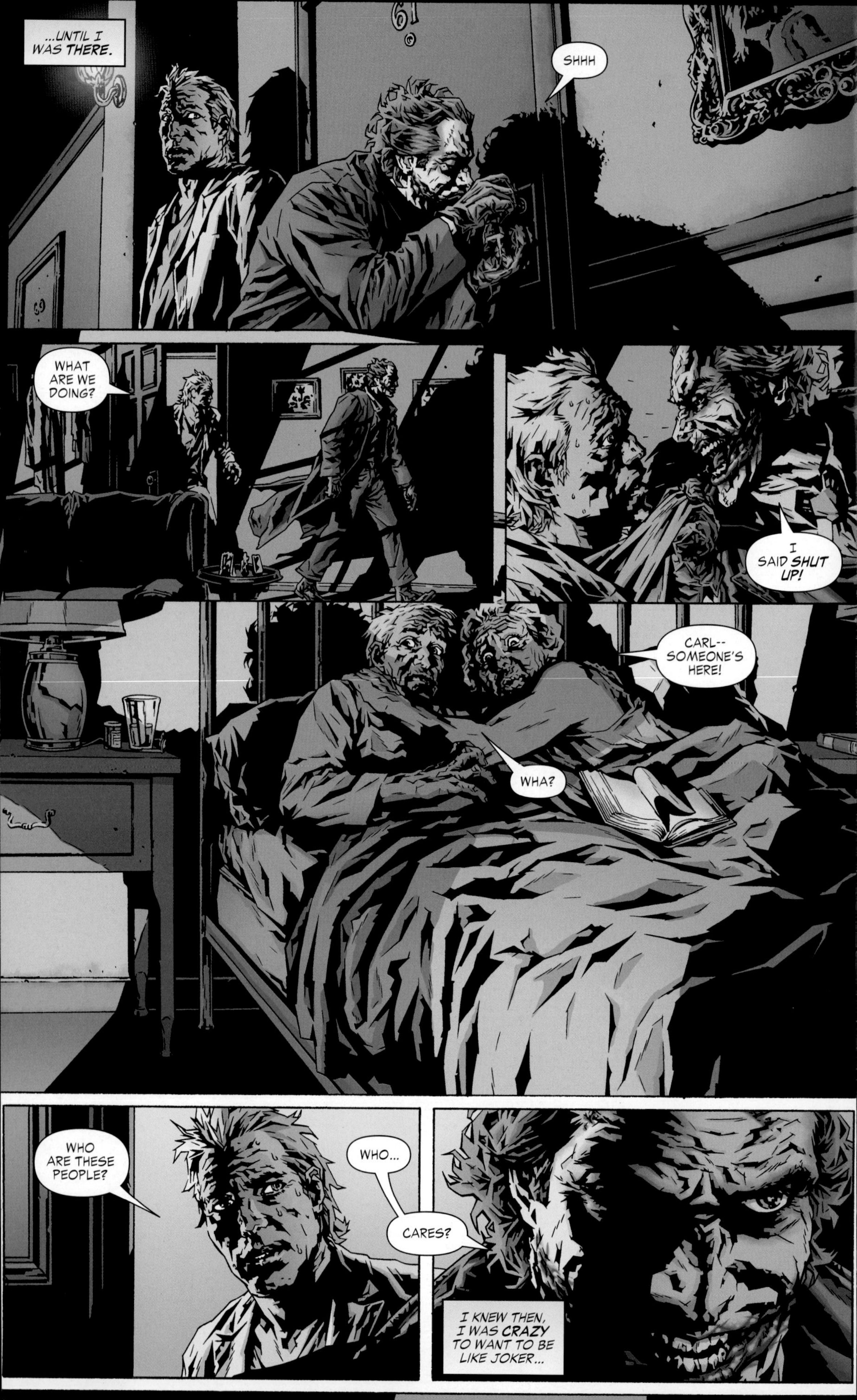
...UNTIL I WAS THERE.
SHHH
WHAT ARE WE DOING?
I SAID SHUT UP!
CARL-- SOMEONE'S HERE!
WHA?
WHO ARE THESE PEOPLE?
WHO...
CARES?
I KNEW THEN, I WAS CRAZY TO WANT TO BE LIKE JOKER...

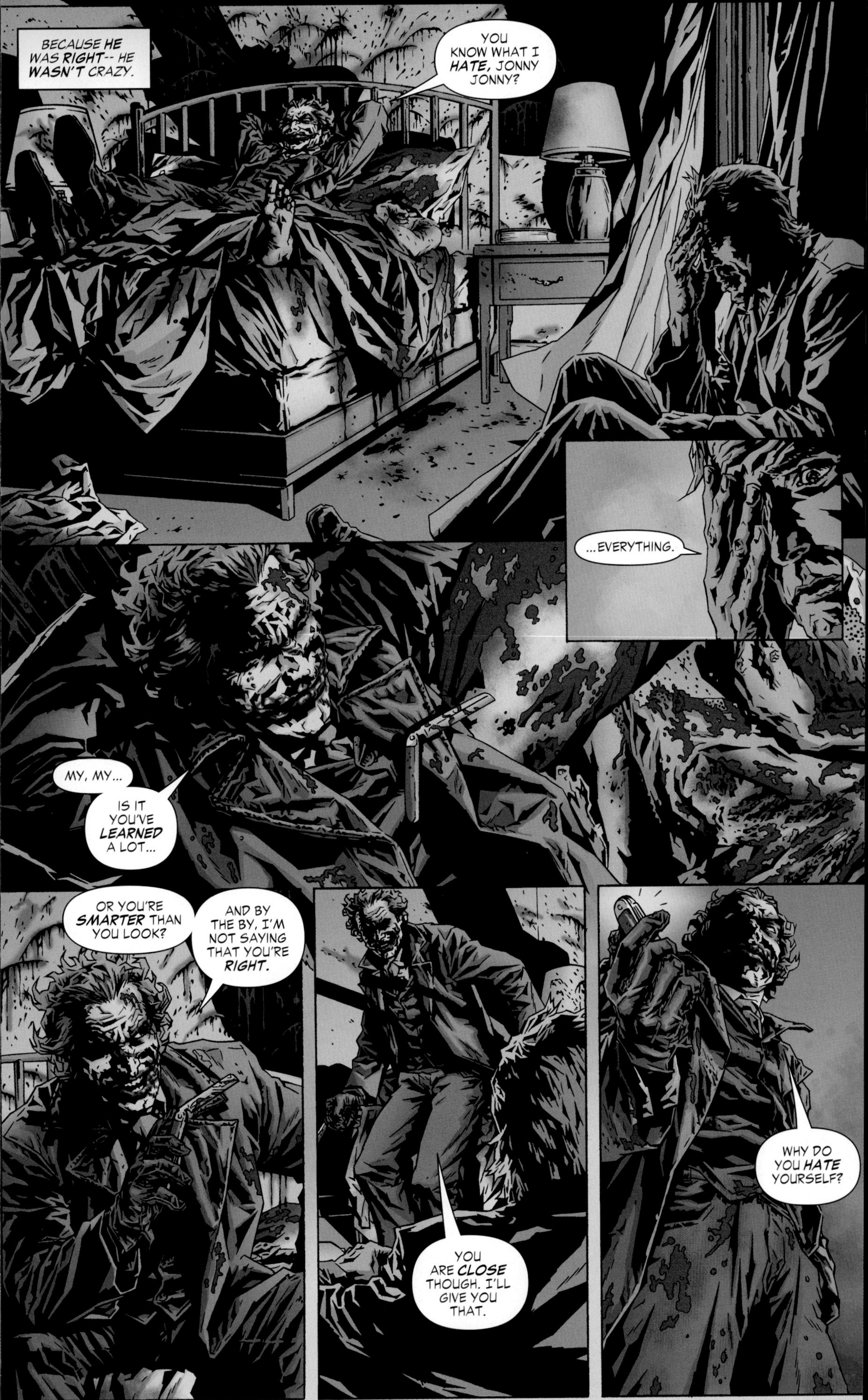
BECAUSE **HE** WAS **RIGHT**-- HE **WASN'T** CRAZY.
YOU KNOW WHAT I **HATE,** JONNY JONNY?
...EVERYTHING.
MY, MY...
IS IT YOU'VE **LEARNED** A LOT...
OR YOU'RE **SMARTER** THAN YOU LOOK?
AND BY THE BY, I'M NOT SAYING THAT YOU'RE **RIGHT.**
YOU ARE **CLOSE** THOUGH. I'LL GIVE YOU THAT.
WHY DO YOU **HATE** YOURSELF?

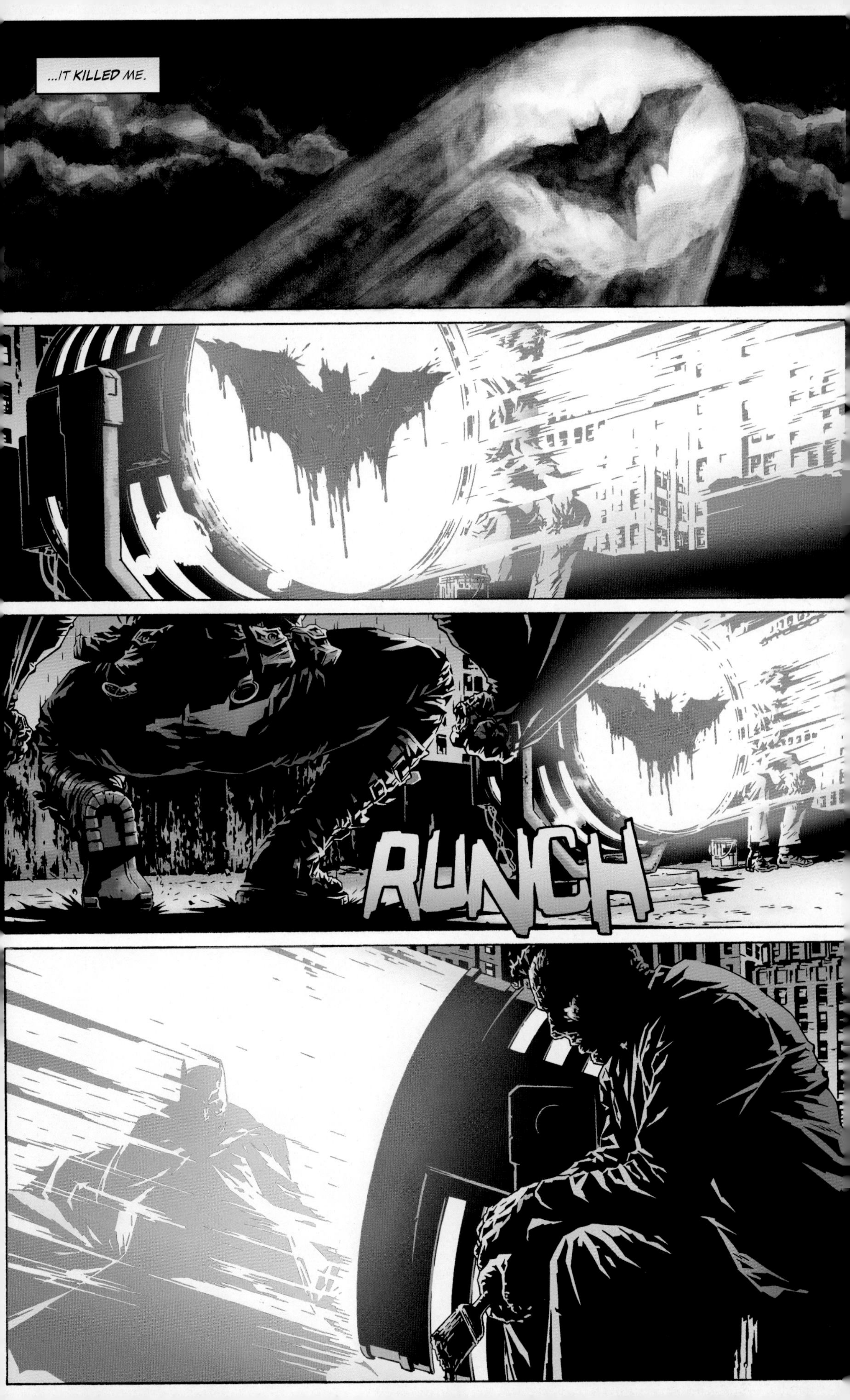
...IT KILLED ME.
RUNCH

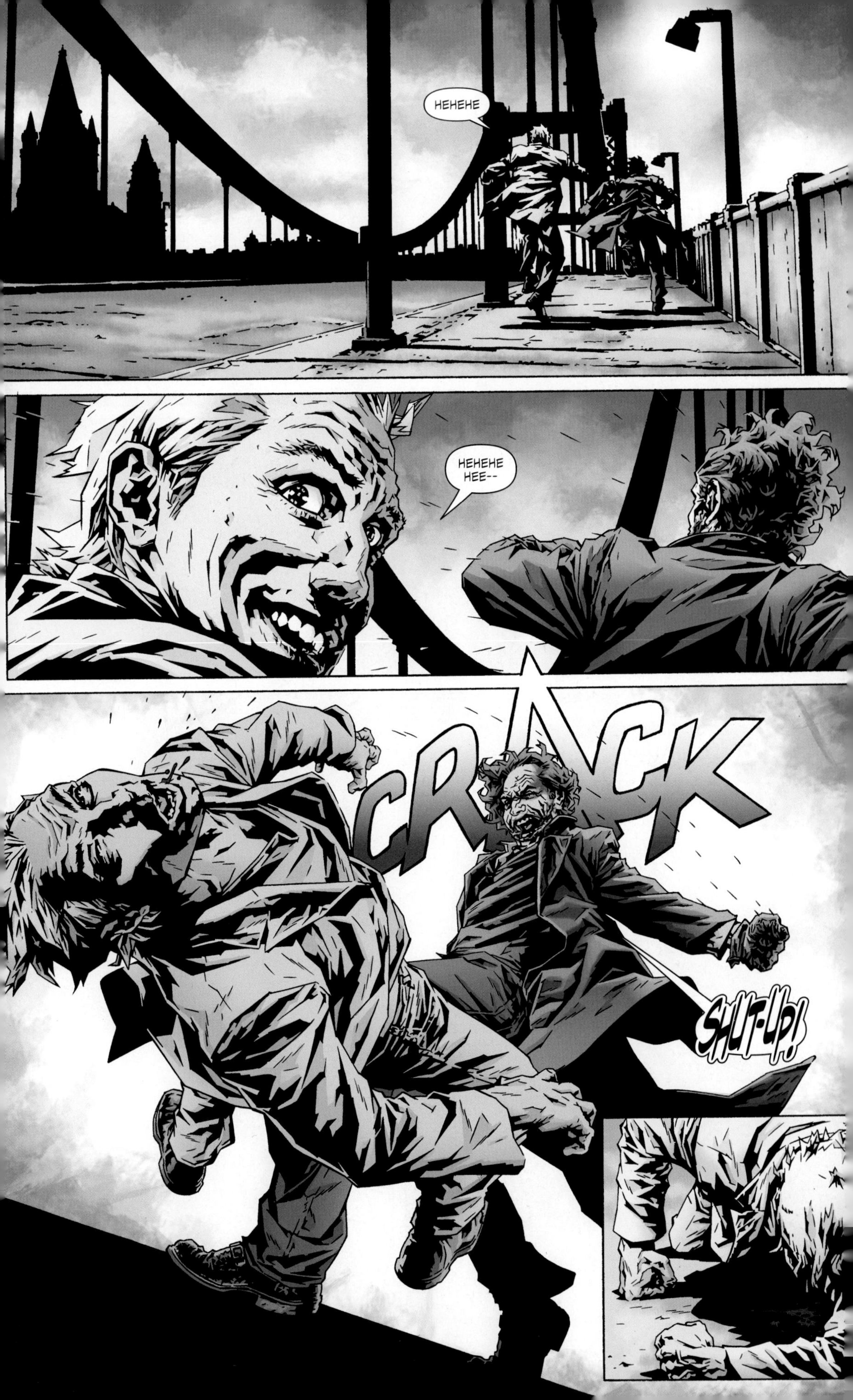
HEHEHE
HEHEHE HEE--
CRACK
SHUT-UP!

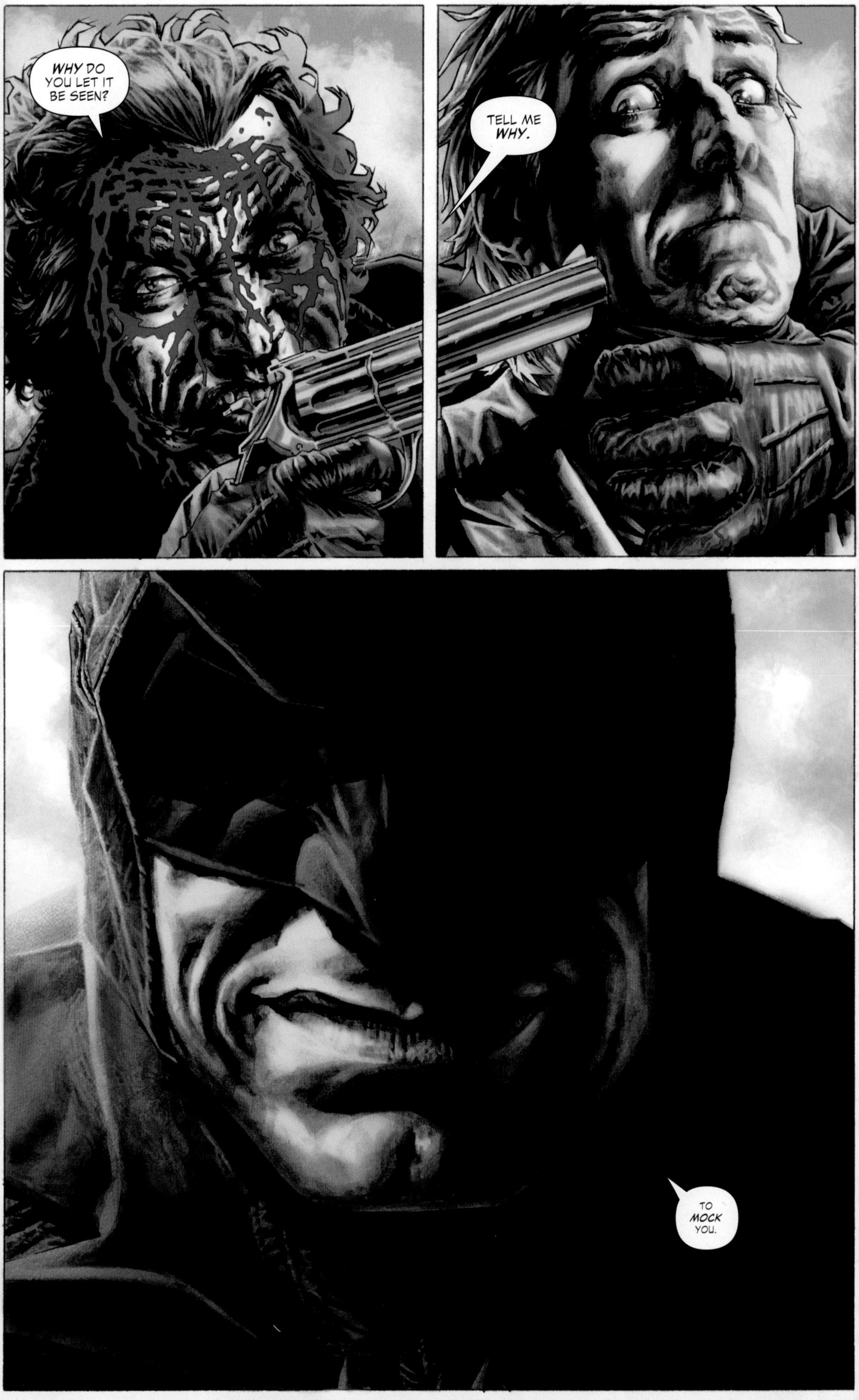
WHY DO YOU LET IT BE SEEN?
TELL ME WHY.
TO MOCK YOU.

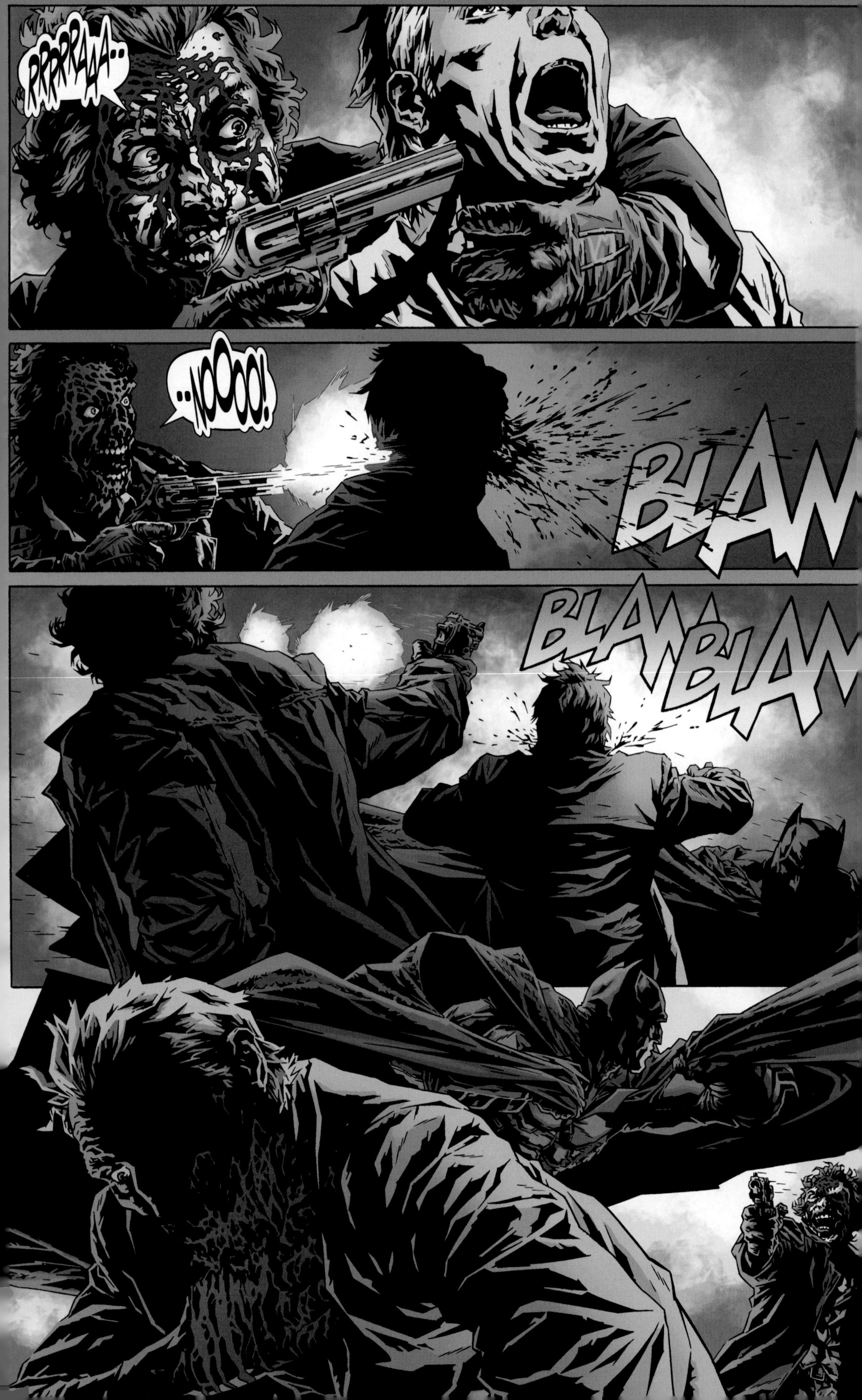
RRRRRAAAA..
..NOOOO!
BLAM
BLAM BLAM

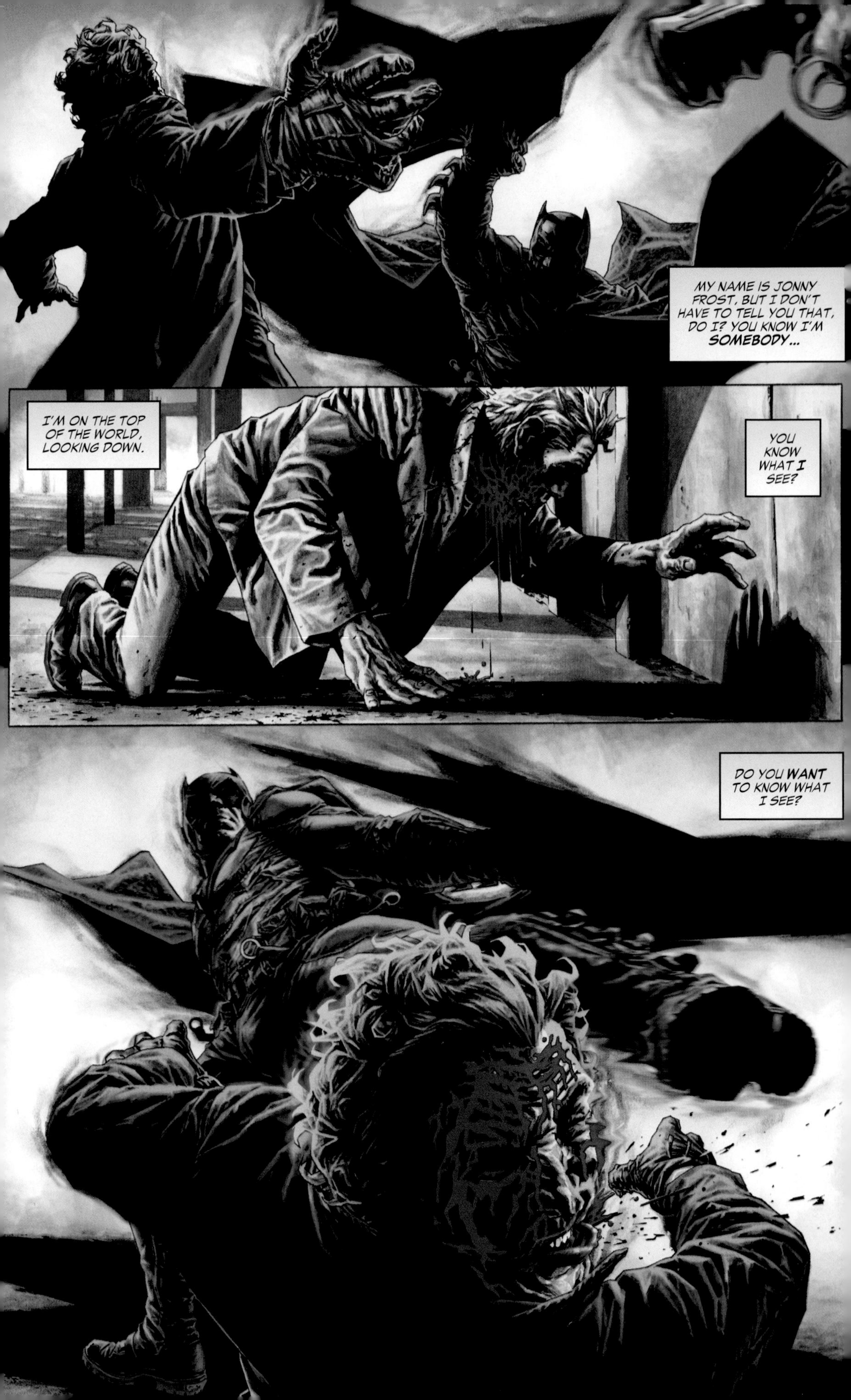
MY NAME IS JONNY FROST, BUT I DON'T HAVE TO TELL YOU THAT, DO I? YOU KNOW I'M SOMEBODY...
I'M ON THE TOP OF THE WORLD, LOOKING DOWN.
YOU KNOW WHAT I SEE?
DO YOU WANT TO KNOW WHAT I SEE?

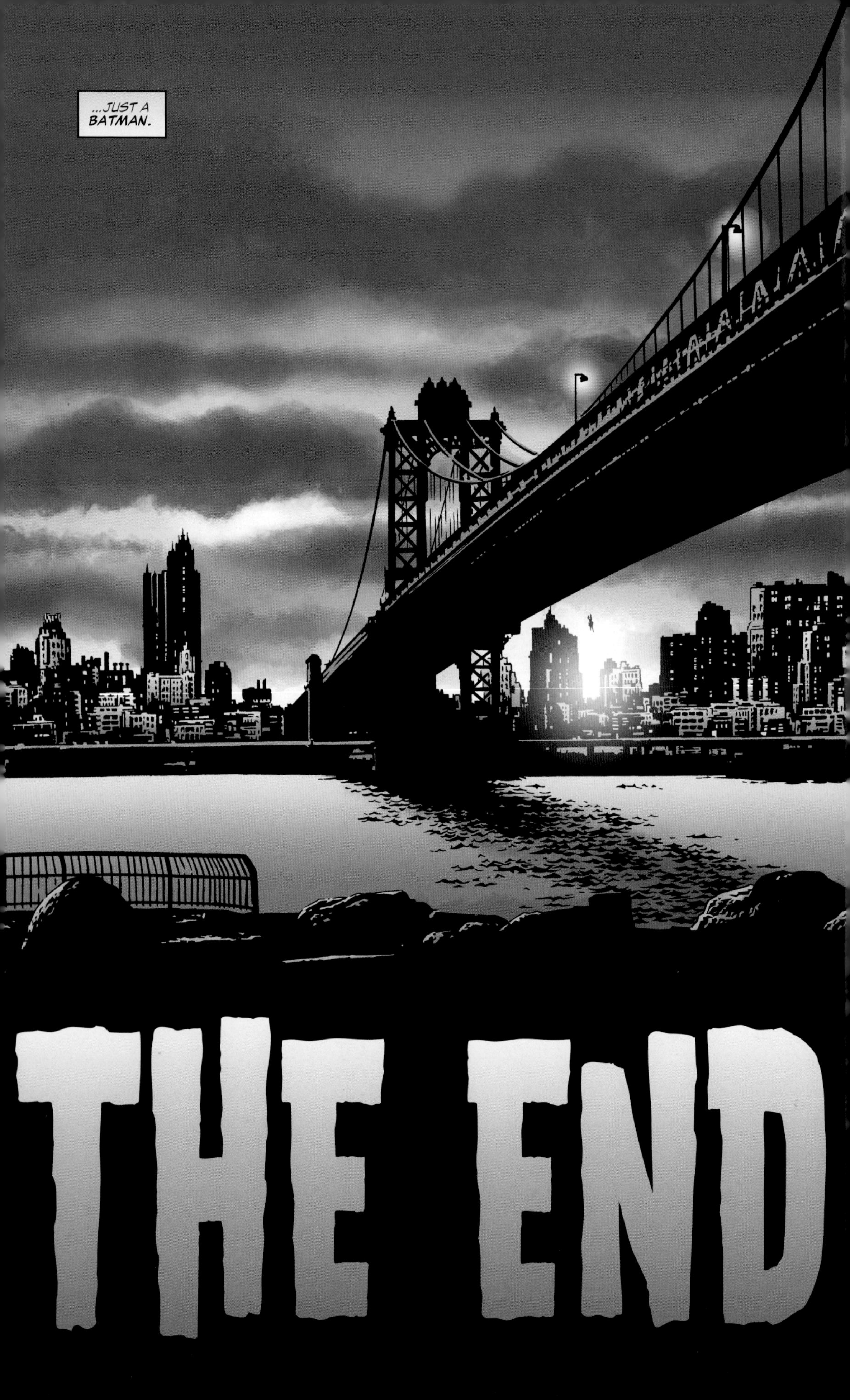
...JUST A BATMAN.
THE END

BRIAN AZZARELLO

Brian has been writing comics professionally since the mid-1990s. He is the writer and cocreator with Eduardo Risso of the acclaimed Vertigo monthly series 100 BULLETS, which has won multiple Eisner and Harvey awards.

Brian's other writing credits for DC Comics include BATMAN and JONNY DOUBLE (both with Risso), SUPERMAN (with Jim Lee), SGT. ROCK: BETWEEN A HARD PLACE AND HELL (with Joe Kubert), LEX LUTHOR: MAN OF STEEL (with Lee Bermejo), DR. 13, and an Eisner-nominated run on HELLBLAZER. He has also written FILTHY RICH for the VERTIGO CRIME line.

He has been cited as one of Wizard magazine's top ten writers and has been profiled and/or reviewed in Entertainment Weekly, GEAR, The Chicago Tribune, and countless other publications. He lives in Chicago with his wife, artist Jill Thompson, and he finally has a website.

LEE BERMEJO

Lee began drawing comics in 1997 for WildStorm Studios in San Diego at age 19. This project marks the third collaboration with Brian Azzarello, the first being BATMAN/DEATHBLOW: AFTER THE FIRE, followed by LEX LUTHOR: MAN OF STEEL. He has also done a number of other short projects, including GLOBAL FREQUENCY with WARREN ELLIS, SUPERMAN/GEN13 with Adam Hughes, and HELLBLAZER with Mike Carey. Recently, he has worked primarily as a cover artist, doing covers for HELLBLAZER for Vertigo and The Stand and Daredevil for Marvel Comics. Currently, he's writing and drawing a graphic novel for DC Comics. In 2003 he moved to Italy, where he hopes to eventually earn enough money to get away from it all. He can't keep doing this work with these..... people.

MICK GRAY

Mick Gray grew up wanting to be an artist and car designer. At the suggestion of his father, Mick became a draftsman, getting on-the-job training at 16 and an Associate's Degree in Technical Illustration at 20. In 1988 his best friend suggested him to local comic book publisher Slave Labor Graphics. On a whim, Mick brought down his portfolio of technical illustrations. He was instantly hired to ink backgrounds like buildings and cars...and he's been busy ever since.

Mick is an Eisner Award-winning inker and has worked continuously for DC comics on such projects as SON OF SUPERMAN hardcover (J.H. Williams III), SUPERGIRL AND THE LEGION OF SUPER-HEROES (Barry Kitson), ZATANNA (Ryan Sook), PROMETHEA (J.H. Williams III) and most recently BATMAN CONFIDENTIAL (Rags Morales), TEEN TITANS GO! (Alexander Serra) and JSA (Dale Eaglesham).

PATRICIA MULVIHILL

Patricia Mulvihill began her professional career as a book jacket painter and graphic designer before unwittingly detouring into comics. Projects include WONDER WOMAN, BATMAN, LOVELESS, and 100 BULLETS. When not working she is often devising plans to slip away and travel. She is an Eisner Award winner and has been a colorist for DC Comics for over a decade. Trish lives in New York City.

FROM EISNER AWARD-WINNING WRITER

BRIAN AZZARELLO

WITH LEE BERMEJO

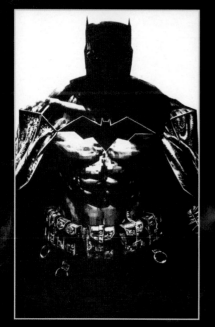

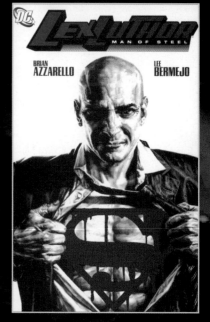

BATMAN/DEATHBLOW: AFTER THE FIRE

LEX LUTHOR
MAN OF STEEL
BRIAN AZZARELLO
LEE BERMEJO

LEX LUTHOR: MAN OF STEEL

BRIAN AZZARELLO JIM LEE SCOTT WILLIAMS
"Taut, gripping." —Library Journal
FOR TOMORROW

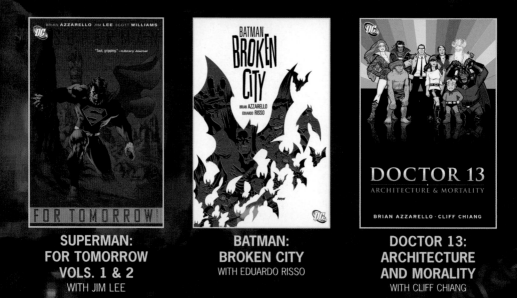

SUPERMAN: FOR TOMORROW VOLS. 1 & 2

WITH JIM LEE

BATMAN
BROKEN CITY
BRIAN AZZARELLO
EDUARDO RISSO

BATMAN: BROKEN CITY

WITH EDUARDO RISSO

DOCTOR 13
ARCHITECTURE & MORTALITY
BRIAN AZZARELLO · CLIFF CHIANG

DOCTOR 13: ARCHITECTURE AND MORALITY

WITH CLIFF CHIANG

SEARCH THE GRAPHIC NOVELS SECTION OF **DCCOMICS.COM** FOR ART AND INFORMATION ON ALL OF OUR BOOKS!